LIVING *in the* FACE *of* DEATH

THE TIBETAN TRADITION

LIVING *in the* FACE *of* DEATH

THE TIBETAN TRADITION

Translated, edited & introduced by

Glenn H. Mullin

Snow Lion Publications
Ithaca, New York

Snow Lion Publications
P.O. Box 6483
Ithaca, New York 14851 USA
607-273-8519

Printed in Canada on recycled paper

ISBN 1-55939-100-6

Library of Congress Cataloging-in-Publication Data

Mullin, Glenn H.
    Living in the face of death: the Tibetan tradition/ translated, edited & intro-
duced by Glenn H. Mullin.
        p.   cm.
    Rev. ed. of: Death and dying, 1986.
    Includes bibliographical references and index.
    ISBN 1-55939-100-6
    1. Death--Religious aspects--Buddhism. 2. Buddhism--China--Tibet. I. Mullin,
Glenn H., Death and dying. II. Title.
BQ4487.M84 1998
294.3'423--dc21   98-14199
                                                                    CIP

Contents

Foreword

by Professor Huston Smith

Death is the most important question of our time, as Yale psychiatrist Robert Jay Lifton has suggested, in good part because we refuse to face it. For some time now social historians have pointed to the way it has replaced sex in our social taboos. Whereas nineteenth-century Victorians whispered about sex behind closed doors and were publicly obsessed with death, with us it is the opposite; our iceberg of unmentionables has capsized. We splash sex across our billboards and every other channel of display, and confine death to the embarrassment of private grief. Arnold Toynbee called death un-American, but it is more than that. It is an affront to the entire Promethean West in its countermand to our will to power—the lid it places on our insistence on having our way and retaining control.

The present book appears amidst Western medicine's many recent programs attempting to lift that lid with technology. The appropriateness of such heroic measures, as we have come to refer to drastic elongations of the death process, could turn importantly on our attitude toward their alternative, the death that would follow if we declined to put them to use. For if we continue to think of death in military terms, as 'the enemy' toward which heroic postures are indicated, two things will happen. The lives that extraordinary measures prolong will be of dubious quality for being lived in fear of the enemy's inexorable advance. And we will suffer the skewed allocation of resources that war always occasions. Social inequities will increase as the cost of dying rises and issues of death are taken increasingly to court. And across the board, moneys and energies that should be directed to life's enhancement will be diverted to slowing the death process that must eventually come whatever we do.

The moral of this is not a moratorium on medical technology. Rather, it is balance that we need: a readiness to assist the body when such assistance is appropriate, coupled with an equal readiness to 'drop the body,' as the Indians say, when its purpose has been fulfilled. It is difficult to achieve this balance when we regard death as a wall to be avoided as long as possible—literally at all costs because it is the ultimate personal disaster. And this is where Asia can help us. Having escaped the mechanomorphic view of reality that modern science seemed in its infancy to decree—it no longer does, but our thought forms have not caught up with that fact—Asia has been spared the impact of death as a blank wall and continues to approach it as we too once did, as a doorway through which one passes into a different kind of existence. If we think of that existence as a simple continuation of our present life, we underestimate the subtlety of the notions this book will unfold. There may be only a single metaphor in our present repertoire that is applicable, an abstract spatial one. In ways that must currently elude us completely, the life-after-death, we are told, will be a larger one. Ultimately, though for most persons not at once, it will be like removing a tight shoe.

Asia as a whole has retained its grip on this life-after-death, but nowhere has the grasp remained firmer than in Tibet and its outlook as preserved in exile since the Chinese invasion. For it is in Tibet that the archaic (not to be confused with naive) perspective has remained most completely intact—right down to the middle of the present century, we can note in near disbelief. Because tribal societies lack written records, Tibet is our last living link to the civilizations of the distant past. The mystery cults of Egypt and Mesopotamia are gone, and India and China have been eroded by waves of westernization. But modernity passed Tibet by. To meet her mountains and people, one had to cross oceans, traverse subcontinents, and climb steep defiles, only to enter wastelands of black gulfs and white summits. Set in the absolute coldness of the sky, Tibet seemed not to belong to our earth and was ignored—a society left on the shelf as if set in amber.

For our present, potential profit is the point that interests us here. Because the Promethean dream never touched her, Tibet was able to retain toward death a wakeful watch. Visions of 'life extension through kryonic suspension'—with their undertow of psychological denial,

Ernest Becker's *The Denial of Death* has helped us to see—never occurred to her. This enabled her to keep her eye on death undistractedly. She did not lose sight of its cosmic context.

Some of the realizations that she retained will be familiar to us. In reading her reflections on the way a vivid awareness of one's personal death can bring the present to sharp focus, showing it as the unearned gift it undeniably is, we may be reminded of the Psalmist's plea that we be taught 'to number our days that we may apply our hearts unto wisdom.' Or Heidegger's point may occur to us: if we were immortal everything could be put off till tomorrow. Those who remember Thomas Kelly's assertion that 'eternity is at our hearts, pressing upon our time-worn lives, warming us with intimations of an astounding destiny, calling us home to its self' will not be surprised by the size of the setting in which the Tibetans find death situated.

There will be other points in these pages though that will seem foreign. As such they will carry the shock of novelty, but with it the excitement that attends the possibility of truths that have not before occurred to us. Only this last can explain the sensation *The Tibetan Book of the Dead* created when it hit the West in Evans-Wentz's translation in 1927. Nothing can detract from that book's importance, but it was a single text that needed to be supplemented. This study performs the service of presenting the Tibetan understanding of death as a whole; circumambulating it, as we might say, to view it in the round. The author/translator has selected key texts to address the many aspects of the Tibetan view of death; he has chosen wisely, but equally important is his love for the Tibetan people and his respect for their culture—this shines through his introduction to the book as a whole and the leads he provides for its individual texts. The result is a study that realizes admirably its projected intent.

Earlier, in *The Wheel of Death*, Philip Kapleau gave us a useful summary of the Zen perspective on death and dying. Glenn H. Mullin's addition of the Tibetan perspective gives us a second approach to the Buddhist view and in doing so introduces the dimension of death that binocular vision affords. For this he deserves deep gratitude. When the Prophet Muhammad counseled his followers to 'Seek knowledge, even in China,' he was saying obliquely, 'Look for it everywhere; wherever it can be found.'

Preface

by Elizabeth Kübler-Ross

The rich culture and spiritual wisdom of Tibet are evident in its extraordinary diversity of literature about death and dying. To this day Tibet is one of a few countries that have not been influenced by the Western conception of death as an enemy, as something that has to be postponed at any cost or feared. Rather, these admirable, highly spiritual people look on death as a threshold, as an entrance to a different existence. And for centuries they have taught people to conduct their lives so as to be prepared for this most important and significant transition.

Some twenty years ago, when I began my research on the process of dying, I reached into the Tibetan traditions, having been made aware of them through Evans-Wentz's *Tibetan Book of the Dead.* I have been touched by Buddhist thought, especially the concept of karma—the theory that all our actions, be they positive, negative, or neutral, leave an impression in our consciousness. Accordingly, a person who commits an evil act will plant in his or her subconscious a strong trend towards cruelty. Conversely, a person who effects something good through loving, considered, and friendly action, will increase his or her positive tendencies further.

How does this outlook differ in comparison with Christian teaching, which says that we will reap what we have sown? When we sow hatred and negativity, they will return to us exactly the same, like a boomerang. When we have expended our energy in loving, in caring for others, and in sympathizing with them, this also comes back to us.

This is truly a universal law taught by all great religions, yet it seems so difficult for us to understand it and live by it.

This is not a book that can be read lightly like a novel. It requires time for study chapter by chapter. Even though I have learned very much in my work with thousands of dying patients in the last twenty years, this book is still instructive reading, and reminds me how similar we all are and how we reach the same result, though by different paths. The truth appears to be universal, in spite of all the differences of language and concepts.

The reason for working with dying patients, who are preparing for their journey into another life, is to help them to rid themselves of any negative attitudes, to complete any unfinished work in their relationships with others, and to become free of all negativity. By learning to love themselves and those close to them truly and unconditionally, a patient can be ready for the last farewell without fear, and can anticipate a joyous transition into a different realm of existence.

To practice the spiritual path, we must know which of our tendencies we need to develop and which to conquer—and I do not need to stress that it is our own responsibility to accomplish this task. Our inner progress depends solely on our own endeavors and our discipline. This is the reason why I feel that two points are extremely important in the education of our children: unconditional love combined with a strict, definitive discipline.

This book presents the lives and the teachings of many great masters. It is not easy to find such teachers in the West. However, I have observed how many of my patients have become deeply spiritual and were allowed, just as I was, to have spiritual experiences with teachers like Stephen Levine and others; in a comparatively short time they were able to look within and ultimately be ready and able to see death as an evolutionary step as the Buddhists do.

No matter what our social status in life may be, we all have the same opportunities to develop love, compassion, understanding, and wisdom. These are the qualities that count at the moment of death, not any titles or the material possessions we have accumulated. If at the moment of death we are rich in love and compassion and free of fear and confusion, we have lived our life correctly.

My greatest teacher was a hospital cleaning woman who had never finished high school. She had weathered many storms in her life and lived in poverty—a circumstance that was directly responsible for the death of her child—and yet she used every experience to better understand and to feel for others. Without words she radiated a measure of serenity and love to the dying patients whose rooms she cleaned, so that one could almost say she was practicing "transformation of consciousness," and thus she enabled my patients to complete their transition in peace and calmness. If ever I had a guru, it was this woman who taught me about life and death and who gave me the inspiration for our later seminars on death and dying at the University of Chicago.

Only very few people in the West strive consciously for enlightenment or even think about it, though some individuals comprehend that only through constant practice and hard work on oneself is it possible to reach this goal within a single lifetime. However, most of us understand that the seed of perfect wisdom lies always within each of us, and ever more people in the Western world are deciding to take active steps to learn how to understand this better. This book may contain some foreign words and concepts, but it can help you in your search, until you experience the fruits of your labors. During more than twenty years of work with dying patients I have learned much about the things written of in this excellent book; thus much of what stands behind some of the difficult words rings at the same time true and familiar.

I am grateful to the author for the immense labor he has put into this masterpiece. It leads the people of the West to the spiritual wisdom of the people of the "Land of the Snows" and contributes to bringing us closer to one another—to build a bridge between the religious teachings of East and West, and ultimately to reach the insight that we humans are all one.

Acknowledgments

Tibetan literature is rich in materials on the subject of death and dying. The present volume is an attempt to give the Western reader a glimpse of the breadth and nature of these. It grew out of my twelve years of study and research at the Library of Tibetan Works and Archives, Dharamsala, and my experiences in the Tibetan refugee communities in India. None of the work involved was done officially for or with the Tibetan Library; rather, it represents some of the extracurricular activities that came up around my researches there. Yet it would be unkind of me not to acknowledge the fatherly guidance of Mr. Gyatso Tsering, Director of the Tibetan Library, whose generosity to all Tibetologists who wandered into the Shangri-La of Dharamsala was extraordinarily consistent since the Library opened its doors to Western scholars in 1971. In addition, I would like to mention the untiring assistance of the numerous tutors at the Library who helped me over the hurdles of learning Tibetan language, literature, philosophy and religious practice: Geshe Ngawang Dargye, Chomdze Tashi Wanggyal, Ven. Doboom Tulku and Ven. Amchok Tulku.

I was originally introduced to the Tibetan tradition on death and dying by Geshe Ngawang Dargye, my first instructor in Dharamsala. Geshe Dargye had been appointed by His Holiness the Dalai Lama to set up the Buddhist Studies program at the Tibetan Library, and in the early 1970s gave several courses on the Buddhist concept of death. In 1976 a German friend by the name of Michael Hellbach and I approached Geshe Dargye with a request to give us a private discourse on the overall schemata of the trainings in death meditation practiced by Tibetan Buddhists; we were planning a German periodical, and this discourse eventually appeared as an article in it (*Aus Tushita* vol. I, Duisberg, Germany, 1977). Part of this same article is used in chapter two of the present volume.

In 1978 a British film-maker by the name of Graham Coleman asked me to work as a consultant for three documentary films he was engaged in making, which were released as *Tibet: A Buddhist Trilogy* (Bath, England: Thread Cross Films). One of these centered on a death ritual performed by a Tibetan monastery in Ladakh, and my researches for it led me to numerous interesting facets of the Buddhist tradition on death. Chapters five and eight draw strongly on materials I encountered at this time. Coincidentally, when my mother passed away in 1979 the Junior Tutor to the Dalai Lama recommended that I have the same ritual done for her as was documented in the above film. This ritual is the focus of chapter eight. I originally read it with Tsering Don-drub.

Another friend to draw me into a study of the Tibetan literature on death and dying was Mr. David Lewiston, for whom I worked as a field associate in the production of the Tibetan recording *Shedur: A Ghost Exorcism Ritual* (New York: Nonesuch Records, 1978). This introduced me to several unusual aspects of the Tibetan view of the after-death experience. A few years later David asked me to help him with some materials for a project he was doing on Lahoul. He had been accompanied by Tashi Tsering, research scholar at the Tibetan Library, on an excursion he made through Lahoul in 1982, and they had acquired a copy of Terton Dulzhug Lingpa's collected works. Tashi had marked several of these as being of interest to David's purposes, and I was asked to translate them. One of these caught my attention and impressed me as worthy of closer study. It is included in chapter five. I translated it with the assistance of Tsepak Rigzin, a young lama who also helped me with the Tibetan materials in chapters one, five and seven.

In 1982 I read through the collected works of the Thirteenth Dalai Lama and translated one of his early discourses, a portion of which I used in an article for *The American Theosophist* ('The Thirteenth Dalai Lama's 1921 Sermon at the Great Prayer Festival,' Illinois, March 1983). In chapter one of the present volume I have used the entire sermon, translated with Tsepak Rigzin. In it the Thirteenth Dalai Lama provides an excellent introduction to the nature of the Buddhist trainings in death meditation and how these relate to the complete Buddhist path.

Another fascinating work that revealed a range of materials on the

Buddhist view of life and death was the First Dalai Lama's commentary to the methods of divining the signs of death, producing longevity and training in consciousness transference at the time of death; I read this with Ven. Artsa Tulku of Magadha University, Bihar, during the winter of 1982. This led me to the Second Dalai Lama's commentary to the longevity yogas that I have included in chapter six, and also the elucidation of consciousness transference in chapter seven. The former of these was translated with the kind assistance of Ven. Amchok Tulku and the latter with Tsepak Rigzin. I quote liberally from the First Dalai Lama's commentary in my preambles to these sections.

During the spring of 1978 the present Dalai Lama gave an open discourse in the main temple at Dharamsala to several thousand devotees and yogi/scholars. At the conclusion of it he read a number of short scriptures and poems, commenting briefly on them. One of these, which I later translated with Ven. Chomdze Tashi Wanggyal, was Lama Gungtang's *A Conversation with an Old Man*, here included in chapter three. On the same occasion His Holiness read several Seventh Dalai Lama poems, one of these being *Meditations on the Ways of Impermanence*, which I have used in the concluding chapter. It seemed the perfect note on which to close this collection.

I would like to thank Ms. Hilary Shearman, who assisted with the editing in the final stages of the manuscript; and also both Pierre Robillard and Jan McDonald of the Kampo Gangra Buddhist Meditation Center, Toronto, for helping in numerous points of detail.

Glenn H. Mullin

Introduction

That time of year thou mayst in me behold
When yellow leaves, or none, or few, do hang
Upon those boughs which shake against the cold,
Bare ruin'd choirs, where late the sweet birds sang.
In me thou see'st the twilight of such day
As after sunset fadeth in the west,
Which by and by black night doth take away,
Death's second self, that seals up all in rest.
In me thou see'st the glowing of such fire
That on the ashes of his youth doth lie,
As the death-bed whereon it must expire,
Consum'd with that which it was nourish'd by.
  This thou perceiv'st which makes thy love more strong,
  To love that well which thou must leave ere long.

—Shakespeare, *Sonnet LXXIII*

The subject of death and dying has fascinated human beings from time immemorial, ever since intelligence developed to the point where we could realize that the laws of impermanence, so obvious in our surroundings, also applied to our own stream of being.

Yet like all things that make a strong statement to us but provoke more questions than ready-made answers, our response to the constantly pressing reality of death has changed with the trends of the passing centuries. Thus we have seen great civilizations, such as that of Egypt, with entire religious traditions centered on the concept of death.[1] Intricate and sophisticated philosophies of death and dying

have filled volumes of learned European writings.[2] Poets have attempted to convey its meaning in subtle rhyme, and painters have
tried to capture its poignancy on canvas.

Our own age, on the other hand, has constantly attempted to gloss
it over. The decline of religion at the turn of the century, and the replacement of God and the religious attitude with the doctor and the
almighty medical machine, resulted in death and dying being taken
out of the community and placed in the hands of 'professionals.' The
old are taken from us and hidden in special homes, where they can
receive 'the help they really need.' The terminally ill are wheeled to
secret death beds on the upper levels of sterile hospitals, where the
only witnesses to their silent, drugged passing are the ultramodern
machines that tick, bleep and hum in the background, recording the
steady decline of the heartbeat, blood pressure and respiration. When
the corpse is eventually given back to the relatives, it appears not in
the guise of a proof of death, but with chemical blood that absorbs the
deathly odor and prevent its escape, a lace job to provide a beatific
expression of being merely asleep and lost in a sweet dream, and a
well-pressed suit of clothing like that of a person being sent off to a
formal dinner party.

The Occident has progressed technologically and materially to a
tremendous degree, yet perhaps future generations who look back
upon us may still find some aspects of our culture rather humorously
primitive. Ours is the great cosmetic civilization, and nowhere is this
quality of our age so obvious as in our attitudes and habits regarding
death and dying. We can witness cosmetic death on television in our
living room hundreds of times a day. Veritable armies rise and fall on
the screen before our eyes, yet for some mysterious reason the reality
of death must be hidden from our immediate environment. Imagi-
nary death is somehow enticing and entertaining, yet real death is
made to seem disgusting and fearful.

Sickness, aging and death have become taboo subjects in our society.[3]
We are under constant pressure to hide from the very thought of our
own death. People are made to feel guilty about their increasing years,
and to ask them their age becomes almost an insult, like clumsily men-
tioning a disabled person's handicap at an inappropriate moment.

Ours is a society that worships youth and young life, and in this
worship makes every effort at imitation. Billions of dollars a year are
spent on facelifts, hair dyes, body creams, endless varieties of
cosmetics and countless other tactics for projecting an image of being

younger and healthier than we really are. These methods of camouflage are not only acceptable to supposedly mature human beings but are encouraged and hyped up as being normal and necessary. To think about our own death is considered to be dangerously morbid, and to talk of it in public is frowned upon as being in extremely bad taste.

The last few decades, however, have seen major breakthroughs in the serious study of death and dying. Modern psychology is beginning to peel off the taboos concerning death much in the same way that Freud almost a century ago removed the stigmas surrounding sexuality. Research specialists like Dr. Kübler-Ross, Dr. Raymond Carey, Dr. E. Haraldsson, and Dr. Ernest Becker have made monumental contributions to the field known as 'thanatology,' the study of death and dying. Because of their clinical observations of death and their work with the dying, even the most conservative sciences are beginning to recognize that, although death cannot be seen through a microscope, it nonetheless can be observed as a psychological phenomenon that has more implications to the individual than the mere termination of his/her physical body.

Perhaps the most important discovery by modern studies on death comes from the psychiatric research undertaken by Dr. Kübler-Ross and others that reveals an understanding and awareness of our impermanent nature to be mandatory to our psychological well-being. Just as Freud proved, amidst tremendous opposition and controversy, that an understanding of our own sexuality is necessary to our psychological maturation, so amidst considerable hullabaloo modern thanatologists have brought forth significant documented evidence to support the theory that awareness of death and of our own impermanence helps us to live a healthy, balanced and harmonious life.[4] The connection between Freud's work with sexuality and the present work with death and dying may be more related psychologically than we care to acknowledge. In an essay entitled 'The Pornography of Death' by Dr. Geoffrey Gorer[5] we read:

> In the twentieth century there seems to have been an unremarked shift in prudery; whereas copulation has become more and more mentionable, particularly in Anglo-Saxon societies, death has become more and more unmentionable.

It is certainly true that Freud's work with sexuality took half a century to filter from his clinic to the mainstream of established society; we may well expect that the present work with death and dying could take the same length of time to influence public perception.

In Freud's time both sex and death were illicit topics. By the middle of this century only death remained so. Dr. Robin Denniston writes in his foreword to Arnold Toynbee's *Man's Concern with Death*,[6] 'Some five years ago...the discussion of death really did seem like the new pornography—a secret and shameful matter totally opposed to the life-enhancing virtues of sex, love, freedom and immortality....' And Dr. Richard Kalish writes:[7]

> Death is blasphemous and pornographic. We react to it and its symbols in the same way that we react to any pornography. We avoid it. We deny it exists. We avert our eyes from its presence. We protect little children from observing it and dodge their questions about it. We speak of it only in whispers. We consider it horrible, ugly and grotesque.

In fact, our sexuality and our proneness to death are closely related to one another, like opposite poles of a magnet. One gives us the strength of life and the ability to procreate, making us significant, meaningful, powerful and real. The other condemns us to destruction and renders us insignificant, meaningless, powerless and unreal. Both are inseparably connected with the animal side of our nature. One makes us feel strong, the other teaches us humility. In terms of our life, one is ultimate creativity, the other ultimately negative. One makes us aggressive and outgoing, the other makes us passive and withdrawn.

Understanding our sexuality helps us to realize the aggressive, powerful aspect of our nature. Understanding our mortality causes us to realize the passive, humble aspect, balancing our sense of aggression and power. When this balance is not present, problems of sexual expression arise, ranging from impotency to sadomasochism.

It is perhaps the ethereal romanticism of the eighteenth and nineteenth centuries and the dualism between body and mind this period advocated that have caused us to enter the present century unable to relate realistically to either our sexuality or our mortality. In the romantic view, the mind was holy and the body profane. Thus the body and its qualities of sexuality and proneness to death were to be ignored or suppressed. Societies that exhibited a strong body culture were to be labeled as savage and degenerate, and were to be reformed by military strength or to be obliterated.

Freud's work with sexuality produced a veritable cultural and social revolution in the West: who knows if today's work on death and dying will have an equally powerful impact on our society over the following decades. To understand our mortality is to get back in touch with our humanity, something from which we have managed to alien ate ourselves.

Certainly the immediate threat of death is a very powerful stimulant, at least as powerful as the sexual instinct. Nothing gives us quite as much energy as a sudden threat to our life. If our life is in danger and we have the choice of escaping or indulging in sex, we would undoubtedly opt to escape.

The Indian Buddhist sage Shantideva wrote:[8]

> The prisoner condemned by a king merely to have a limb amputated as a punishment for a crime totally panics. His mouth goes dry, his eyes bulge and he trembles with fear. How much more terrified is someone threatened with death?

In fact, we are threatened by death at every moment, just as our own sexuality influences our motivations at all times. To ignore either side of our nature is to permit the mind to live under the darkness of ignorance and illusion concerning the nature of our being. This ignorance can only harm us in the end. It may feel comfortable for a while, but eventually ignorance leads to confusion and pain.

The creative potential of an understanding of our impermanence not only to us as individuals but also as a complete society is stated very strongly and optimistically by Dr. Kübler-Ross in her most successful book, *On Death and Dying*,[9] in which she writes:

> If science and technology are not to be misused to increase destructiveness, prolonging life rather than making it more human, if they could go hand in hand with freeing more rather than less people for individual person-to-person contacts, then we could really speak of a great society.... We may achieve peace—our own inner peace as well as peace between nations—by facing and accepting the reality of our own death.

This view clearly harmonizes with that of the Buddhist world, wherein an understanding of death and our impermanent nature is held to be of paramount importance to our spiritual well-being. Buddha himself said,[10] 'Of all footprints, that of the elephant is supreme. Similarly, of all mindfulness meditations, that on death is supreme.' The range of benefits of meditating on death daily, and the disadvantages of not doing so, are discussed at length in the work translated in chapter two, *Tibetan Traditions of Death Meditation*.

Tibetan Buddhism is tremendously rich in materials on death and dying, more so than the many other forms of Buddhism. This is not surprising, for Tibet, although not large in population, produced more literature than any of her far more populous neighbors. It was not uncommon for a Tibetan writer to pen as many as a thousand titles of varying lengths. Perhaps it was the duration and intensity of the Himalayan winter, perhaps the crisp clarity of the atmosphere on the Roof of the World, or perhaps the stimulation provided by the extraordinary amount of butter tea the average Tibetan consumed; but something in the chemistry of Tibetan life caused her to become one of the most literarily prolific nations the world has known. No thorough consensus of Tibetan literature has ever been made, and now that the Chinese invasion has resulted in the destruction of the thousands of monastic libraries in Tibet no complete analysis will ever be possible, but without a doubt the number of titles measured in the millions.

Like most ancient cultures, Tibet produced a predominantly spiritual literature. Fiction existed only as spiritual allegory. To the Tibetan author, writing was an instrument to record the lives of religious people and events, communicate spiritual experience, elucidate spiritual practice and in general further the causes of philosophy, art, medicine, religion, history and the various spiritual sciences. The subject of death and dying ranked with importance among these, and most Tibetan authors contributed at least one essay, meditation guide, ritual manual, poem or prayer containing their personal insights or reflections.

It is not possible to say when Buddhism first began to infiltrate the snowy ranges of Tibet, although it existed on the southern and western foothills almost from the time of the Buddha himself. But not until the mid-seventh century was Tibet to become officially Buddhist, when King Songtsen Gampo married two Buddhist women, one from Nepal and the other from China.[11] The gentle spirituality of these two ladies deeply moved him, and in their honor he ordered the construction of the Jowo Temple (known to the West as the Central Cathedral of Lhasa). At his instigation the minister Thomi Sambhota and two dozen assistants were sent to India to study and to devise a special Tibetan script for the translation of Buddhism from Sanskrit.[12] Renditions of several Indian scriptures were prepared, and the basis for a government-organized importation of Buddhism was laid. This work was to blossom a century later, during the reign of King Tri-song Deutsen, who brought the tantric adept Padma Sambhava and the monk Shantarakshita from India to found the first government-sponsored monastery.[13] Under these two masters, translation teams were drawn up from

Tibet's twenty-five principal scholars and the work of rendering the principal Indian Buddhist scriptures began in earnest. From this time until the destruction of Buddhist India by the invading Muslim hordes six centuries later, the systematic translation of Buddhist Sanskrit texts into Tibetan continued almost without a break, save for the brief interruption that occurred during the reign of King Lang Darma in the late ninth century.

Here it should perhaps be noted that although Tibet became officially a Buddhist nation, nonetheless a small fraction of the people did remain faithful to the pre-Buddhist tradition, known as Bön. Possibly this ancient lineage of spirituality—a combination of Persian, Mongolian, Tibetan and Indo-Burmese shamanism—had its own script and literary tradition prior to the advent of Buddhism, but most scholars believe it was exclusively an orally transmitted culture. Be this as it may, the new script introduced by Thomi Sambhota was to become adopted by the Bön almost overnight, and has remained until today. Thus in Tibetan we have both Buddhist and Bön writings, although the Buddhist materials obviously greatly exceed those of the Bön in terms of sheer volume. In this study of the Tibetan tradition of death and dying, however, I am only including the Buddhist scriptures. The Buddhist tradition in Tibet was a comprehensive system that thrived independently of the Bön; Tibet was largely a tribal nation, and the few Bön tribes that existed kept very much to themselves, perhaps saving themselves from extinction by their isolationist policy.[14] Not that there was any serious animosity between the two, but distances in Tibet were great and it was easy for the peoples of a valley kingdom to go for months or even years without seeing the peoples of a neighboring valley.

As for the Buddhist literature, a distinction must be made between what Western scholars call 'the Tibetan canons' and indigenous Tibetan writings. The former category refers to the two collections of translations from Sanskrit—the *Kan-gyur*,[15] or translations of Buddha's original discourses, and the *Ten-gyur*,[16] or translations of the works of later Indian Buddhist masters. These translations preserve more than 6,000 of the most important Buddhist scriptures to appear in ancient India. They communicate Buddha's essential message of the Hinayana, Mahayana and Vajrayana levels of training.[17] It is upon the philosophy and general attitudes expressed in these scriptures that all later independent Tibetan literature is based, at least within the Buddhist tradition. The last of this translation work was done in about the mid-fourteenth century, when Buddhism disappeared in India. Although a certain amount of indigenous Tibetan literature had appeared before this time, while Buddhism thrived in India the main emphasis had been on the study and analysis of the Indian Buddhist tradition. The Tibetan literary arts thus did not come into their own until after this time.

Buddhism in Tibet underwent three major phases: the early and later periods of the propagation of the Dharma, which were mainly eras of translation and transition,[18] and the period after Buddhism in India had disappeared, when the Tibetan sects were becoming more stable and were beginning to concentrate more upon defining themselves as traditions, and the Dalai Lama incarnations were to appear.[19]

The early period refers to the various Buddhist movements that formed prior to the eleventh century. The sects that arose during this time are collectively referred to as the Nyingma, or Ancient Ones. As the centuries passed these sects became more and more related to one another, until today the Nyingma is considered to be a single sect. A principal characteristic of the tradition is that the language of their scriptures is strongly influenced by that of the early pre-Buddhist Bön culture. This is not to say that they were directly influenced by Bön trends in thought or practice; rather, the situation of this early phase of Buddhism in Tibet is similar to the early stage of Buddhism in the West, where the translations were rendered into nineteenth-century Christian idiom.

The later phase of translation began in the mid-eleventh century with Rinchen Zangpo of Western Tibet. This marked the second stage of Buddhism in Tibet, and it sparked off a renaissance in the Land of Snows. Early Buddhism had been translated into the language of old Tibet; in this new phase, the trend was to update and review all the old translations into the language that had developed in a Tibet now evolved philosophically and linguistically by several centuries of Buddhist experience. Again many Tibetan scholars began to travel to India to study there and retranslate the holy scriptures, and Indian masters were invited to come and check out the various Buddhist monasteries of Tibet. Numerous new sects were to be formed on the basis of this work, but three were to become lasting pillars: the Sakya, Kargyu, and Kadam. Over the following centuries the smaller movements were to amalgamate themselves with one or another of these three.

The four principal sects that formed during the first two stages of the development of Buddhism in Tibet all had direct roots with particular Indian masters: the Nyingma with Padma Sambhava and Shantarakshita; the Sakya with Dharmapala and Virupa; the Kargyu with Naropa and Maitripa; and the Kadam with Atisha. By the close of the fourteenth century these traditions were to be established, well-organized entities operating in relative independence of one another, each specializing in those lineages popular with their respective founders. The scene was set for Tibetan Buddhism's third phase.

It was at this time that the great lama Tsongkhapa,[20] guru of the First Dalai Lama, appeared. Rather than join one or another of the four earlier sects, or travel to India and initiate another Indian-based sect, he spent the first thirty-five years of his life travelling the length and breadth of Tibet, studying with the most important teachers of his time in the four traditions. In all he trained under forty-five Tibetan masters, collecting together all the fundamental Buddhist lineages that had found their way from India into the Land of Snows. He has often been called a reformer of Tibetan Buddhism, but this is inaccurate. He made no attempt to reform any of the four sects. Rather, his aim was to collect together all the Hinayana, Mahayana and Vajrayana transmissions that existed in Tibet and to house them under one roof. In other words, he was a synthesizer of lineages, not a reformer of established schools. The monastery that he founded, Ganden, became a prototype, and dozens of monasteries modeled on it were to spring up over the next generation. Within a hundred years his tradition had become the largest and most popular in the country.

The four sects that formed during the first two phases of Buddhism in Tibet are sometimes called 'the Red Hat sects,' for all of them used a red pointed hat in their monastic rituals. Tsongkhapa was to change the color of the ceremonial hat to yellow, and thus his tradition, the Geluk, or Wholesome Way, was to become known as 'the Yellow Hat sect.'

In fact, according to Tibetan oral tradition the ceremonial monastic hat in early India had been yellow, the color of the earth, symbol of discipline and the foundation from which all good things are born. However, this had become changed to red, symbol of fire and victory, after the Hindus began gaining the upper hand over the Buddhists in public debate.[21] The mystical tactic apparently worked, and the hat remained red thereafter. The tradition carried over in Tibet during both the early and late phases of the spread of the doctrine, but Tsongkhapa felt that the main threat to Buddhism in Tibet was not unsuccessful public debate with non-Buddhists, as it had been in classical India; rather, it was the general laziness and lack of discipline of the Tibetan practitioners. Therefore he changed the color of the hat back to the original yellow, bringing it back to the earth element and the firm foundation required for successful engagement in the higher practices.

The Yellow Hat order thus became not so much a new sect of Tibetan Buddhism but a fusion of all the earlier sects. However, the language adopted in the monastic course of studies was that of the later translation period, i.e., that of the Sakya, Kargyu and Kadam traditions. In this sense it was linguistically and philosophically closer to those sects. Nonetheless it did incorporate many of the tantric lineages of the Nyingma, or earlier phase, and in the transmission of these lineages naturally used the terminology associated with the specific lines of transmission.[22]

Sometimes a twofold division of the Tibetan sects is made into the old and the new. When this is done, some scholars take the dividing line as the mid-eleventh century; this divides the sects according to the translation periods, and reflects the difference in the language used in the scriptures of the orders. In this case the Nyingma represent the old tradition, and the Red Hats of the later translation period, together with the Yellow Hats, comprise the new sects. However, because the Yellow Hats are as large as all other Tibetan sects combined and are clearly demarked by their yellow hat, other scholars make the division of old and new as the Red Hats and the Yellow Hats. This division is more superficial, having no reference to doctrine or textual content.

The Yellow Hat order founded by Lama Tsongkhapa was to grow at a tremendous rate, and within a hundred years had become the largest sect in Tibet. In 1578 the Mongolians under Altan Khan also adopted the Yellow Hat tradition as the official state religion, and it quickly spread through what is now Inner and Outer Mongolia, as well as much of Siberia.[23]

The founder of the Yellow Hat order, Lama Tsongkhapa, had five principal disciples. The youngest of these was Gyalwa Gendun Drub, to be known posthumously as the First Dalai Lama. He was to become the most famous of the five, and when he passed away at the age of eighty-three his disciples extracted from him a promise to return to them.[24] Thus after his death a search was begun for his reincarnation. Soon a child was found who exhibited the signs of being an exceptional incarnation. He was submitted to rigid tests, and convinced those who participated that indeed he was the reincarnation of Gendun Drub. The tradition was continued at the death of each subsequent Dalai Lama, until today we have the fourteenth in the line of reincarnations.

The Dalai Lamas have always been Yellow Hat adherents by monastic ordination, but in terms of study and practice they have had tutorage from masters of the various traditions. In addition, the Yellow Hat order is itself a fusion of the earlier sects. It is perhaps this trans-sectarian aspect of the Dalai Lamas that made them so popular in Tibet and caused their lineage to rise to the forefront of spiritual and secular leadership in Central Asia. The fifth in the line of Dalai Lamas united the three provinces of Tibet in 1642, and under the guidance of the successive Dalai Lamas after him the various Tibetan traditions were encouraged to preserve and develop their individual lineages without partisanship.[25]

Within the diverse orders of Tibetan Buddhism there of course exist philosophical and doctrinal differences, but the essential substance of each of the traditions is the same. All are based on Buddha's Hinayana teachings of the four noble truths and three higher trainings, the Mahayana teachings on the cultivation of the bodhisattva aspiration and the six perfections, and the Vajrayana methods of the two stages in tantric yoga. The differences lie more in the manner of expression of these teachings. Each lineage developed at a different time and in a different part of the country, and thus each preserves variations in language and style. Each advocates the applications of all three *yanas*, while emphasizing different aspects of the teachings and giving slightly different philosophical interpretations to the various scriptures.

The sects nonetheless have more in common than in conflict. As the present Dalai Lama said to me in an interview in 1976, 'All Tibetan traditions transmit and preserve the same essential message of the Buddha and all have the ability to guide the trainee to enlightenment in one lifetime. The difference is more in the nature of stressing different points in the teachings in order to suit the individual needs and spiritual propensities of specific practitioners.'

This study of the Tibetan tradition of death and dying draws largely from the writings of the various Dalai Lamas, rounding out these materials with the writings of some of Tibet's most famous authors. In total I have incorporated nine illustrative works. Three of these are from the pens of the early Dalai Lamas. Two are by well-known Red Hat lamas, and the remaining four by famous Yellow Hat authors. The materials are carefully selected in order to show the essential fibre of the thought, practice and attitudes that run through all traditions of Tibetan Buddhism—the basic elements that constitute the flesh and bones of the Tibetan tradition on death and dying.

As I pointed out earlier, Tibetan Buddhism has a richness of literature beyond that with which most Western scholars credit it. We in the West tend to have a very romantic view of Tibet—and it no doubt had its romantic aspects, with nomads, yaks[26] and towering monasteries—but we often think of it as being more primitive and illiterate than in fact it was. Quite to the contrary, every family aspired to produce at least one scholar/yogi, and the study period to accomplish this would require between twenty and thirty years of intensive discipline.[27]

In Tibet, writing has for centuries been the great national pastime. While we in the West were floundering in the dark ages and then racing manically around the world to colonize and seize other people's lands, the Tibetans were sitting in their caves and monasteries on the Roof of the World sipping butter tea, chewing yak cheese and generally keeping themselves out of trouble by occupying themselves with study, meditation and literary composition. At the time of the Norman invasion of England, Tibet's national budget was tied up in bringing Indian masters such as Atisha to Tibet, building monasteries and libraries, publishing scriptures and so forth. This was the era of Marpa the Translator, Milarepa the Yogi and Rva Lotsawa the Sorceror, the time when the great Sakya lamas were popularizing the study of poetry, medicine and composition, and making them into national subjects in the educational system. While the Spanish were raping and pillaging in South and Central America, and England was doing the same in North America, the Third Dalai Lama was inspiring the Mongolian hordes to turn from their warlike ways and convincing them of the superiority of a spiritual life. Later, the Fifth Dalai Lama was busily introducing the world's first system of national health care and national education to his people. I do not wish to overly idealize Tibet, for there certainly were also faults and shortcomings; human failing and tragedy exist in every society and at all times to some degree, but an objective observer certainly must admire the spirituality of this tiny Himalayan nation in a time when the rest of world was thinking of little else but military adventure and international piracy.

Tibet was a small nation only as regards her population. Its high, dry climate could not support a large populace, but its land mass equalled that of the entirety of Western Europe, and was more than half of classical China. Yet she was to be important neither for the number of her people nor the size of her borders, but for her distinction as a cultural fountainhead to numerous Himalayan valley kingdoms that ringed her frontiers on every side. Tibetan has for centuries served as the spiritual and academic language of the numerous regions that line India's north, including Ladakh, Lahoul, Spiti, northern Nepal, Sikkim, Bhutan and Assam. All these lands traditionally have sent their best scholars to Tibet for higher learning. Similarly, the spiritual cultures of both Inner and Outer Mongolia, as well as much of Siberia and Western China, have long been deeply rooted in Tibetan Buddhism. Tibet as a piece of real estate was itself of considerable size; as a culture it comprised the whole of Central Asia.

It has been said by numerous Western scholars that the Buddhism of Tibet has been strongly influenced by Tibet's pre-Buddhist religion, or Bön. Undoubtedly there would have been some cultural overlapping, for the language and attitudes of a people will affect the interpretation of any religion brought in from a foreign country and translated from a foreign tongue. Yet as Dr. Evans-Wentz[28] and Lama Govinda[29] point out, the Bön that survived the Buddhist influx seems to have absorbed far more from Buddhism than Buddhism did from Bön. Very few Western scholars realize the extent and intensity of the contact between Tibet and Buddhist India during the classical years of the great translation work. Tibet shares a land border with India and Nepal of some 2,000 miles, and the absorption of Buddhism went on for almost 1,000 years. Tibetan scholars in the early days were expected to spend at least ten years in one of the great monasteries of India, and several of these monasteries, including Nalanda itself, had department houses just for Tibetan students.[30] Hundreds of Indian masters travelled to Tibet, and many stayed for years. Thus the chance for Tibetan Buddhism to have become overly deviated by pre-Buddhist trends is remote. The 6,000 texts in Tibetan that are translated from the Sanskrit would further indicate the intensity of Tibet's efforts to acquire and retain a respectable degree of purity.

The attitudes toward death and dying that formed in Tibet thus were essentially Buddhist ideas. Consequently it is not really possible to understand the Tibetan tradition on death and dying without first acquiring at least a basic comprehension of the Buddhist view of the role of the individual, the nature of the mind and the concept of evolution in the world of samsara, or cyclic existence.

Fundamental to Buddhist thought is the idea of karma and reincarnation.[31] The word *karma*, in Tibetan *las* (pronounced *lay*), literally means action or deed. The theory is that every action we create, be it positive, negative or neutral, leaves an impression or instinct on the mind that will later act as a subconscious predisposition. A person who creates evil will cause his/her mind to become laden with a heavy subconscious predisposition to cruelty. Conversely, a person who creates goodness through acts of love, wisdom and kindness will increase his/her predispositions toward these qualities. Thus karma or action affects our mind and personality in this life, and consequently also influences the patterns our life will take. But more importantly, at the time of our death the karmic seeds we carry within the mind strongly affect our future evolution.

In the Buddhist view, when the body dies the mind enters the *bardo*, or state between death and rebirth, taking with it the karmic instincts it has generated during life. These instincts will be of both positive and negative values, and usually whichever predominates will determine what kind of rebirth we will receive. Generally speaking, people with heavy negative karma will die in negative states of mind, and those with much positive karma will die in positive states, but people with equal positive and negative karma could die in either state of mind. The content of one's mind at the moment of death is said to be of extreme importance in determining one's next rebirth. If we enter the bardo in a negative state of mind we trigger the negative karmic instincts and are led to a miserable rebirth; similarly, to enter the bardo with positive thoughts triggers positive instincts, and results in a positive rebirth. As in a dream, we are led in accordance with the mental content of the moment.

Buddhism speaks of the six realms: the hells, the ghost realms, the animal world, the human plane, and the heavens of the demigods and of the gods. Each of these in its negative aspect corresponds in nature to one of the six root delusions, and whichever of the six predominates at death will determine into which of the six we are to be reborn. For example, the nature of the hells is violence, and this corresponds in nature with the delusion anger. Thus to die in a state of anger produces a mental content similar to the hells and results in a rebirth in hell. Similarly, the nature of the ghost realms is unfulfilled craving, and this corresponds with the delusion attachment. Thus to die with heavy attachment leads to rebirth in the ghost world. The nature of the animal world is suffering due to lack of intelligence, and consequently dying in a state of stupidity, mental cloudiness or narrow-mindedness leads to a rebirth as an animal, insect, etc.

Generally speaking rebirth in the upper realms is of two basic types: that produced from good karma stained by delusion, and that produced by good karma and auspicious mental frameworks.

The former produces a positive rebirth with negative conditions, the latter a positive rebirth with auspicious conditions.

The delusions associated with a negative rebirth in the upper realms are egoism, envy and pride. When these twist the positive karma producing a high rebirth, they cause the auspicious form to be directed in vain and meaningless directions. These three delusions respectively cause negative rebirths as a human, a demigod and a god. The positive karma throws the being to an auspicious realm, but the presence of the delusion causes the happiness of the realm to be misused or withheld.

The Buddhist scriptures speak of karma in different ways. One division is into contaminated and non-contaminated, the former being the seed placed on the mind by any action—good or bad—of an ordinary person. The latter form of karma, non-contaminated karma, is the nature of karma produced by a saint. This type of karma leaves no samsaric seed on the mind; for the saint, being free of karmic compulsions and from delusion, abides in wisdom that does not grasp at the true existence of the act, the performer of the action, or the object of the deed. His action is non-contaminated and places no further instinct on the mind. His karma is enlightened activity.

The contaminated karma is of three principal types: positive, negative and meditative. These are the three roots of samsaric evolution. Together with delusion, they provide the fuel for the ever-burning fires of cyclic existence. Negative karma results in rebirth in one of the three lower realms; positive karma produces rebirth in the human, demigod or sensual god worlds; and meditative karma brings rebirth in the higher heavens of form and formlessness.

Yet in the Buddhist concept a rebirth in any of these realms, no matter how high or pleasurable, is of limited benefit. The ultimate aim is the attainment of the wisdom of enlightenment free from all worldly existence; anything less is ephemeral. Even a high rebirth, when directed by the contaminated karma produced by grasping at true existence, will one day end and the being will fall back to ordinary states of being. In this way we wander on the wheel of life endlessly, being born and dying again and again in accordance with the twelve links of interdependent arising.

Sometimes we hear it said that the theory of karma is fatalistic and promotes nihilism. This attitude can only arise from a misunderstanding of the general principles of the teachings. At every moment we have the choice of action, and as such have the ability to mold our future. The principles of karma are negative when we do not apply self-control, and when we live cruel, harmful lives. They are positive when we use them positively, cultivating love, compassion and wisdom, and generating actions based on these motivations.

Nor is it the case that we necessarily become condemned by our actions. Should we engage the four opponent powers, any degree of negative karma can be overcome. These four are disappointment without negativity, resolve to avoid it in future, relying upon refuge and the bodhimind (see page 50) as forces able to turn away evil, and counteracting the negative karma by means such as meditation upon emptiness, recitation of purification mantras, and so forth. When we apply these four, even the most intense karma is purified.

The spearhead of the theory of karma, the main thrust of the argument for it, is self-responsibility in all we do, say and think. Actions of body, speech and mind are our principal vehicles of interaction and transformation. When we take responsibility for our own actions of body, speech and mind we come to grips with the pivotal point of our being. Without this sense of personal responsibility, there is no hope for us to progress along the Buddhist path. In all three Buddhist vehicles—the Hinayana, Mahayana and Vajrayana paths—it is necessary to accept responsibility for one's karmic flow in order to work with the various levels of training.

Therefore Buddha himself said, 'We are our own worst enemy or we are our own savior.'[32] When we accept karmic responsibility for our own lives and actions we take in our very hands the reins of the horse of our fate. There is nothing fatalistic or nihilistic being expounded in this concept. The theory of karma is rich and dynamic. It is not, as is sometimes said, a means of using the past as an excuse for the failings of the present; primarily it is an attitude of discipline in action as a means of enriching our sense of the past, our lucidity in the present, and our continued growth in the future.

Nor is the concept of reincarnation something totally alien to our own culture. Socrates in his last discourse as recorded by Plato sets forth the highest Greek logic to clarify the reasoning behind his own belief in reincarnation.[33] There is evidence that the early Christians, particularly the Essenes, believed it to be true, and that the theory was not excluded from Christianity until the Council of Nicaea in A.D. 325.[34] Unfortunately, once Rome decided to outlaw the doctrine it became nearly extinct within the known world of the West; yet glimmerings of it nonetheless survived, and the burst of literature on it in the last century of Catholic liberalization would suggest that the underlying sentiment in its favor is perhaps stronger than is acknowledged.

The idea of death, dying, the in-between state and rebirth applies not only to the end of life and what follows. In the Buddhist conception, it occurs every single moment of our lives, and also in every daily cycle. Each moment's consciousness is said to be a product of the fading out and re-arising of a previous moment's consciousness. The present mind is thus a unit born from the death of the last moment's mind. This is an important concept in Buddhism, and because of it enlightenment is possible. It is due to this continual death and rebirth of the mind on a moment to moment basis that change and transformation can operate within our personality. Because of it the mind can either degenerate or improve. Our consciousness can become more subtle and light, or become more gross and heavy. In addition, the split instant between the two thought moments is very important, as it is the primordial nature underlying all mental activity; awareness of it becomes a powerful antidote to delusion.

Each daily cycle also provides us with an experience of death, bardo and rebirth. The moment of falling asleep gives us an experience of clear light like the flash of clear light at the moment of death. The dream state is similar to the bardo and its visions, and the body of a dream similar to the bardo body. Consequently, dream yoga is important in the tantric training; when we can control our thoughts and visions in the dream state we are close to being able to control our mind in the bardo experience.[35] Finally, awakening from a dream is like rebirth; our dream body dies and we arise in a different form than we had conceived of only moments before in our dream.

The study of the mind is of paramount importance in Buddhism. Buddha himself said, 'The mind is the forerunner all events. Like the horse gives directions to the cart, so our mind directs all actions of our body and speech.'[36] The essential purpose of a study of Buddhism is therefore nothing other than a study of the mind and how to cultivate it spiritually.

Death and dying is included in Buddhist studies out of necessity. The death experience is primarily an inner, psychic phenomenon. At death everything we have done and learned during life is put to the supreme test. As the body fails in strength and we fall into ever more subtle levels of consciousness, the degree to which we have spiritually trained ourselves becomes increasingly relevant.

The Tibetan literature on death and dying is therefore essentially inspirational and instructive in nature. Its principal aim is to encourage the seeker of knowledge to embark upon the spiritual quest with full intensity, and to advise us on how this quest is accomplished.

The methods of accomplishing the Buddhist path are threefold: Hinayana, Mahayana and Vajrayana. The training in death awareness is practiced in all three of these, albeit in a different manner in each.

The essence of the trainings of the Hinayana vehicle, firstly, is to develop a sense of moderation and non-attachment. Death awareness is important for this because it provides us with a more real and panoramic view of ourselves and our activities. Normally the untrained mind tends to exaggerate the events of our lives; things and people that give us pleasure are made to seem exceptionally good, and those that have harmed us or threaten us with unpleasantness are made to seem very dark. This respectively gives rise to attachment and aversion, and from these spring forth a host of negative karmic actions. Training in death awareness causes us to see things in a more calm, undisturbed and unaffected light, providing us with a deeper sense of moderation in interaction.

Secondly, death awareness is useful in the general Mahayana trainings. The essence of the Mahayana is great compassion, and when the trainee has a deeply rooted awareness of death it is easy for him/her to feel patience toward the harms caused by others, and to feel love and compassion toward them. Seeing their impermanent nature, he/she responds with great compassion toward any act based on ignorance. An awareness of the impermanence of others, of their proneness to death and dying and their oblivion to it, strengthens the bodhisattva's resolve.

Thirdly, in the Vajrayana, and especially in Highest Yoga Tantra, the trainee is able through meditation to experience the stages of death just as at the time of actually dying. This is the ultimate training in death awareness, providing the practitioner with the ability to enter the death experience during meditation and know precisely what occurs after death. Here the principal topics are the subtle energy channels, energies and points of the subtle body, the manipulation of the sexual substances and the invoking of the most refined bodily energies and levels of consciousness. This is the path that provides the practitioner with the powers to accomplish full Buddhahood in one lifetime.

Not a great deal of the vast reserves of Tibetan materials on death and dying has been translated into English to date. The first to appear was *The Tibetan Book of the Dead*, translated by Lama Kazi-Samdup and edited by Dr. W. Y. Evans-Wentz (Oxford: Oxford University Press, 1927). This work remains as one of the most remarkedly inspired renditions of a Tibetan scripture to appear in the Western world to date, due in no small measure to the charm and wonderful sensitivity that underlay all of Dr. Evans-Wentz's literary endeavors. This work attained such a high level of popularity that it went through numerous reprints and was translated from the English version into most major European tongues. The Tibetan title of the work is the *Bardo Toedol*,[37] or 'Liberation by Hearing [when entering] the Bardo.' Evans-Wentz used the title *The Tibetan Book of the Dead* due to the popularity of *The Egyptian Book of the Dead*[38] and the similarity of the two texts. The text is one of many such Tibetan works in the cycle of literature known as the *bardo ngo-tro*[39] or 'introduction to the nature of the bardo.' Thus a more appro-priate title would perhaps have been *A Tibetan Book of the Dead*. The main difference between the various Tibetan texts in this genre is length, and the mandala deities the text is associated with. *The Tibetan Book of the Dead* is complicated by the fact that it is written in connection to the mandala of the 108 peaceful and wrathful deities of the Zhitro (i.e., 'Peaceful and Wrathful') Cycle,[40] a factor that has confused and baffled most Western readers, to whom these forms mean nothing whatsoever. Nonetheless, the remainder of the text does give us one of the most comprehensive descriptions of the bardo experience, and has intrigued students of Tibetan Buddhism since it first appeared in 1927.

Strangely enough, although *The Tibetan Book of the Dead* was tremendously well received, no further translations of any major Tibetan work on death and dying were to appear for more than fifty years, when Ven. Lati Rinpoche and Professor Jeffrey Hopkins brought out *Death, Intermediate State and Rebirth in Tibetan Buddhism* (London: Rider & Co., 1979), a presentation of a masterful little text by the eighteenth-century Yellow Hat mystic Yangchen Geway Lodro.

The present volume is an attempt to look into the range of Tibetan materials on death, not in terms of giving a bibliographical survey of what exists there but by taking a number of works illustrative of their genre of literature and informative of typical Tibetan attitudes and practices. The aim is not to set forth an array of theories and philosophical interpretations, but to show how the tradition of death and dying works as a living system of practice. It does not seek out the most rare of materials, nor the most abstruse, but rather attempts to reveal the substance of the literary tradition on death and dying as

an embodiment of the sentiment, attitudes and practices that per-
vade Tibetan culture.

The Tibetan materials on the subject number in the thousands, but
they may be categorized within a few characteristic themes or genres.
For my analysis I have chosen nine texts to illustrate seven principal
categories of literature on death and dying. These seven are as follows.

(1) Instructive manuals for the purpose of guiding trainees in death
meditation during this lifetime. These may cover materials from either
the Hinayana, Mahayana or Vajrayana techniques discussed earlier. The
first two of the nine chapters in this collection are of this nature. By the
Thirteenth Dalai Lama and Geshe Ngawang Dargye respectively, the
first of these deals mainly with the Sutrayana, or Hinayana and general
Mahayana methods; the latter surveys both Sutrayana and Vajrayana
methods, giving special attention to the Vajrayana techniques for actually simulating the death experience.

(2) Poetry and prose to inspire us in practice. Chapters three and
nine, by Lama Gungtang and the Seventh Dalai Lama, are used to
illustrate this genre of writing. I chose these two largely due to their
lasting popularity with Tibetan audiences, and because I felt they convey something of the wit of the original (not always possible in a translation).

(3) Inspirational accounts of the deaths of great yogis, meditators
and saints. Nothing is considered to be a more powerful teacher of
death and impermanence than is the passing of one's own guru. It is
said that Buddha passed away in the manner that he did solely in
order to point out the reality of death to his disciples. His last words
were, 'All things are impermanent. Work out your own salvation.' The
Tibetans developed a cycle of literature centered around the deaths of
accomplished practitioners in order to demonstrate the sentiment with
which death should be faced. Chapter four illustrates this type of writing, being a relatively modern account (1954) of the death of a twelfth-
century mystic. Although written not that long ago, it follows the
classical Tibetan style.

(4) Occult materials on the methods of divining prophetic signs of
untimely death. The Tibetans enthusiastically adopted the Indian traditions of divination, amongst which were those methods for determining a danger to one's natural life span or the end of life. The former
divination method was used in order to know when the longevity
yogas were to be applied; the latter to know when death was inevitable
and one should begin the training in the methods of consciousness

transference. Chapter five is a divination manual of this category, being from the pen of the fifteenth-century mystic Karma Lingpa, author of *The Tibetan Book of the Dead*. This type of work is perhaps difficult for a Western audience to appreciate, at least at first glance. But the literature on thanatological divination in Tibet was very popular. The First Dalai Lama himself wrote a treatise on the tradition. I chose the version of Karma Lingpa because it throws light on the inner experiences of the final moments before death, and because it ties in well with the earlier material in chapter two.

(5) Methods for achieving longevity by yogically turning away the advent of untimely death. This has been a pet theme of many Tibetan authors. Literature of this nature often takes the form of meditational guides or ritualistic manuals. Numerous longevity techniques came to Tibet from India, such as those associated with the *Tara-tantra*,[41] the *Ushnisha-vijaya-tantra* and so forth. In chapter six I have used a brief work by the Second Dalai Lama based on the system of the *Amitayus-tantra*, which had been popularized in Tibet by the famous yogi Milarepa during the late eleventh century.

(6) Methods for training the mind in *po-wa*, or consciousness transference at the time of death. Adopted from the general Mahayana and Vajrayana traditions of classical India, these yogas provide the practitioner with a method for training the mind in how to focus at the time of death in order to achieve optimal conditions. There are numerous systems of this yoga, but all are similar in the type of attitudes they advocate as beneficial at the time of death. In chapter seven, I have incorporated a work by the eighteenth-century master Tsechokling, who was the guru of the Eighth Dalai Lama. It is an excellent example of this genre of writing, being clear yet sufficiently detailed to give the reader an understanding of the principles of the technique.

(7) Ritualistic texts to be read in aid of a deceased person. *The Tibetan Book of the Dead* belongs to this class of literature. I have here used a popular manual associated with the *Vajra-bhairava-tantra*, a fundamental yogic method to be applied by a ritualist in order to guide the deceas-ed and encourage him/her to maintain positive attitudes. The work is by the nineteenth-century sage Lama Mahasukha. It is one of the most popular manuals of this class, and conveys succinctly in moving imagery the sentiments to be inspired within the deceased.

I have limited my presentation of the Tibetan tradition on death and dying to these seven principal themes. There are also a number of other classes of literature on the subject outside of these, but as they are not directly related to the living practice tradition I have not incorporated them here. Lati Rinpoche and Jeffrey Hopkins' book *Death, Intermediate State and Rebirth* is in one such category, and there are numerous works of this nature in Tibetan dealing with the doctrinal analysis of the process of death, dying and rebirth. I have not used a manual of this type here because the above-mentioned work is comprehensive and accurate, and any text of this nature would require a volume in itself. In this collection I have tried to stick with literature related directly to practice and the tradition of death and dying as a living spiritual tradition, the religious and mystical writings that have shaped and toned the character of the Tibetan attitude. I would, however, highly recommend *Death, Intermediate State and Rebirth in Tibetan Buddhism* as an excellent supplement to this volume, giving an overview of the processes involved.

Another interesting category of literature on death is the *day-lok*, or 'returned from the dead' material.[42] These are the various accounts of people who have died and mysteriously come back to life. There are hundreds of these in Tibetan of differing lengths, although most are hundreds of pages long. They are somewhat reminiscent of early Greek accounts of people who died, went to Hades and returned. Usually the dead person meets with deceased relatives and friends, as well as with famous personages of old, and is asked to take back messages to the living. After coming back to life the person is often moved to embark upon the life style of a wandering prophet, travelling from place to place relating his/her experience and warning those who will listen to take heed and avoid evil, the cause of suffering in the hereafter, and to cultivate goodness, the cause of happiness. I have not included a work of this nature in this collection as the formidable length of the texts available to me convinced me that any serious study of these would require a separate publication in itself.

Throughout my efforts in bringing together the ideas and Tibetan materials that form the substance of this book, my main interest has been to bring to light those aspects of the Tibetan literature on death and dying that will provide the reader with an insight into the system as a whole, as a way of perceiving the world and our position and function in it. For example, I have also avoided exotica, such as the manuals on methods of mummifying the dead[43] (also quite popular in Tibet), wrathful methods of bringing the dead back to life, shamanic methods of animating corpses, and other such facets of the Tibetan literary tradition that, although fascinating, do not make any realistic contribution to the modern world. My aim has been to try and deal with the human elements, the traditions that reach out across times and cultures, in the hope that something in the tradition may add a degree of stimulus, some small input, into the present studies of death and dying. Tibet had one of the few very ancient cultures of the world to come into the present age intact, unaffected by the colonial era and the destruction of the great wars that have plagued the materialistic societies of the last two centuries. It is possible that this very ancient sentiment coupled with the lofty spirituality that was poised in the hearts of the Tibetan Buddhist mystics on the Roof of the World may still today carry some meaning to a planet at a crossroads of self-destruction and the dawning of a new renaissance. Certainly Tibet had a marvelously complex culture, and as such it belongs the world's cultural reservoir; and if tapping some of its waters somehow enriches our collective perception, purifying the polluted rivers of a time overwhelmed by fear, aggression and materialistic grasping, or even if but a few living beings find some real and beneficial spiritual meaning in these ancient texts by some of the greatest masters of the Land of Snows, then my purpose in compiling this work will not have been in vain.

Concerning his efforts to preserve the Tibetan cultural tradition in the face of the Chinese invasion of Tibet and attempts to eradicate the Tibetan spiritual legacy, His Holiness the Dalai Lama has stated:

> If there is something in our tradition of benefit to mankind, it is our responsibility to preserve it in the face of any obstacle. Spiritual culture is a thing that transcends race, national borders and even time. Worldly culture, no matter how quaint, has no lasting value; but spiritual culture does. Therefore those aspects of Tibetan culture which were merely qualities of the time and place of old Tibet need not be saved. But if there are traditions that are truly beneficial to mankind now and in the future, we would be weak, foolish and irresponsible to let them become lost or destroyed. I believe our ideas and methods for knowing the nature of the mind and cultivating the spirit belong to the category of what is useful to mankind. They do not belong to the Tibetans; we are merely their safekeepers. Therefore I and my people are making every effort to see that these facets of our culture are not lost with the loss of Tibet as a nation. They must endure for our children and our children's children, and those in the community of mankind who are able to benefit from them.[44]

Buddhism has been the religion of almost half the world's population at some time or another, and Tibet served as a repository of classical Indian Buddhism as did no other nation. It is not impossible that something from within these ancient teachings will be of relevance to modern people. Our technology has changed somewhat, as have the toys with which we amuse ourselves, but the fundamental nature of the human body and mind are much the same as they were in the time of Buddha. The nature of consciousness, the eye, and the world seen by the eye consciousness have not changed in fundamental nature. We may live a decade or so longer than most people did in the time of Buddha—although Buddha himself lived to the age of eighty-two— but we still meet with a death that is no less real than was the death of the peoples of old.

The present age is a time in which the world is becoming increasingly small, and the various world cultural centers are interchanging knowledge with one another at an amazing rate. Tibet was one of the four great cultural centers of Asia, but due to its natural geographic isolation from the Western world it is one of the last to enter the international arena. This isolation also had the advantage of permitting it to enter the present time in relative cultural purity. We owe it to ourselves to take a look at what the master philosophers and meditators of this profoundly spiritual land had to say, and to search and sift through the Tibetan cultural treasury to examine whether or not there is anything that can help humankind along the road to understanding. The East is presently learning all it can from the West, and will reap the according rewards. From our side, we should overcome our cultural snobbery and see if perhaps there is not something in the East to serve of benefit to us. The key to learning and development is openmindedness and intelligent curiosity. Intellectual or spiritual vanity have never helped anyone progress. The Tibetan tradition has fostered a deeply thought spiritual culture for many centuries now, and has served as the Mecca of Mahayana Buddhists for longer than the Americas have even appeared on European maps of the known world. Its past speaks for and gives evidence to its greatness. We owe it to posterity to look at the findings of the Tibetan masters, and to test their ideas in the light of modern thought.

The preparation of this book has been a tremendous joy to me. I hope that there are those who will also take a joy in reading and studying it. Death and dying is only a morose subject at face value; it also has its wonderful and amazing side. The Tibetan thinkers developed a unique way of looking at and into it, a way that laughs and cries a little with each glance. They appreciate the darkness and tragedy of death, but they also see light and freedom in it. Their sentiment carries a sense of both idealism and realism, hope and sadness. In my twelve years with the Tibetan refugees in northern India I witnessed the deaths of numerous lay people and masters, and saw the reactions of those involved. The depth with which this culture lives the philosophy it expounds is truly moving. One year in Bodh Gaya the Dalai Lama gave a week of teachings and initiations, and over 100,000 people came from the various Himalayan kingdoms. Babies were born in this time, and several old people died. One night I saw an old man sitting under a tree. He sat in peace and serenity, quietly saying his prayers and rejoicing in his good fortune at having made it to the holy place of Bodh Gaya at such an auspicious time. He looked over at the group I was with and beamed us an enormous smile. A few minutes later he leaned back against the tree and, still sitting in the meditation posture, passed away. His face expressed perfect contentment. When his family noticed that he had died, they sent out for the family lama, who came with a small group of colleagues and began reading prayers beside him. They let him sit there all night, as they sat beside him chanting and meditating. At dawn they took him on a palanquin and carried him down to the banks of the river. There, with the family in attendance, they cremated his remains. After the cremation the family gathered his ashes and scattered them under the trees that grow near the great temple at Bodh Gaya, watering them with a few silent tears. That afternoon they were back at the Dalai Lama's sermon, almost as though nothing had happened; yet as they listened to the Dalai Lama talk, one could sense their awareness of the loss of their grandfather, an awareness that bore the loss with a beauty, strength and dignity that equalled the expression of contentment that had been the old man's last message to his people.

The Tibetan race is a strong, hearty and robust lineage, and their culture one of the most spiritual that the earth has seen in our recorded history. It gives me great pleasure to have lived with them for so many years, a sense of honor to have known the Dalai Lama and his four gurus[45]—all four of whom have since passed away—and a sense of responsibility to have studied for so long with so many of the greatest masters to have hailed from the Land of Snows. It is not possible to express the respect that I feel toward this rare species of mankind, nor to repay the kindness they showed me over the years, but as an act of respect and a token of my profound gratitude, I dedicate this work to them. I also dedicate it to the late Dr. W.Y. Evans-Wentz, who first brought forth accurate translations of Tibetan materials to the West and laid the foundations for much of what since has come to pass in the field of Tibetology.

In closing I should also add a note on the system of transliteration of Sanskrit and Tibetan terms and names. I have not used the diacritical marks on the Sanskrit words in the text itself; these appear only in the notes at the end. My own feeling on these is that they provide only irritation to the general reader, who never knows what to make of them, and that the Sanskrit scholar to whom they will be meaningful in fact has no need of them, as he/she usually knows the original Sanskrit of what is being said.

Tibetan words always create a problem in transliteration. Throughout the text I have given them only as they are pronounced. The literal spellings are used only in the notes and glossary. Tibetan abounds with silent prefix, suffix, superscript and subscript characters, and the rules on what they do to the sound are exceedingly complex. 'Blo-bzang-grags-pa,' for example, is pronounced simply as 'Lobzang Drakpa'; 'bsTan-pa' simply as 'Tenpa.' The silent letters only confuse the uninitiated.

Sir Winston Churchill, as noted a grammarian as he was a politician, once wisely commented on the use of the hyphen, 'It is a blemish on the English language. Except when nature revolts, dispense with it.' Even though I generally agree with this view, I have nonetheless used the hyphen in Sanskrit and Tibetan words when not to do so runs a high risk of mispronunciation. It occasionally seems to be the only safe way of handling the extraordinary length of some Sanskrit terms and names, and the only way of solving the problem of groups of consonants that so often begin and end Tibetan syllables, e.g. Wang-gyal, Sang-gye, Song-tsen. Also, when the letter 'g' appears at the beginning of a syllable I transliterate it in the text as 'g,' but if at the end of a syllable then usually as 'k,' this being more true to pronunciation.

Chapter One
Death and the Bodhisattva Trainings

*Then it is a fact, O Simmias, that true philosophers make death and dying
their profession....*

—Socrates in Plato's *Phaedo*

TRANSLATOR'S PREAMBLE

The material in this first chapter is taken from the volume of sermons
given by the Thirteenth Dalai Lama, Gyalwa Tubten Gyatso, on the
occasion of the first full moon of each Tibetan New Year.[1] This annual
discourse represents the climax of the Great Prayer Festival of Lhasa,
a religious fête that begins on the day before the new moon of Febru-
ary and lasts for fifteen days, culminating in the sermon of the full
moon.[2] The tradition of the Great Prayer Festival was initiated by Lama
Tsongkhapa, guru of the First Dalai Lama, early in the fifteenth century, and has continued to the present day. The present Dalai Lama
maintains the tradition in Dharamsala, India.

Throughout the centuries the full moon sermon of the festival has
been delivered by the Dalai Lama incarnation or, in his absence or mi-
nority, an appointed high lama. The sermon that I have selected for this
chapter was delivered in the spring of 1921, when the Thirteenth Dalai
Lama was in the last year of his three-year retreat. In this discourse he
chose as his theme the Kadam lineage of meditation upon death, probably due to the trans-sectarian nature of this transmission. This tradition had been brought to Tibet in A.D. 1042 by Jowo Atisha, who was

invited to the Land of Snows by the king of Western Tibet and remained there until his death some thirteen years later. To show the lineage and subject of the sermon to follow, the Thirteenth opens with a verse from Atisha's writings that refers to death and impermanence.

The Atisha lineages did not remain confined to any one order of Tibetan Buddhism. Within a century of his demise they had spread to all regions of the Land of Snows and had influenced all Tibetan sects. They became the basis for the Kargyu order as outlined in Gampopa's *The Jewel Ornament of Liberation*,[3] the Sakya as embodied in *Separation from the Four Attachments*,[4] the Nyingma as reflected in *Instructions on the Great Fulfillment*,[5] and the Geluk as presented in *The Great Exposition of the Stages in the Path to Enlightenment*[6] by Lama Tsongkhapa.

The Thirteenth Dalai Lama's discourse thus serves as an excellent opening chapter, providing us with an inside view of a tradition of death meditation that is fundamental to all schools of Tibetan Buddhism. Thus we get to see it not as an isolated spiritual exercise but in context to the path as an organic entity.

The Thirteenth was the first of the Dalai Lamas to be known intimately by Western people. His era was not an easy one. Wedged by British India on the south, expanding Tsarist Russia on the north and the unstable Manchu Dynasty on the east, Tibet was a continual target for the intrigues of these three superpowers. At the turn of the century it seemed as though Lhasa might go pro-Russian, so the British, always jealous of Russian designs in Central Asia, launched an invasion into Tibet in 1904 from India.[7] This event, known to history as the Younghusband Expedition, resulted in the victory of British power in Central Asia, and the following summer a treaty was drawn up in which Tibet was forced to leave its foreign policy under the suzerainty of British-influenced China, a move the British felt would remove Tibet sufficiently from Russian influence while not angering Russia to the point of confrontation (as placing Tibet directly under the British umbrella would have). Strangely enough, Lt. Col. Young-husband, leader of the British forces, fell into a mystical trance when in Tibet, an experience that was to transform his life, and soon thereafter he returned to England, retired from the military and dedicated the remainder of his life to writing on spiritual affairs!

But Tibet was not content with the proximity to China that she had been forced into, and attempted to assert her independence to the world. China, on the other hand, was encouraged by the British policy and felt that the time had come for her to show a strong hand with the

Tibetans. She launched an invasion in 1909, but fate would prove her move to be ill-timed, and a year later civil war erupted in China proper The Chinese forces in Tibet, cut off from supplies and reinforcements, surrendered to the Tibetans in 1912. To add insult to injury, the Thirteenth had them march to Calcutta and return to China by ship, rather than directly via the overland route. No Chinese were allowed in Tibet from this time until after the Thirteenth's death in 1933.

Matters of state thus set in order, the Thirteenth returned to a quiet spiritual life after the China affair had been settled. In 1918 he entered the traditional three-year retreat, which he completed in 1921, the year in which this discourse was given. Several British officials were in Lhasa from the time of the expulsion of the Chinese. Among them, Sir Charles Bell, who had been Britain's liaison with the Dalai Lama from 1910-1912, visited in 1921, and became a close confidant of the Tibetan leader. Sir Charles' excellent biography of the Thirteenth, *Portrait of a Dalai Lama*,[8] gives us a wonderfully clear picture of life in Tibet during these crucial years. It is a tribute to the Thirteenth that he was able to guide his people through these troubled times without a major mishap. Unfortunately after his death in 1933 Tibet suffered from internal turmoil, but then, this seems to have been a worldwide disease during the 1930s and 1940s.

The Thirteenth Dalai Lama had been born in 1876 of peasant stock. Perhaps due to his humble background he always remained a 'people's Dalai Lama.' Many of his sermons were given openly, and his students came from all walks of life. The discourse that forms the basis for this chapter was just such a sermon, having been delivered to a mixed audience of more than 20,000 of his disciples. Because it was directed at both learned scholar/yogis and the most simple of listeners, it combines profundity and simplicity with a lucid charm that characterizes many of the Thirteenth's works. It provides the reader with an easy access to a view of the Tibetan tradition of death meditation and a perspective on how this tradition relates to the general system of Buddhist training.

DEATH AND THE BODHISATTVA TRAININGS

by Gyalwa Tubten Gyatso, the Thirteenth Dalai Lama

As was stated by Jowo Atisha, crown ornament of all the Buddhist sages of India and source of all the Kadampa oral transmissions:

> This life is short
> And the objects of knowledge many.
> Moreover, when we shall die
> Is something unknown to us.
> Be therefore like the swan,
> Which can separate milk from water.[1]

We living beings are in a difficult situation. Helplessly overpowered by the three psychic poisons of attachment, aversion and misknowledge, we are propelled and guided largely by negative karma and afflicted emotions. In our constant craving for samsaric indulgence in the repeated cycle of birth and death since beginninglessness, we have again and again drawn ourselves into situations of frustration, suffering and pain. Again and again we have died and taken rebirth on the basis of ignorance and the twelve links of causation.

However, amidst the suffering and confusion that predominates in the lower forms of life, we humans have managed, as a product of previous positive karmic instincts, to find an auspicious life form capable of spiritual endeavor. In short, the ripening effect of our positive karmic seeds has provided us with a very special and precious life form: that of a human being blessed by the eight freedoms and ten endowments.[2]

Not only have we been reborn as humans, we have also met with spiritual teachings and thus have the opportunity to accomplish the paths to higher being, enlightenment and eternal happiness. Yet this auspicious human form that we have found will not last for long. Even the Buddhas themselves were unable to prophesy the length of life of each individual human being.

Although we bring forth scriptural quotations from the sutras and tantras taught by Buddha, or set out a great display of reasoning, or rely upon other conventional means of persuasion, nonetheless our lives will not last forever. Before long our existence as part of humanity shall cease.

As our lives will be short, we should be like the swan, which if given milk mixed with water can, due to a special faculty of its beak, separate the two and drink only the milk, spitting out the water. When we know how to practice the spiritual path, each day provides us with the ability to extract the milk of goodness and joy and to spit out the ways of negative being that lead to frustration and misery.

At present we have the inner and outer conditions by which the path to enlightenment and everlasting happiness may be accomplished. We should not let the opportunity slip by, thinking, 'I will practice tomorrow or the next day.' Do not be deceived even for a moment by the laziness of self-indulgence, which becomes entranced by the alluring images of the eight worldly concerns and loses sight of the spiritual path in its attachment to the ephemeral, transient pursuits which benefit this life alone.

One should strive with utter concentration to take the essence of this precious human incarnation by accomplishing the path to enlightenment and higher being. Then when the time comes for us to die we will be able to do so with confidence and serenity instead of regret and confusion, and thus will be able to find our way to a conducive rebirth. We should make our prime concern the accomplishment of the spiritual path and, to this end, should endeavor to practice the Dharma as intensely and purely as possible.

The practices to be accomplished are collectively known as the Dharma. It is said that the Buddha, seeing that the living beings were afflicted by 84,000 delusions and emotional disturbances, expounded the 84,000 aspects of Dharma as a remedy to these.

In terms of the written word these 84,000 teachings are subsumed under the three categories of scripture: the *Vinayapitaka*, *Sutrapitaka* and *Abhidharmapitaka*, or, respectively, the 'Collection on Discipline,' 'Collection of Discourses' and 'Collection on Metaphysics.' In terms of actual content they are subsumed under the three higher trainings of discipline, meditation and wisdom.

Another way to divide the Doctrines of Buddha is into the twofold category of Hinayana and Mahayana vehicles. In this context the Mahayana Vehicle includes the teachings of both the exoteric Perfection Vehicle, or *Paramitayana*, and the esoteric *Vajrayana*, the tantric path.

Both of these Mahayana vehicles take as their main gateway the altruistic bodhimind, the aspiration to gain enlightenment as the best means of benefitting the world. For all Mahayanists, the bodhimind is the key point in practice.

When Jowo Atisha was asked about his teacher Serlingpa[3] [the Indonesian master Dharmakirti], he touched his hands together in a gesture of reverence, tears came to his eyes and he replied, 'Whatever Mahayana spirit I have attained is due only to the kindness of that great guru.

Even when I would see him ten times in a day he would each time ask me, "Is the spirit of enlightenment, the bodhimind, blended in with your thoughts? His emphasis upon the cultivation of the bodhimind was always first and foremost.'

Thus although the Buddha taught 84,000 practices, we as Mahayanists should always make our foremost concern the cultivation of the bodhimind, the bodhisattva spirit of enlightenment, the mind of equanimity, love, compassion and empathy, which seeks full omniscience for the benefit of all living beings. Progress in all other Mahayana practices depends upon progress in the cultivation of the bodhimind.

Concerning the nature of the bodhimind, the text *Seven Points for Training the Mind*,[4] which embodies the oral tradition given by the Indonesian master Serlingpa to Atisha, states:

> The bodhimind is like a diamond scepter,
> The sun and a medicinal tree.

In spiritual training, the bodhimind is like a diamond. Just as a diamond can eradicate poverty and fulfill all needs, the bodhimind eradicates spiritual poverty and fulfills all spiritual needs. Just as a fragment of a diamond outshines all other ornaments, even a partial development of the bodhimind surpasses more complete achievements in lesser practices. A tiny piece of diamond is far more precious than a large piece of a lesser gem.

The bodhimind is like the sun in dispersing darkness. When the sun rises, how can darkness remain? A sun rising over an entire continent illuminates the entire land. In the same way, the generation of the bodhisattva spirit within ourselves is like the rising of the sun of the mind.

The bodhimind is also likened to a medicinal tree. The tree as a whole is an effective antidote to all 404 types of diseases, and also its individual components such as leaves and berries have their own individual healing abilities, their unique powers to cure specific diseases. Similarly, if we develop the bodhimind within ourselves we become cured of every spiritual affliction, thus attaining full enlightenment. Even if we only develop a few small branches of the bodhi-sattva spirit, these will have their own spiritually reviving effects.

To have generated merely the foundations of the altruistic bodhimind is to gain the title of 'bodhisattva,' the Awakening Warrior. One may extensively cultivate other spiritual qualities, such as concentrations and formless absorptions resulting from the training in higher wisdom, and through these practices may even gain the exalted states of a *shravaka arhat* or *pratyekabuddha*,[5] yet anyone who has trained in the bodhisattva spirit will always surpass these lesser adepts purely by means of the essential nature of his/her path.

The bodhimind has the inherent ability to remedy the inner darkness of emotional afflictions and delusions, such as falsely grasping at the nature of the self and phenomena. As it has the power to cure the mind of the roots of cyclic suffering—the product of delusion and compulsive karmic patterns—it is indeed a supreme medicine, having both conventional means for curing conventional afflictions and ultimate means for dealing with deeper spiritual problems.

This is what is meant by the expression 'method and wisdom combined.' There is the training in the conventional bodhimind practices of patience, love, compassion and so forth; and also the training in the ultimate bodhimind, which is the wisdom of emptiness that realizes the most profound and essential nature of the mind, body and world around us. When we accomplish the ultimate bodhimind, we attain everlasting emancipation from the imperfect world of suffering and confusion. We then become an Arya, a High One, a transcended being who is free from samsaric claws. When this is achieved on the basis of a training in the conventional bodhimind, we go on to actualize fully omniscient knowledge and the complete powers of a Buddha's body, speech and mind. This provides us with the ability to fulfill the bodhisattva spirit by manifesting in the world as is most effective in the uplifting of sentient life, while ourselves retaining complete abilities to maintain absorption in the vision of highest truth. Thus the bodhimind is a most precious method, and one should make every effort to accomplish it in its two aspects of conventional and ultimate.

How does one approach the trainings in the two levels of bodhimind? This is stated as follows in the text *Seven Points for Training the Mind:*[6]

First train in the preliminaries.

In the beginning one must seek a qualified teacher possessing a valid lineage, and from him/her must receive the transmission teachings. Here it is said that one should carefully select one's teacher, and that after entering training should try to cultivate the attitude that regards the guru as an embodiment of all the Buddhas. He/she is to be seen as all enlightened beings, who manifest as ordinary people in order to train persons such as oneself. Practicing constant mindfulness of how the guru shows the kindness of unveiling the path to us, try to please him/her in the three ways: by making the threefold offering of respect, attention and sincere practice of the teachings.

The cultivation of an effective working relationship with a spiritual master is the foundation of all other trainings. It is the very life of the path to enlightenment. If we wish to become great bodhisattvas, we must first learn the methods of achieving the bodhisattva stages. Then we must accomplish the practices under competent guidance. If our own attitudes are not conducive to training, progress will be difficult. Consequently trainees are advised to regard the teacher as an embodiment of all the Buddhas. This is in fact the function the guru performs in our life.

The next important preliminary is meditation upon the precious nature of human life. We must learn to appreciate the special qualities of human existence and the spiritual opportunities with which it provides us. The scripture *A Collection of Everything Valuable*[7] states:

> By means of spiritual training
> One leaves behind the eight bondages
> Which share the nature of animal existence,
> And by training one always gains
> The eight freedoms and ten endowments.

The eight freedoms enjoyed by humans are set in contrast to eight states of bondage. Four of these are likened to four nonhuman states: the continual pains of the hells, the constant craving of the ghosts, the vicious stupidity and shortsightedness of the animal world and the sensual indulgence and spiritual apathy of the samsaric divinities who have gained all worldly perfections. The remaining four are undesirable human states: being born as a barbarian in a land where spiritual knowledge is nonexistent; having imperfect sensory powers, such as being retarded or demented; being born at a time when spiritual teachings are unavailable; and living under the influence of extremely negative views contrary to the nature of the spiritual path.

These are the eight states of bondage. If we have freedom from them, we may count ourselves as fortunate indeed.

The ten endowments are in two sets, personal and environmental. The former of these are given as follows in a verse by Nagarjuna:[8]

> Being born as a human being
> In a spiritually civilized land,
> Having full sensory capacities,

Not having committed severely negative karmas,
And having interest in spiritual practice—
These are the five personal endowments.

These five personal factors provide one with an effective inner basis on which to strive for enlightenment.

Nagarjuna then states the five environmental endowments as follows:

Being born in an era when a Buddha has manifested,
When the holy Dharma has been taught,
When the Doctrine is still in existence,
When there are practitioners of the Doctrine,
And being shown supportive kindness by others—
These are the five environmental endowments.

These five factors provide us with the external prerequisites of practice. They are called environmental endowments as they are qualities of the world in which we find ourselves rather than personal qualities directly connected with our own body or mind.

Any man or woman who possesses these eight freedoms and ten endowments is in a position to attain full and perfect enlightenment in one short lifetime. This is not an opportunity known to lesser forms of life. If we direct our lives to intense training, we can attain utter spiritual perfection, not to mention being able to fulfill every conventional aim. Human life is most precious, and we who have gained it should make every effort to take its essence. We should again and again meditate upon the eight freedoms and ten endowments, until intense appreciation of the human potential is constantly blended into our stream of being.

Consider also how rare is the human life form in comparison to the immeasurably large number of animals, insects and so forth. At the moment we have all the opportunities of human existence at our disposal, but if we ignore them for transient, worldly pursuits, there is not much hope that after our death we will regain an auspicious rebirth. Those who die bereft of spiritual training have little hope of happiness in the hereafter.

Once one has developed a solid appreciation of the human potential, it is important to take up meditation upon impermanence and death. In the Atisha tradition coming from Guru Serlingpa of Indonesia, this means practicing meditation upon three subjects: the definite nature of death, the uncertainty of the time of death, and the fact that at the time of death nothing except spiritual training is of any real value. These are known as 'the three roots.' Each of these three root subjects in turn has three lines of reasoning to support it, and finally there are three convictions to be generated. Therefore the meditation is known as 'three roots, nine reasonings and three convictions.' This is the principal method of meditating upon death as handed down from the great Kadampa masters of old.

The first subject is the definite nature of death. Three lines of reasoning are to be contemplated. (1) The Lord of Death comes to us all sooner or later, and at that time nothing can be done to turn him away. (2) There is no way to extend our life span indefinitely, and our time is continually running out on us in an unbroken stream. (3) Thirdly, even while we are alive we find very little time to dedicate to spiritual practice.

To speak of these three points in more detail: (1) The Lord of Death shall definitely come one day to destroy us. No matter how wonderful a body we may have, it does not pass beyond the reaches of death. 'The Chapter on Impermanence' in *The Tibetan Dhammapada*[9] states:

> The Buddha himself, as well as his disciples
> The mighty shravaka arhats and pratyekabuddhas,
> Have all left behind their bodies.
> What need be said of ordinary mortals?

Just before passing away Buddha told his monks, 'O spiritual aspirants, take heed. It is rare to meet with an enlightened being. All phenomena are impermanent. This is the final teaching of the Tathagata.' Having spoken these words the Master passed into the sphere of *parinirvana*.

Similarly in India and Tibet many masters, yogis, great religious kings, scholarly saints and so forth have appeared in history, but without exception all have passed away. We can read the details in their biographies. All the kind teachers of ancient times demonstrated the drama of passing into *parinirvana* in order to impress the reality of impermanence upon the minds of those to be trained. How, then, can we mere mortals who are so attached to our contaminated samsaric aggregates hope to be beyond the laws of impermanence and death? There is not a single sentient being who has lived since the beginning of the world without passing through the cycle of repeated birth, death and rebirth.

It is said in *The Sutra of Advice to a King*:[10]

> The four great sufferings of birth, sickness, age and death destroy
> all achievements, just as four mountains crumbling into one

another destroy all foliage in the way. It is not easy to escape by running, exerting physical force, bribery, magic, spiritual practice or medicine.

When the time of death arrives one may take the most expensive medicines, or may make elaborate ritual offerings to the most powerful guardian angel, yet death will not be turned away for long.

(2) There is no way to extend our life span indefinitely, and our time is constantly passing. The time that has already passed since our birth has mostly been dedicated to meaningless activity. Of what remains, this is steadily being eaten up year by year, the years by months, the months by days and the days by moments. Before we are ready for it, death will be upon us.

The Seventh Dalai Lama, Gyalwa Kalzang Gyatso, sums up our situation as follows:[11]

> From our very birth, life pauses not for a moment
> But races onward toward the great Lord of Death,
> Life is a walk down a wide road leading to death,
> A melancholy scene, a criminal being led to his execution.

Like water dripping steadily from a container, and like a ball of wool constantly being unraveled, our life continually approaches its end, which moment by moment comes ever more near.

(3) Moreover, even while alive we dedicate very little of our time to spiritual endeavor. *The Sutra on Entering into the Womb*[12] states:

> Ten years are given to childhood, and during our final twenty years the body and mind are not strong enough to embark upon the spiritual path with any great degree of success.

During the first twenty years of one's life, thoughts of the spiritual path are rare, and during the last twenty years one's powers of memory and penetration are too weak to accomplish much. Moreover, it is difficult to have confidence in the belief that one will live to see old age. Many people do not.

Of what remains of our life, half goes to sleeping, eating, collecting the requisites of life, and so forth. As the illustrious Kadampa master Geshe Chekhawa once said:

> A person who lives until the age of sixty will, after subtracting the time taken by sleeping, eating, gathering requisites and other such distracting activity, have only five years or so left for the practice of the spiritual path. And much of this will be lost to impure practice.

This is the nature of our situation. Therefore we should decide to practice the spiritual path now, without procrastination. As is stated in *A Letter to King Kanika:*[13]

> The merciless Lord of Death
> Kills all beings without discrimination.
> Hence for so long as he has not come,
> The wise live in mindfulness of him.

When we plan to travel to a foreign country, we first gather the necessities of the journey. As it is definite that we must travel to the land of death, we should prepare ourselves through study, contemplation and meditation upon the path. We should generate a firm conviction to engage single-pointedly in spiritual endeavor, and to gain the inner qualities that give birth to the power to die with confidence.

These are the three lines of reasoning contemplated in conjunction with the first topic, the definite nature of death.

The second topic, the indefinite nature of the time of death, also is supported by three lines of reasoning.

(1) The life span of those living on this planet is not fixed. Legend relates that the life span of the humans on the mythological planet Draminyen is 1,000 years in length, but we on Earth have no set life span.

Vasubandhu's *An Encyclopedia of Buddhist Metaphysics*[14] states:

> Human life has no fixed span. At the end of an aeon the average life span is only ten years in length, and at the beginning it is thousands.

It does not matter whether one is young, old or middle-aged. Death can come to us at any time. As is said in *The Tibetan Dhammapada:*[15]

> Of the people seen in the morning,
> Many are not seen [alive] at night.
> And many people alive at night
> Are no longer alive the next morning.
>
> Boys and girls meet with death,
> And adolescents meet with death.
> What youth can say that
> Death will not come to him soon?
>
> Some die in the womb,
> Some die just after birth,
> Some die as infants
> And some in their later childhood.
>
> Some die in old age, some in youth
> And some in the prime of life.
> Death comes to all
> Whenever the appropriate conditions ripen.

Just as death can come to others at any time, we can be sure that we ourselves live under the constant threat of sudden death.

(2) The causes of death are many and the forces supporting life few. *The Precious Garland*[16] states:

> The conditions bringing death are many,
> The forces sustaining life are slender
> And even these can cause death.
> Therefore constantly practice Dharma.

There are countless causes of death, such as disease, accidents, harmful people and beasts, and so forth. Any of these could strike at any time. In addition, the forces sustaining our life, such as food, shelter, property, etc., can become causes of our death. Food may turn poisonous, our house may fall on us, and other sustaining factors can become causes of death. We can lose our life gathering the requisites of livelihood, or lose it in protecting our possessions. In brief, as Nagarjuna says in *The Precious Garland:*

> We constantly live under the threat of death,
> Like a butter lamp placed in a windstorm.

(3) Our body is in fact very fragile. Nagarjuna writes in his *Letter to a Friend:*[17]

> Earth, mountains and oceans
> Will burn with the heat of seven suns
> And not a trace will remain.
> What then of the frail bodies of mankind?

The most solid external phenomena are impermanent. All living beings share this same transient nature. The slightest change in our environment or internal bodily system can cause our death at any time. It is not enough simply to determine to practice Dharma. As the time when death will fall is unpredictable, we must determine to practice Dharma purely, without procrastination, and without mixing our practice with worldly concerns.

A Letter to King Kanika[18] relates:

> The Lord of Death, without procrastination,
> Strikes suddenly at unexpected times.
> Do not say, 'I will begin practice tomorrow.'
> Engage in the supreme path now.

The third topic to be contemplated is the fact that at the time of death nothing but spiritual training is of value. Once again, three lines of reasoning are to be contemplated. (1) Although we are surrounded by a hundred kind friends, not one of them will be able to accompany us after death. (2) Even if we have wealth and property equal to Mt. Meru in size, we cannot take along a single atom of it. We will have to enter the hereafter naked and alone. (3) Even this body that we have cherished as our own from the moment we left our mother's womb will have to be abandoned and left behind. Nothing will continue but our stream of consciousness and the positive and negative karmic instincts that it carries, the karmic seeds that were developed during our lifetime. If at that time one sees that due to attachment to friends, relatives, property and one's body one has wasted one's life and only generated a great deal of negative karma, the mind will be over-whelmed by regret, like a man who suddenly realizes that he has eaten a lethal dose of poison and it is too late to apply the antidote.

One should firmly determine that from now on even at the cost of one's life one will not fall under the misguiding influence of the eight worldly concerns, such as pleasure and pain, fame and notoriety, etc. Resolve to avoid worldly interests just as you would avoid stepping in excrement.

A Letter to King Kanika[19] relates:

> Except for positive and negative karmic seeds,
> We enter the hereafter with nothing.
> Nobody can accompany us.
> Before that time, become a treasury of spiritual knowledge.

The early Kadampa masters always cultivated five preliminary meditations: the preciousness and rarity of the human life form, death and impermanence, the karmic laws of cause and effect, the general and specific shortcomings of unenlightened existence, and the nature and procedures of taking refuge and entering the spiritual path. These preliminary trainings are very important, for they make one into a vessel suitable for the higher methods.

Some people have little respect for the preliminary trainings, and regard the higher methods with great reverence. However, although generally speaking gold is more precious than water, to a man nearly dead from thirst the water will be the more useful. Only after he has had his fill of water and thus revived himself will gold be of interest to him. We practitioners who are on the initial stages of development, who have been under the influence of the three psychic poisons for countless lifetimes, should first think about how to make firm the foundations of the path while the slender thread of our life span remains unbroken. Until the basis is laid, forget about chasing after the higher practices, such as those of the tantric path, which are beyond our present abilities. Once the foundations are secure, the higher teachings of the sutras and tantras become meaningful. In the beginning it is more important to generate a confident understanding of the preliminaries by receiving direct meditational instructions from a qualified master and then cultivating an inner experience. We should make sincere efforts to fathom the more subtle levels of the basic trainings. Only then can we enter the higher practices with the prescribed degree of competence and maturity.

The text *Seven Points for Training the Mind*[20] states:

> When proficiency [in the preliminaries] is attained,
> The secret teachings can be given.

One should first gain confidence in the method side of practice, such as meditation on death and the cultivation of the conventional bodhimind of love, compassion and the aspiration to highest enlightenment as the most effective means of benefitting the world. Then one can receive the wisdom teachings on the nature of the self, mind and phenomena. The foundations must be made firm before the higher paths can be approached. Otherwise, progress will be obstructed or distorted.

We should take our example from Geshe Chekhawa, the bodhisattva who wrote down the text *Seven Points for Training the Mind*. Although famed for tremendous learning in both the sutras and tantras, he was not satiated and wished to arrive at the heart of practice through following a quintessential oral transmission teaching on the development of the bodhimind. One time when he was visiting Geshe Chakzhingpa he happened to see a verse from the short work *Eight Verses for Training the Mind*,[21] a Mahayana oral transmission written in eight short verses. Most impressed, he asked who had penned the text. Discovering the author to be the renowned Geshe Langri Tangpa, he left immediately in search of this great master. However, when he arrived at Lhasa he learned that Langri Tangpa had already passed away. He also learned that Langri Tangpa's two main disciples were in the area, so he left to try and meet with Geshe Sharawa, the elder of the two. When he arrived at Sharawa's residence the master was in the middle of giving a discourse on Asanga's *Stages of the Shravaka Path*,[22] a well-known Hinayana work, and although Chekhawa listened to the remainder of the discourse he did not hear a single reference to the Mahayana oral transmission text that had so inspired him. Therefore he arranged a cushion near the stupa and, when Geshe Sharawa finished the discourse and came to circumambulate, he requested the teacher to sit and talk with him. The discussion that followed deeply moved Chekhawa, who stood up and prostrated to the guru three times, begging to be accepted as a disciple. Chekhawa remained under the guidance of Sharawa for twelve years, studying the Six Doctrines of the Kadam Tradition and accomplishing the various levels of meditation. Indeed, he uprooted the two prime causes of suffering from within himself: self-cherishing and the belief in a false self. Of Geshe Sharawa's 3,000 disciples, Chekhawa became the principal spiritual heir. In fact, today Chekhawa is one of the most revered gurus of his generation.

We should look to the great practitioners of the past, such as Sharawa and Chekhawa, for our models in practice and, like them, should make the cultivation of the bodhimind our innermost concern. We speak very admiringly of the holy bodhisattvas, but all we have to do to become a bodhisattva ourselves is to resolve to cultivate the bodhimind and to engage in the bodhisattva trainings, such as the six perfections: generosity, discipline, patience, enthusiasm, meditation and wisdom. This makes us into a bodhisattva, a Mahayana trainee.

There are many ways to cultivate the bodhimind. However, the basis of all is the cultivation of love and compassion. Once in a previous lifetime Buddha (as a bodhisattva in training) was wandering in the jungle with some disciples. The group encountered a starving tigress with five newly born cubs. The tigress was so weak with hunger and thirst that she could hardly move, and was just about to devour her own offspring in order to nourish herself. Seeing the terrible karmic repercussions that arise from killing one's own children, the bodhisattva sent his disciples away and offered his own flesh and blood to the tigress, thus saving her life and the life of her cubs. This is how Buddha in a lifetime prior to his enlightenment cultivated love, compassion and the bodhimind. He felt that his life at the time anyway was drawing near its end, and he took the needs of the tigress and her cubs as an omen that the time had come for a meaningful death. Dedicated as he was to the ideals of love and compassion, he could not let the tigress and her cubs die, and as there was no time to use other means, he gave his body to them.

We who have attained a human rebirth and have the opportunity to accomplish the spiritual path should regard ourselves as navigators of a boat able to travel to a fabulous island filled with wish-fulfilling gems. Rather than create an endless host of negative karma by chasing after the small fishes of samsaric achievements, we should without delay dedicate ourselves with renewed vigor to the study and practice of the holy Dharma, and thus guide ourselves to the jewel isle of enlightenment.

Khedrup Choje[23] once wrote:

> Abandon thoughts of home and possessions,
> And resolve to practice the spiritual path.
> Otherwise, distracted by gregarious activities,
> One becomes the fool who renders
> One's own precious human opportunity meaningless.

The world of ordinary life with its samsaric values is a prison giving birth to every form of frustration and discontent. Understanding this, we should transcend worldly interests and engage in spiritual training. If one is a Buddhist, one should become familiar with how Buddha trained and should try to train oneself accordingly.

There are those of us who call ourselves Buddhists, but who don't like to observe the disciplines entailed by the Buddhist path. Such people prefer to waste their time hanging out with friends or wandering around town. Every minute of our lives is precious, and if we cultivate the habit of idly wasting time due to direct or indirect attachment to the eight worldly concerns, before long it becomes a pattern in our lives and robs us of all spiritual progress. We become like the fool who directs his energy to foolish things, and as a result gets only the fool's achievements.

We have to be honest with ourselves concerning our practices. At the time of death we will not be able to hide the nature of our spiritual development. If we do not carry even one ray of religious training within our mindstream, we will be like someone embarking on a long journey without so much as a light to show the way. What can one's destiny possibly be other than lower rebirth? Then we shall wander for countless lifetimes in the lower realms of existence, such as those of the hell creatures, the ghosts and the varieties of animal life. It shall be a long time before we again receive the opportunity of a human rebirth, if this life is devoted to meaningless or harmful pursuits. At death one becomes intensely aware of how one has spent one's life, and this greatly affects how we evolve in the after-death state. This in turn influences the rebirth we will take. Therefore we should spend our lives meaningfully, and not be like the mentally ill person who goes about creating only frustration for himself and others.

Among the world of Buddhist practitioners, the Sangha who dedicate their entire lives to the practice and study of the three categories of scripture and two levels of tantra are especially valuable in the life of the Buddhadharma, just as the life sustaining energy of the body is more fundamental to a person's life than any of the subsidiary energies. Whether or not the Dharma flourishes or diminishes depends to a large extent upon the purity of the monkhood. We who are monks must always bear this in mind. I'm sure that among us there are those who call themselves teachers, abbots, incarnate lamas and so forth, but who, rather than being motivated by compassion and wisdom, are motivated by thoughts of gaining fame, devotion, respect and so forth. To turn one's back on achieving the inner qualities of discipline, learning and intuitive insight while pretending to be spiritually realized is merely a cause of destroying our own happiness in this life and the next.

There are those of you who, like me, sit proudly on teaching seats and preach the holy Dharma, while inside being devoid of a single qualification, like a jackal pretending to be a lion. However, at the time of death it is difficult to be counted as a saint merely for having deceived a few people. It is important to cultivate one's own stream of being before thinking of trying to teach others. To speak of preaching the Dharma to others when one has not overcome at least the coarse aspects of the three psychic poisons of attachment, violence and ignorance from within oneself is like talking about a horn on a rabbit's head. Firstly cultivate spiritual experience within yourself. The establishment of a basis of insight into the teachings through study, contemplation and meditation is the preliminary that becomes a supreme method of teaching others. We should look to the biographies of the illustrious masters of the past and train ourselves accordingly before thinking of teaching Dharma to others.

In order to practice Dharma well we need to know the points and stages in training. We must know what needs to be cultivated and what needs to be eliminated from within our psyche. Then we have to take upon ourselves the responsibility of accomplishing the path. Our progress depends exclusively upon our own efforts. Others may guide us, but they cannot carry us to enlightenment. We must personally understand the teachings and, by integrating them into practice, must accomplish their meaning within our continuum of being. Then when we speak on Dharma it will have some meaning.

We should look at how our own lineage masters lived. For example, take Lama Tsongkhapa, founder of the Yellow Hat tradition. First he studied with numerous qualified masters of the various traditions extant in Tibet at the time. Without any sectarian bias, he learned the sutra and tantra teachings of Buddha. After gaining a thorough understanding of the teachings, he retreated into the mountains and engaged in intensive meditation until he gained realization. Only after this did he begin to teach, establishing the glorious Ganden tradition, or Yellow

Hat sect, which incorporates all aspects of Buddha's teachings and presents the path whereby one individual may practice all aspects in a single sitting and may gain enlightenment in a single lifetime. Tsongkhapa's effect upon all traditions in Tibet was such that after his appearance in the Land of Snows the Dharma shone as brilliantly as it had in India during Buddha's own lifetime.

Throughout his entire period of training Lama Tsongkhapa made the foundation of his practice the guarding of all disciplines and precepts related to the specific level of teaching he was involved in. We who claim to follow his tradition should do the same. Just as children should try to live up to the legacy of their parents, so that when they come of age they are able to receive the responsibility entailed by their position, similarly we must try to equal in practice the greatest masters of the past. We should try to pattern our life styles after theirs, to study and practice as did they. Then we will be able to equal them in attainment.

No matter what our level of training, we should always try to maintain the associated disciplines. At the very least we should try to avoid the ten negative courses of action, such as killing, stealing and so forth.

It is said that the practice of discipline for a single day surpasses the practice of generosity for a lifetime when the generosity is devoid of a sense of discipline; the difference is like the water in a horse's footprint compared to that in a lake. The reason is that when discipline is not present, any practice becomes distorted.

The Indian master Vasubandhu[24] wrote:

> Like the water of a lake
> And the water in a horse's footprint:
> Thus are respectively compared the merits
> Of the practices of discipline and generosity.

A generous gesture is positive, useful and in fact a mandatory virtue for anyone practicing the bodhisattva path, but without discipline one merely uses one's acts of generosity as a means of influencing others for one's personal gain, rendering the activity spiritually meaningless. The bodhisattva cultivates the six perfections—generosity, discipline, patience, energetic perseverance, meditative concentration and wisdom—but these are all interdependent, and discipline is the basis for progress in the other five.

It does not matter whether we practice the Hinayana or Mahayana paths. Discipline is required in both. In the Hinayana the principal method is the threefold application of discipline, meditative concentration and wisdom, or insight. Without discipline, the first of the three, there will be no progress in the two higher trainings of meditation and wisdom. The same applies to the Mahayana, the essence of which is the practice of the six perfections. Without a basis of self-discipline they exist only as words.

When our self-discipline is strong, all the forces of goodness are behind us. As a result we will always be blessed with sufficient requisites of life, such as food, clothing and shelter. As Garak Gomchung, a lord of yogis, once said:[25]

> I have never heard of a meditator
> Dying from cold, hunger or thirst,
> Even when no effort was made
> To gather food or clothing.
> If one does not go down the mountain for food,
> The food will roll up to one's meditation cave.

The basis of our practice should be self-discipline. With it as the foundation, we should apply ourselves to the various levels of study, contemplation and meditation until we gain an undistorted inner experience of the profound nature of the teachings. Practicing as steadily as a river flows, endeavor to take the fruits of accomplishment and actualize the higher states of being. Merely sitting around talking about practice is not a very realistic approach to the path.

The master Vasubandhu[26] wrote:

> Without knowing and applying the teachings,
> There is no way to pacify one's own delusions.
> Those who possess delusions continue to wander
> In the miserable realms of samsaric existence.
> The Buddha taught the Dharma as a direct antidote
> To the delusions that afflict the mind.

To gain control over our stream of being and bring our rougher aspects under control, we require constant mindfulness of the events of our body, speech and mind. Without mindfulness and self-observation there is no way to stay on the spiritual path. Always be aware of your thoughts, words and actions, analyzing them for content and source.

The great Kadampa meditators of old had a saying:

> When sitting alone,
> Watch your mind.
> When in public,
> Watch your speech.

Some people feel that in order to practice Dharma properly one must become a monk or nun. This is untrue. What is necessary to practice Dharma is awareness of and control over the activities of our body, speech and mind. Whether we have taken the robes or not does not matter; this is more a matter of choice in life style. What is important is to be aware of our stream of being and the forces that direct, focus and motivate us, and to use our life experiences as a means to cultivate appropriate inner qualities.

The Fifth Dalai Lama, Gyalwa Ngawang Lozang Gyatso, wrote:[27]

> It may sometimes appear that the people
> Who devote themselves to working in society
> Have no opportunity to practice Dharma—
> This is in fact untrue.
> When a person maintains mindfulness of practice,
> All works become spiritually significant,
> As though touched by an elixir
> Able to turn iron into gold.

From this quotation we can see that whether we are ordained or not, of high or low position in society, rich or poor, does not determine how well we are able to practice Dharma. We can read numerous accounts of accomplished practitioners who were not ordained. Some were kings, others ministers, others totally ordinary in social standing. High and low alike, those who devote themselves to correct training accomplish spiritual progress.

At the time of death it does not matter whether one is a monk or layperson, rich or poor. What really counts is the state of one's mind. If at the time of one's death one has managed to generate a state of mind possessed of clarity, control, love, wisdom and so forth, our life has been well spent. Should confusion, attachment, helplessness, fear, aversion and dark instincts predominate in our mindstream, this is a sign that our life was spent meaninglessly. Those who die in a state of spiritual backwardness and ignorance, be they high or low, rich or poor, monk or layperson, will fall into the lower realms of being, regardless of their social standing during their lifetime. When the mind has been dragged down with the weight of negative deeds and evil tendencies, one is swept helplessly away.

Every moment of our life we are presented with a choice. On the one hand there is always the opportunity to waste time, or, even worse, to engage in negative activity. On the other hand there is the constant opportunity to engage in spiritual practice. I myself, for example, who am called the Thirteenth Dalai Lama, could quite easily lead a lazy, indulgent life style. As the religious and secular head of the country I could easily do nothing but sit around inventing ways to amuse myself. But because I feel that there is something I can do to benefit the practice of Buddhism within people, and also feel I have something to offer to the country by accepting some social responsibility, I make any possible efforts I can in these directions, in the hope that I can at least reach up to the dust on the feet of the early Dalai Lamas.

Human life is very precious, and we who have attained it should turn our backs on the eight worldly concerns and instead make our primary concern the cultivation of spiritual goals. If we have met with a spiritual master and have received his instructions, we should make every effort to practice well.

All living beings carry the Buddha-nature, the seeds of enlightenment, within their own mental stream. *The Sutra of the Noble Wisdom Warrior* states:[28]

> The mind is the fountainhead
> From which wisdom is born.
> Do not look for Buddha
> In any other place.

The seed of perfect wisdom is always within us. When fertilized by the forces of creative being and watered by the refreshing liquids of study, contemplation and meditation, the laws of causation and evolution encourage it to unfold and blossom. Those who exert themselves with utmost energy and skill can attain full enlightenment in one lifetime. Those who train more moderately will see their practice increase lifetime after lifetime, until eventually all excellent qualities have been generated and they attain enlightenment.

As I said earlier, the principal Mahayana endeavor is the cultivation of the bodhimind. Therefore before beginning any action we should think, 'May this work produce benefit and illumination for the sake of all living beings.' This transforms all activities into bodhisattva deeds. During the action we should meditate upon the bodhimind spirit of enlightenment and upon the emptiness nature of the three circles: the doer, the deed and the object of the deed. Finally, when the activity is complete we should seal it with the bodhisattva dedication: 'May this action produce happiness and illumination for the uplifting of the world.'

Lama Tsongkhapa wrote:[29]

> The altruistic bodhisattva spirit is a supreme method
> And turns all virtues into causes of enlightenment.
> Viewing the three circles of action as pure
> Is the very life of the path.
> Therefore seal actions in the beginning, middle and end

With the motivation of the bodhisattva's compassion
Conjoined with the view of emptiness which is free
From all grasping at 'is' and at 'is not '

We should try to dwell constantly in the bodhisattva spirit of love, compassion and the wish for enlightenment as a supreme means to benefit the world. However, in order to actually achieve enlightenment we must also cultivate the view of emptiness, the non-inherent nature of all phenomena. We should always simultaneously practice these two aspects of Buddha's teachings with energy and care, not wasting a moment, as steadily as a river's flow.

I have spoken here on a wide variety of Buddhist topics, though mainly on the subject of death awareness and how it relates to the bodhisattva trainings. I pray that it may cause some of you to engage in the bodhisattva practices with full intensity, with constant awareness that the Lord of Death could strike at any moment and rob you of the golden opportunities afforded by the precious and rare human incarnation. Now that we hold the jewel of humanity in the palm of our hand we should make full use of it and achieve perfect enlightenment. Procrastination leads to further procrastination, and in the end death strikes and leaves us empty-handed. Alternatively, if we grab the opportunity while we have the chance, the essence of a meaningful life can become ours.

But who am I, you may ask, to talk of such serious matters amidst a world of great philosophers, meditators and practitioners? How can I have confidence to express myself on these affairs?

It is true, I may not be anything especially great. However, I do nonetheless carry upon my head dust from the feet of many enlightened gurus whom I served with intense devotion in order to receive their teachings, and even though I may not have accomplished much myself, they were all perfect Buddhas and I thought that it may be beneficial to pass on to you some of the essential instructions with which they entrusted me. My motivation, therefore, is simply to show what of their teachings was most beneficial to my own practice, with the hopes that something from within it may be of value to others.If you feel that anything in it could be of benefit to you, please take it into your hearts and lives.

The colophon: Notes from a sermon delivered by the omniscient Thirteenth Dalai Lama, Gyalwa Tubten Gyatso, in the holy city of Lhasa, on the occasion of the full moon of the Great Prayer Festival in the Iron Bird Year.

Chapter Two
Tibetan Traditions of Death Meditation

This world nys but a thurghfare ful of wo,
And we been pligrymes, passynge to and fro.
Deeth is an ende of every worldly soore.

—Chaucer: *The Knight's Tale*

TRANSLATOR'S PREAMBLE

This second chapter is drawn from a series of talks given by Geshe Ngawang Dargye, a lama from Sera Monastery of Central Tibet (now relocated in South India). He came to Dharamsala to meet with the Dalai Lama and to ask for blessings to enter a three-year retreat. The Dalai Lama, however, had other plans for him, and instead asked him to remain in Dharamsala and open a study program at the newly formed Library of Tibetan Works and Archives. I met him a year later, in 1972, when I came to Dharamsala to join the program.

In 1976, Michael Hellbach, a German friend, and I undertook the task of preparing a periodical in the German language. Entitled *Aus Tushita*, the publication was to deal with Tibetan spiritual culture. One of the subjects we wanted to cover was the Tibetan attitude toward death and dying, as well as related practices and beliefs. To this end we approached Geshe Dargye and requested him to give us an oral account of his own reflections on the topic. He agreed, and over the month that followed dedicated two evenings a week to the project. The material of this chapter is edited from these sessions.

The opening section of his analysis draws from the outline of death meditation given by Pabongkha Rinpoche, root guru of both (late) Senior and Junior Tutors of the present Dalai Lama. Pabongkha was one of the most famous teachers of the last century, and his text on practical meditation[1] is one of the most popular of such manuals with present-day lamas. After presenting Pabongkha's outline, Geshe-la diverges into his own views, covering the full range of death-related practices: a summary of the differing means of the systems of Hinayana, Mahayana and Vajrayana treatments; the stages of inner and outer signs that manifest during the final phases of the dying process; the traditional means of disposal of the corpse; attitudes to be maintained during the dying process by both the afflicted person and those who are present; what those close to the deceased can do to benefit the dead friend or relative; and so forth.

As is the Tibetan custom, throughout his talk Geshe Dargye quotes from the Indian Buddhist scriptures to illustrate the source of the practices being discussed. The Tibetan intention is always to follow the lead established by Buddha and the Buddhist masters. Here he does so to demonstrate that this is being done in his presentation of the crucial topic of death and dying. Thus scriptural quotes are given in abundance. I have edited some of these out where they were more illustrative than informative, and have also tailored the material so as to fit with and supplement that in chapter one.

Some of the topics covered by Geshe Dargye are technical and in need of further elucidation for the general reader. Among these are the process of taking the three *kayas* as the path—transforming the clear light of death into the *Dharmakaya*, the bardo visions into the *Sambhogakaya* and rebirth into *Nirmanakaya*—and also the manner of working with the subtle energies, sexual drops and psychic channels of the body. Some of these points are dealt with in subsequent chapters of this book, and when this is the case I have indicated it in the notes. Geshe Dargye also deals with the consciousness transference method, which is covered further in chapter seven. Thus he manages to discuss a tremendous amount of material in a rather short space, introducing us to many of the ideas that are to be elucidated in detail in the chapters to follow.

I witnessed Geshe Dargye at work as a teacher for almost twelve years in Dharamsala. Rarely have I met anyone with such a love for life and a sense of the sanctity of the living. It is truly inspiring to behold this raw vivacious quality in someone so acquainted with death and dying. In 1975 one of my best friends in Dharamsala died, a British student of Geshe Dargye. I sat with this friend in the Swiss hospital in the Tibetan Children's Village for three days as his strength gradually failed. An hour after his death Geshe Dargye arrived to perform the transference of consciousness. He always regarded his disciples as his own children, and the death of one of them was a tremendous blow to him. He sat in the room for an hour or so meditating and reciting prayers. His face seemed cheerful enough, but every few moments a tear would fall from his half-closed eyes and mark the robe on his lap. He dedicated the remainder of the day to the arrangement of the prayers and rituals that are to be performed for the deceased, including an astrological reading to determine the most favorable manner for the disposal of the corpse (in this case cremation was prescribed),[2] the performance of a ritual of caring for the dead (as described in chapter eight of this work), and the reading of prayers for auspicious conditions to arise. He himself participated in most of the rituals and saw that everything was done in accordance with tradition. The next day he delivered his usual three hourly lectures in the Tibetan Library, although we heard later that he did not sleep the previous night, but stayed up until dawn performing prayers and meditations for the deceased student.

After Geshe Dargye had given his discourse to us on the Tibetan traditions of death and dying we had one more session with him of questions and answers related to points that had come up in his talk or that were of special import to us at the time. I have included some of these at the end of the chapter when it seemed to me that Geshe's answers fall within the scope of this book.

TIBETAN TRADITIONS OF DEATH MEDITATION

by Geshe Ngawang Dargye

To be born as a human being in this world system is held by Buddhists to be a great blessing. The human life form is very powerful, able to cultivate all perfections of the spirit. As humans we have the chance to become a Buddha within our lifetime. This is a most rare opportunity not known to lesser forms of life.

Yet not many humans take advantage of the human situation. Once Buddha was asked, 'How many people use their lives meaningfully?' He scratched the earth with his fingernail and, pointing to the dust

that he had picked up under the nail, replied, 'This many as compared to the weight of the world.'

To dedicate our lives solely to materialistic or worldly pursuits is to
reduce our human status to that of a rat, who also has no spiritual sense.
It would be like a beggar who finds a wish-fulfilling gem but, rather
than using it, just throws it away. Our life can be useful to both ourselves and others; to throw it away on worldly concerns is foolish.

One of the most important meditations for encouraging the mind
to follow the spiritual path is meditation upon death. Through always
keeping the thought of death present in our mindstream, life becomes
increasingly meaningful. To understand life we must appreciate it in
context to impermanence and death, which is its final nature. Not everything dies at death, only the body and the works of this life. The
mindstream, together with the instincts cultivated during life, continue
into the bardo, the hereafter, and then into our future cycle of lives.

Thus it is extremely important to emphasize the cultivation of spiritual traits in our mindstream while we are alive—traits such as love,
compassion, wisdom, patience, understanding and so forth. To generate such qualities is the most meaningful thing we can do. If we die
with a mindstream refined with positive qualities such as these, we
will have harvested life's most wonderful treasure. The result will be
a positive rebirth conducive to progress on the spiritual path. On the
other hand, when we generate only negativity with our life, the future
will hold only negative rebirths, such as a denizen of hell, a ghost or
an animal.

There are many people who study and practice Dharma in words,
but who never bring the essence of practice into their hearts. Their
Dharma remains in their mouths. This is because they have not spent
enough time meditating upon death and impermanence.

The disadvantages of not regularly contemplating the reality of
death are numberless; yet they can be summarized under the following six topics.

(1) If we do not meditate on death we will not be mindful of our
Dharma practice. All of our time will be lost in mundane pursuits.
One of the early Kadampa masters commented:

> If on waking up in the morning one does not meditate on death,
> the entire morning will be wasted. If we don't meditate on it at
> noon, the afternoon will be wasted. Similarly, if we don't medi-
> tate on death in the evening, the night will be lost to meaning-
> less pursuits.

In this way most people waste their entire lives.

(2) Even if we practice some Dharma, our practice will largely be mere procrastination. There are numerous Tibetans who have told their gurus that they will soon do a retreat. But, not meditating sufficiently on death, they put it off year after year. In the end they die before they ever get around to the retreat.

(3) One's practice remains impure and becomes mixed with worldly ambitions, such as the eight worldly concerns. Many students of Buddhism have their eyes fixed more on becoming scholars and celebrities than on attaining spiritual realization. Atisha was once asked,[1] 'If someone wishes for the happiness which is of this life alone, what shall he gain?' Atisha replied, 'Just what he wished for.' 'And what shall he gain in the hereafter?' the disciple asked. 'Rebirth in one of the lower realms,' was the answer.

It is said that in order to practice Dharma well, one must abandon this life. What does this mean? Not that one must abandon one's present life style, home, possessions or position. What it means is that we must transcend the eight worldly concerns: wishing to experience wealth, fame, praise and pleasure; and wishing to avoid poverty, notoriety, criticism and discomfort. To differentiate between a true spiritual practitioner and a false one is simple. The former has abandoned the eight worldly concerns; the latter has not, and thus lives under their restrictive control.

Geshe Potowa once asked Lama Drom Tonpa,[2] 'What is the line between religion and non-religion?' Lama Drom replied, 'That which contradicts the beliefs of worldly people is religion. That which agrees with worldly views is non-religion.'

(4) Our practice will lack stamina. Although we take up a practice, at the first setback we will give it up. A small thorn bush grew outside the cave of Kadampa Geshe Kara Kunjung. Every time he came or went from the cave its thorns would tear at his flesh. This thorn bush remained there until he died, for this great meditator practiced with such intensity that he never wished to waste the few moments necessary to cut it down. He had realized the fruit of meditation upon death.

(5) We will continue to create negative karma. Without a continual awareness of death, attachment to the things of this life persists. Friends and relatives are held as more worthy of respect than are strangers and enemies. This emotional imbalance gives rise to an endless string of mental distortion, which in turn results in the generation of much negative activity. In this way the happiness of this life as well as of all future lives is lost.

(6) One will die in a state of regret. It is certain that death will come. If one has not lived in mindfulness of it, it will come as a surprise. At that crucial moment one will realize that all of the materialistically oriented attitudes one had cultivated during one's lifetime are of no value whatsoever, and that one's wealth, friends and power are useless. When death strikes, nothing but one's spiritual realization is of value, but, having neglected the meditations on death, one consequently neglected all the other spiritual practices and now stands empty-handed. Regret fills the mind.

The Indian master Shantideva wrote:[3]

> When grasped by death's agents,
> What value are friends?
> What value are relatives?
> At that moment, the only protection
> Is the force of one's own goodness;
> But this I never cultivated.

The Kadampa Geshe Karmapa once remarked that we should fear death now, while there is still time for us to act, and at the time of death we should be fearless. The situation is reversed for ordinary beings. When strong and healthy they never give a thought to death, yet when death comes to them they clutch at their breasts in utter terror.

Most practitioners never begin to really practice. Every day they procrastinate. Then, lying on their death-beds, they pray for just a few more days of life, hoping to do the practices they so long ignored. But then, lying between the jaws of death, the time for practice is only a memory. It is like a piece of meat which we held in our hands but, not eating, let slip from our fingers, and fall to the floor, and is now in the belly of a dog. It can never be brought back again. Although regret is pointless, regret arises.

The advantages of meditating on death are also limitless. Yet sometimes we see them condensed into six categories.

(1) Life becomes purposeful. It is said in *The Sutra of Buddha's Entering into Parinirvana*:[4]

> Of all footprints,
> That of the elephant is supreme. Similarly,
> Of all mindfulness meditations,
> That on death is supreme.

If one properly practices death meditation, one's mind will yearn to seek a deeper understanding of life. We can see this in the biographies of the past saints. Buddha himself was turned away from attraction to mundane existence by seeing firstly a sick man, then an old man and lastly a corpse. The yogi Milarepa was inspired to renounce black magic and to search for a more purposeful path when he witnessed his magic-teacher's reaction to the death of a patron.

(2) Meditation on death is an extremely powerful opponent to the delusions of the mind. The strongest opponent to delusion and afflicted emotions is meditation upon emptiness, the highest nature of phenomena. Death awareness is second to this alone. If one recollects death whenever attachment or anger arises, that delusion is instantly dispelled, just as a stone is crushed by the blow of a hammer.

The yogis and mahasiddhas of ancient India ate their food out of bowls made from human skulls and blew on trumpets made from thighbones. Similarly, monks often painted skulls on the door to their washrooms. This was not done to scare people, but to maintain awareness of death. Even nowadays many Buddhist temples hang a painting of the Lord of Death holding the entirety of cyclic existence in his mouth. This image is usually placed near the main entrance of the temple, not as a decoration, but to instill thoughts of death and impermanence in the minds of all who may visit. In tantric practice, cemeteries filled with corpses and so forth are visualized as surrounding the mystic mandala.

(3) Meditation on death is important in the beginning of each practice as it inspires us to enter the training and to do so well.

(4) It is important in the middle of every practice as it inspires us to continue our efforts with intensity and purity.

(5) It is important in the end of every practice as it inspires us to complete and perfect the training.

Thus it is valuable in the beginning, middle and end, helping us to undertake, maintain and complete our practices.

Some people who take up the practice of meditation on death for the first time have such an intense reaction to it and develop such a heavy sense of renunciation that they lose their perspective of the path and, unready, jump into long meditational retreats with the hope of instant enlightenment. But after a few months their enthusiasm wanes and they yearn to return home, yet they are too embarrassed to break the retreat schedule that they previously announced so proudly. Not wanting to stay but unable to go, they end up cursing their renunciation, which they now see as a source of trouble and irritation.

Thus meditation on death is very powerful. But we must be careful in the beginning to be moderate and not to be overwhelmed by our response to it.

(6) We will die happily and with no regrets. While maintaining an awareness of death while alive, our life spontaneously begins to incline toward goodness and the practice of the enlightenment path. Death will not come as a surprise and will bring neither fear nor regret.

It is said that persons who practice to the best of their abilities will die in a state of intense bliss. The mediocre practitioner will die happily. Even the initial practitioner will have neither fear nor dread at the time of death. We should aim at achieving at least the smallest of these results. Milarepa once said:

> Terrified of death, I fled to the mountains. Now through meditation
> I have realized the ultimate nature of mind, and no longer need fear.

If we practice as intensely as did Milarepa, there is no reason for us not to attain an equal state of realization. We have the same life form and mental capacity as did he, and the various methods that he used in order to attain enlightenment have all come down to us today in an unbroken lineage. In a way, our opportunities for enlightenment are even greater than were his, for a number of oral transmissions not available to Milarepa are available to us today.

These, then, are the disadvantages of not meditating regularly on death and the advantages of performing the death meditation. We should contemplate them every day as a preliminary to formal meditation on death.

How does one meditate on death? There are a number of methods in both the sutra and tantra vehicles. In the sutra system two popular techniques are those known as (1) 'the three roots, nine reasonings and three convictions,'[5] and (2) 'the death simulation process.'

(1) The first of these, that known as 'the three roots, nine reasonings and three convictions' is the Kadampa method expounded in Tibet in scriptures such as Gampopa's *The Jewel Ornament of Liberation*[6] and Tsongkhapa's *Great Exposition on the Path to Enlightenment.*[7]

One begins the session by contemplating the six disadvantages of not meditating on death and the six advantages of performing death meditation, as outlined above. The meditation then continues by bringing the mind to the first root, the definite nature of death, and then reflecting on the three supporting reasonings: death has come to everyone in the past; our life is constantly passing, and there is no way to halt the passing of our time or extend our life span indefinitely; and that our life is made of transient factors, few of which are even related or dedicated to Dharma practice. This brings us to the first conviction: to practice the spiritual path and take life's essence.

We then bring the mind to the second root, the indefinite nature of the time of death or the extent of our life span. This is contemplated in conjunction with the three supporting reasonings: human life span has no specific length; the causes of life are few and the opportunities for death many; and our body is very frail and easily destroyed. Reflecting on these three reasonings brings us to the conviction to practice Dharma immediately.

Finally we move on to the third root, the fact that at the time of death only our spiritual achievements are of value. Here we reflect on the three lines of reasoning that friends and relatives are of no help to us at that time; our wealth, property or worldly power is of no help to us; even our cherished body, left behind like a pile of garbage, is of no value to us then. This causes us to generate the third conviction: to practice Dharma purely, without staining our efforts with the worldly concerns.

One should train in both contemplative and absorbed meditation. In the former of these one glances over all of the points in the meditation, taking only a few minutes for each point. In absorbed meditation one fixes the mind on one of the points for a half hour or so. A popular tradition in Tibet was to apply contemplative meditation on the subject for the first month or so of a particular meditation training. After familiarity with the procedures had been gained, one would then use the glance contemplation as a preliminary to the meditation session, and each day focus on a successive point in the procedure.

In the death meditation, this would mean taking a specific point in the nine-point technique, changing every day until all nine topics had been covered. In this way one would contemplate the entire method as a preliminary to each session, and then dedicate the main part of the session to absorbed meditation on an individual topic, rotating through the points of the technique over a period of a week or so.

To conclude each session one would quickly glance once more through all nine reasonings, generate the three convictions and recite a prayer of dedication, such as the following verse:

By the power of this practice,
May I quickly achieve perfect Buddhahood.
Then may I help all sentient beings
Receive that same state of eternal goodness and joy.

(2) The second technique of meditation on death is that known as 'the death simulation process.' This can be done in both exoteric and esoteric ways.

In the exoteric or general method, there are both external and internal ways of practice. An external technique is to dwell in a charnel ground and observe the stages of decomposition of the corpses in it, while keeping the mind fixed on the thought that these corpses represent the final destiny of one's own body.

An internal means is to visualize oneself as lying on one's deathbed awaiting the approach of death. Visualize that your parents, relatives and friends surround you, lamenting and upset. The radiance of your countenance has faded and your nostrils have sunk back. Your lips are dry, slime begins to form on your teeth, and all grace leaves your body. Bodily temperature drops, breathing becomes heavy, and you begin to exhale more deeply than you inhale. All the negative deeds created during your lifetime arise within your mind and you become filled with regret. You look to all sides for help, but help does not come.

The esoteric technique for meditating on death in the simulation process is much more complex. The method is common to all Highest Yoga Tantra systems of all sects of Tibetan Buddhism. Being thus connected with the secret Vajrayana, it is to be practiced by initiates only.[8]

The source of this method is the generation stage yoga of Highest Yoga Tantra. In the generation stage yogas an important phase is that known as 'taking the three *kayas* as the path.' This phase has three steps: taking the clear light of death as Dharmakaya; taking the bardo, or state between death and rebirth, as the Sambhogakaya; and taking the rebirth process as the Nirmanakaya. These three *kayas* refer to the three aspects of Buddhahood: the Truth Body, Beatific Body and Emanation Body, respectively. In the generation stage yogas one visualizes transforming death, intermediate state and rebirth into them. This lays the seeds for the completion stage yogas, wherein one actually experiences death in meditation and executes the actual transformation.[9]

Thus the esoteric method of simulation of the death process is related to the generation yoga phase of taking the clear light of death as the path of the Dharmakaya, or Truth Body. Only a limited portion of the meditation can be taught openly. The explanations concerning the mandala, the five Buddha-families, the clear light yoga and so forth must be left out.

As said above, in the generation stage yogas one plants the seeds that are later ripened into the attainment of clear light realization by the completion stage yogas, which work with the subtle energies and energy centers of the body.

The esoteric method of meditation on death spoken of here deals with the dissolution of the twenty-five coarse substances, an important topic in tantric practice. What are the twenty-five substances? These are the five psychophysical aggregates of form, feeling/response, distinguishing awareness, volitional formations and primary consciousness; the four elements of earth, air, fire and water; the twelve entrances, that is, the objects of sight, smell, taste, hearing, touch and thought, together with the sensory powers enabling the perception of these objects; and the five imperfect wisdoms: the wisdoms called mirrorlike, equality, accomplishing, discriminating and *dharmadhatu* wisdom. These wisdoms are called 'imperfect' because they are mentioned in reference to someone who has not yet attained Buddhahood.

When death comes naturally to a being, it comes as a process of gradual disintegration. The first stage of this process is the simultaneous disintegration of the psychophysical aggregate of form, the imperfect mirrorlike wisdom, the earth element, the sensory power which sight relies upon and the objects of sight. An outer sign manifests as a result of the disintegration of these five attributes, respectively, as follows: the body withers and loses vitality, the eyes blur, one can no longer move the limbs, blinking ceases and the radiance of the body fades. These are outer signs and can therefore be witnessed by others.

With the disintegration of these five, the dying person beholds an inner sign. This can only be seen by the dying person; others present will not perceive it. This sign is a miragelike appearance that seems to fill all space.

The second stage of the dying process is the disintegration of the psychophysical aggregate of feeling/response, the imperfect wisdom of equality, the element of water, the sensory power on which hearing relies and the objects of hearing. Again, there is an outer sign accompanying the disintegration of each of these five attributes. These are, respectively: one loses discrimination as to whether sensations are pleasant, unpleasant or indifferent; the lips dry; perspiration stops and the blood and semen coagulate; outer sounds can no longer be heard; and even the subtle humming of the ears ceases. The dying person experiences the inner sign of a smokelike appearance filling all space.

The third stage is the disintegration of the psychophysical aggregate of distinguishing awareness, the imperfect wisdom of higher discriminating awareness, the element of fire, the sensory power on which

smell relies and the objects of smell. The five outer signs that manifest: one can no longer recognize the meaning of anything said by
those who surround one; memory of even the names of parents, relatives and friends is lost; bodily heat lessens and the powers of diges-
tion and food assimilation cease; exhalation is strong and inhalation
weak; and the power to recognize smells fades. The dying person experiences an inner sign of a subtle flamelike appearance filling all space.

The fourth stage is the disintegration of the psychophysical aggregate
of volitional formations, the imperfect wisdom of all-accomplishment,
the element of air, the sensory powers on which taste relies and the
objects of taste. The five outer signs which accompany these are: all
physical abilities fail; all purposes are forgotten; the major and minor
energies of the body dissolve into the heart; the tongue turns bluish in
color; and all powers of taste fade. The inner sign is that of a flickering
light, like that given off by an oil lamp.

At this point in the process the doctor would declare the person to
be dead. However, as consciousness still abides in the body, this is not
really the situation as of yet. At this point in the process the loss of the
supporting subtle bodily energies causes the primordial drops of one's
body to move. What are these drops? In the tantric tradition it is said
that cells from the original sperm that had come from one's father at
the time of conception are stored in the crown chakra, and cells from
the original ovum from one's mother at the time of one's conception
have been stored in the navel chakra. When the energies supporting
these substances fail, they slip from their seats in the chakras.

Firstly the white substance slips from the crown chakra. It flows
down through the central channel and comes to the heart. Due to its
passing through the knots at the chakras, a vision of snowy whiteness
is experienced. Then the red substance in the navel chakra moves up
to the heart. A vision of redness is experienced.

The sperm and ovum now come together at the heart. An appearance of darkness is experienced, as when the sky is completely over-
cast with thick clouds.

Ordinary persons here lose consciousness and fall into a faint. But
for the tantric yogi this is an excellent condition for special meditation.

Eventually the heart gives a slight tremble and consciousness passes
out of the body. There is an appearance of clear light, as at the coming
of dawn on a moonless morning. This is the clear light consciousness
of death, the occurrence of which indicates that the death process is
complete.

For the majority of beings these experiences are totally uncontrolled and terrifying. Because of the preparations made during life, however, the tantric yogi has complete mastery over the mind at this time and uses the situation very much to advantage. Many practitioners who have failed to attain complete Buddhahood during their lifetimes can use the dynamic impact of the death experience to attain the final stages.

The two most important topics in Highest Yoga Tantra are the subtle bodily energies and the subtle levels of consciousness that arise from these under yogic training. The energies and states of consciousness of our being in fact exist simultaneously within us in both subtle and coarse forms. At the time of death the coarse energies dissolve into the subtle, and the subtle levels of consciousness arise automatically. The purpose of tantric practice is to create this experience in meditation during our lifetime. Through dissolving the coarse energies into the subtle by means of the yogic techniques, we are able to experience the stages of dissolution and disintegration just as happens at the time of death. The yogi who gains this experience during his/her lifetime is well prepared for death, and is able to maintain control throughout the death process. Then when the subtle energies and levels of consciousness arise, he/she is able to transform them into the *kayas* of a Buddha. Consciousness transforms into the Dharmakaya, or Truth Body, and energy into the Rupakaya, or Form Body. For an accomplished yogi, at the time of death the clear light experience is transformed into the Dharmakaya, the bardo experience into the Sambhogakaya, and the rebirth experience into Nirmanakaya.

The real palace of the mind is the heart. Here, mind resides in the undying drop, or male and female substances. The tantric path lays a great deal of stress on the subject of this undying drop, of which it is said there are two types, coarse and subtle. The coarse drop is the physical drop formed by collecting together the male and female substances evolved from the semen and ovum of our father and mother. The subtle drop is the collection or combination of the subtle levels of consciousness with the subtle physical energies. The former is called 'undying' because it endures from the moment of our conception until the moment of our death. The latter is 'undying' because it endures throughout all our lifetimes from beginningless time until our eventual attainment of full enlightenment. Meditation on the death process in the esoteric, tantric tradition involves meditation on both of these types of drops.

Death meditation is of paramount importance. It was Buddha's first teaching when he taught the four noble truths at Deer Park near Benares, and it was also his final teaching, for he died to impress the idea of impermanence upon the minds of his disciples.

Buddha once said:[10]

> Everything in the three worlds
> Is impermanent like autumn clouds.
> The birth and death of living beings
> Are like the scenes in a theatrical play.
> Human life is like a flash of lightning
> And like the waters of a mountain stream.

If a dog rushes out to bite you, there is no value merely in experiencing fear or apprehension. To be of value, this apprehension must be used to propel you into moving into action and avoiding being bitten. Similarly, there is no point merely in fearing death. We should use the apprehension of death as a prodding rod to inspire us in the practice of Dharma.

If we meditate regularly on either of the two death contemplations outlined above—'the three roots, nine reasonings and three convictions,' or 'the death simulation method'—there is no doubt that we will be benefitted.

We should try to practice Dharma, to practice it right away, and to practice it purely. Dharma is the map whereby we can learn the ways of accomplishing realization of the conventional and ultimate modes of existence. It is food to nourish pilgrims on the path of life and knowledge. It is the guide that leads us through the hazardous passes on the road to enlightenment.

Dharma practice has many levels, of which the most basic is the cultivation of a good heart, the mind of love and compassion. Even if we cannot find the strength or time to take up the higher meditation practices or philosophical studies, at least we should try to maintain a sympathetic attitude toward our fellow beings, an attitude which never harms but only helps others. If we do this, negativity will slowly leave our mindstream. The delusions and afflicted emotions will fade away, and our life will steadily improve in quality. Then, at the time of death, we will be able to maintain a sense of peace and serenity, and to have confidence in meeting the future with skill and competence. This is the consciousness transference practice for the person of minimal Dharma training.

A more ambitious Dharma practitioner tries to develop renunciation, the three higher trainings of discipline, meditative concentration and wisdom, and the bodhisattva attitude of seeking enlightenment as a means of benefitting all sentient beings. Once a degree of maturity in these trainings has been acquired, one enters the ocean of tantric methods in order to fulfill these ambitions in the quickest way possible; for only through tantric practice is it possible to attain Buddhahood in as short a period as three years, or in some cases even less.

However, although it is possible to attain full enlightenment in as short a period as a few years, not many people manage to focus themselves strongly enough to do so. Therefore the various methods of consciousness transference have been taught.

Consciousness transference, or, in Tibetan, *po-wa*,[11] refers to the practice of influencing our rebirth by controlling the mind at the time of death. This is because the last thought a person has before dying has a far-reaching influence on the nature of the rebirth he/she will take. Some people live virtuous lives but, not having developed higher spiritual attainments, have no control over their own mind and at the time of death are overwhelmed by fear, aversion or other such afflicted emotions. As a result they take a negative rebirth. There are also cases of people who led somewhat negative lives but, due to a stroke of good fortune, had positive thoughts at the time of death. As a result the nature of their rebirth was beneficially affected. The yoga of consciousness transference takes advantage of this phenomenon. Of course the good or evil a person creates during their life is still stored in the mind of the person in the form of karmic seeds, to be faced in some future life, but the immediate rebirth is strongly determined by the mental framework at the exact moment of death. If we can achieve a rebirth conducive to further practice, there is a chance that the mind may be purified of the karmic stains at that time.

The exclusively Mahayana methods of transference can be divided into two categories: those taught in the sutras and those taught in the tantras.

The principal sutra technique is that known as 'the application of the five powers.' It has this name because five factors are applied at the time of death: intention, the white seed, familiarity, destruction [of negativity] and the power of prayer.[12]

(1) The power of intention. Generate the firm intention not to let the mind become separated from the altruistic bodhisattva spirit, neither during the death process, the bardo experience nor during rebirth.

(2) The power of the white seed. Try to rid the mind of all forms of physical attachment. In order to effect this, give away all wealth, property and possessions to noble purposes, such as the poor and

needy, the sick, educational institutes or hospitals, spiritual institutes, and so forth.

(3) The power of destruction. Try to destroy the stains of any negative karmas collected during your lifetime. This is done by applying the four opponent forces: regret for any negativity created; resolve to avoid fallacious activity in the future; taking refuge in the Three Jewels and generating the bodhimind, the altruistic aspiration to highest enlightenment; and, lastly, purifying the root of the stains by means of meditation upon emptiness, recitation of the hundred-syllable Vajrasattva mantra, and so forth. If you have any tantric initiations, invite your lama and request him to re-initiate you, or, if this is not possible, then personally perform the self-initiation ritual.

(4) The power of familiarity. Generate the bodhimind as intensely as possible, and pass away in the sphere of meditation upon it.

(5) The power of prayer. Here, prayer refers to the aspiration of an actual Mahayanist, which is the wish that the difficulties of others may ripen upon oneself and that they may thus become free of them. This is made in perspective to the bodhisattva aim of achieving full enlightenment as a means to benefit living beings.

One day when Geshe Potowa was sitting on his throne giving a discourse he suddenly sat in meditation for a moment and uttered, 'May I always be a protector to those who are helpless, and a guide to those afflicted by confusion.' Then he passed away.

When nearing death, Geshe Chekhawa told his disciples that he had long been praying to take rebirth in the lowest realms of existence in order to benefit the beings there, but that he had recently received dreams indicating that he would be reborn in a Pure Land. He requested his disciples to offer many prayers to the Buddhas and bodhisattvas that this might be avoided and his prayers fulfilled.

The application of these five powers at the time of death guarantees a rebirth with conditions suitable for continued practice of the Mahayana path.

If you have a tantric initiation, you should try to practice the Vajrayana methods of consciousness transference, which are taught in the tantras. There are various lineages of these tantric methods as taught in the higher and lower tantras. One should choose a system suitable to one's personal karmic disposition. This choice should be made in consultation with one's spiritual teacher. One of the most popular systems among the Tibetan yogis is that expounded in the *Vajrayogini-tantra*. It is said that initiation into the *Vajrayogini-tantra* is like a ticket to a Pure Land, the Land of the Dakinis.

Consciousness transference as taught in the Tantras is called the forceful method because even practitioners on initial levels who have engaged in heavy negative karmas can, through application of purification and the Vajrayana methods for transference, easily take rebirth in a Pure Land.[13]

There are ways to prepare for consciousness transference. These are the yogas whereby one trains in the method to be applied at the actual time of death. The Vajrayana techniques are dangerously powerful, and even during one's life one can project consciousness out of the body by means of uttering the syllable *PHAT*, and then bring it back with the syllable *HIK*.

One pursues this yoga in intensive retreat until the signs of accomplishment appear, such as a small blister that appears over the crown aperture of one's head and emits a few drops of pus and blood. However, it is not possible to teach any of the tantric methods to non-initiates. Buddha Vajradhara himself said, 'One should not pour the milk of a snow lion into a clay bowl.' Not only does the milk turn bad, but as well the clay bowl is ruined. The gateway to the Vajra Vehicle is the receiving of tantric initiation. This plants the seeds that are later ripened by yogic application.

Some people accuse tantric teachers of being tight-fisted. This is a stupid accusation made by those with no understanding of the tantric path. The tantric code of secrecy is not enforced because the teachers are ungenerous. The problem is that teaching the tantric methods to a spiritually immature person is like lashing a small child to a wild elephant. It is for this reason that such great practitioners as the Fifth Dalai Lama have stressed the importance of gaining an experience of the fundamental principles of basic Buddhism before specialization in the Vajrayana techniques.

Question: Is there anything one can do to benefit a dying person?
Answer: It is helpful to recite mantras and prayers into the person's ear. The mantra of Buddha Shakyamuni is particularly useful. The syllables of this mantra—*OM MUNI MUNI MAHA MUNI YE SVAHA*—refer to dwelling within the three levels of control: control over the negative mind, control over attachment to higher sensual pleasures,

and control over the self-complacency of grasping for personal nirvana as an end in itself. As self-control is vitally important at the time of death, the sound of this mantra can encourage the dying person to maintain appropriate attitudes.

The mantra of Avalokiteshvara, the Bodhisattva of Compassion, is also very effective. The levels of meaning of this six-syllable mantra, *OM MANI PADME HUM,* are too vast to be listed. The mantra lays a very favorable impression on the mind of the dying person.

It is also helpful to place an image of the Buddha or one of the bodhisattvas where the person will notice it. Sacred images have a calming effect upon the mind, and this encourages clarity and control.

In particular, if the person is a spiritual practitioner you should recite the name mantra of his/her guru and place a picture of the guru where it can be seen.

The most important thing is to generate and maintain a positive attitude within the mind of the dying person. Do not agitate or anger him/her for any reason whatsoever. Dying with a positive attitude almost guarantees a positive rebirth.

Once the person has died, it is useful to distribute his/her possessions among needy and virtuous causes. Or they can be sold and the money used to have prayers read. The person's spiritual master should be asked to perform special prayers, for the guru-disciple relationship is especially significant, and anything a guru does for a deceased disciple or a disciple for a deceased guru has extraordinarily powerful effects. Parents and friends should also offer prayers, as they too can have a strong influence. There are numerous examples of people who died in negative states of mind and were transmigrating toward a lower rebirth but who, due to the prayers and offerings of loved ones, have taken higher rebirth.

How to deal with a dying or dead person has been spoken of elaborately in Vasubandhu's *An Encyclopedia of Buddhist Metaphysics.*[14]

Question: Should one do the same for Buddhists and non-Buddhists alike?

Answer: The Buddhas and bodhisattvas are universal protectors and therefore do not discriminate. However, if the person is a Buddhist and is close to you, because of the strength of this bond anything you do will be of more impact.

Question: Should a dying person be told of the fact that he/she is dying, or is this sometimes unwise?

Answer: It depends on the person. If he or she is a Dharma practitioner it is better to be directly honest and to tell him/her what is happening. The person will then be able to put all energies into practice, will be unafraid of death and will be able to apply a method of consciousness transference. Otherwise, if the person is not trained in spiritual practice there is perhaps no point in telling him or her. There is no point in merely causing fear and upset.

Question: How long does consciousness remain in the body after a person is ostensibly dead?

Answer: If the person is an accomplished meditator, consciousness can sometimes remain for days or even months. For example, one of the previous Panchen Lamas remained in his body in meditation for almost a year after he stopped breathing. During this time the body showed no signs of decomposition. He died in Kham, Eastern Tibet, but his consciousness did not leave his body until after he had been transported to Central Tibet, a journey of many months.

Even when a person is not a meditator, consciousness may remain in the body for as long as three days. Therefore a corpse should never be moved until after the signs appear to indicate that consciousness has departed. The strongest such sign is a drop of blood and pus being emitted from either the nostrils or sexual organ. A less certain sign is that the corpse emits a foul smell.

If the body is cremated before consciousness has left, it is almost the same as murder. The body should be left untouched until consciousness has departed. If it is touched, the consciousness may leave from the point of first contact. Because it is more favorable for it to leave via the upper than the lower portions of the body, the first place to be touched should be the crown of the head.

Question: Why was burial rare in Tibet?

Answer: It was considered better to offer the body to the birds as a final act of charity. Only when a body was considered unfit for this because of disease or the like was it buried. It was customary for anyone who was religious to have a tantric yogi do a *chöd* ritual,[15] which is a rite in which the body is visualized as being cut up and offered to hungry animals, birds and spirits. When the dying person was an accomplished meditator he/she would perform this ritual; otherwise a yogi would be invited to do it for him/her. Charnel grounds in Tibet had yogis who specialized in this practice, and it is said that however many birds were required for the consumption of the body, that many would be invited by the yogi and only that many would show up.

If the corpse were small and could only feed ten birds, only ten would come. If it were big enough to feed twenty, twenty would come. It is said that birds thus summoned are usually manifestations of the mystical dakinis and follow a special code of ethics while devouring the corpse.

Question: There seems to be a tremendous amount of Tibetan literature describing death and the after-death state. What is the source of this literature?

Answer: It was written by various experienced yogis and meditators who had attained higher levels of consciousness and perception. These texts are not like the books written today. These days people seem to want to write a book as soon as they learn to read and write. The yogis of old wrote only from their own experience.

A great deal was said by Buddha himself about death, dying and the nature of the experiences in the bardo, or state between death and rebirth. He spoke extensively on these topics in both the sutras and tantras. Much of what he said has been condensed by Vasubandhu into his *Encyclopedia of Buddhist Metaphysics*. This was further elaborated upon by the First Dalai Lama in his commentary to Vasubandhu's *Encyclopedia*.

Chapter Three
A Conversation with an Old Man

First our pleasures die—and then
Our hopes, and then our fears—and when
These are dead, the debt is due,
Dust claims dust—and we die too.

—Shelley: *Death*

TRANSLATOR'S PREAMBLE

Lama Gungtang Konchok Dronme was an important contemporary of the Eighth Dalai Lama. The following verse work by him, *A Conversation with an Old Man,*[1] is well known to most Tibetans today, and has received several reprints (in Tibetan) in India. A thousand copies were distributed amongst the audience by an avid patron in search of merit at a discourse being given in the main temple at Dharamsala in 1978 by the present Dalai Lama. The discourse continued for a week (the subject was, if I remember correctly, Nagarjuna's *Precious Garland*[2]) and at the conclusion of it His Holiness read the audience the brief text by Lama Gungtang. I was amongst the members of the audience to have received a copy of the small text, and I kept it in my files as a memento of the occasion. Several years passed, and the item remained in my library without receiving any great attention. However, I kept coming across references to it in other materials I was studying (for example, Pabongkha Rinpoche refers to it several times in his *Liberation in the Palm of Your Hand*[3]), and kept hearing it quoted in discourses by various lamas. Consequently when I decided to put together the materials for this collection on death and dying, *A Conversation with an Old Man* was in the forefront of prospective items to be included. The job of translation was not particularly difficult, as I had already heard the Dalai Lama give a reading with a brief commentary to it, and also had heard many of the sections in references and quotations by my other teachers.

In fact, as I learned from a friend at about the same time, a translation of both this poem and also another by Lama Gungtang had already been published in both German and English, together with the Tibetan in both the classical script and Romanized transliteration.[4] The English of this version did not do the original poem any great justice, although the German translation was somewhat better. The Tibetan was a useful means to check the accuracy of the text already in my possession, which contained several errors. In addition, the Tibetan Library in Dharamsala had a copy of the complete collected works of Lama Gungtang, and I was able to balance the discrepancies against this edition.

Irony, disdain and sarcasm are popular attributes in Tibetan comedy, and this poem, although serious in subject matter, is essentially an attempt to look at the funny side of old age and the blindness that youth has toward it. The old man firstly presents himself as a pitifully aged and decrepit being, catching the youth's attention and overwhelming him with disgust. But then he begins to demonstrate his inner strength and humor, turning the tables on the youth and shaking the latter's arrogance. In the end he reveals himself as a yogi, winning the youth's confidence and convincing him of the importance of taking life seriously. The youth is deeply moved, abandons the worldly life and joins the old man in meditation in the forest.

The theme is a classical one in Buddhism, coming from the example set by Buddha's own life. It is said that witnessing four great signs turned Buddha from the life of a prince with three wives and 500 concubines to that of a renunciate in search of enlightenment. The first sign was sickness, the next old age and the third a dead person. When Buddha beheld these, his mind became overwhelmed by grief at the unsatisfactory nature of cyclic existence and the ephemerality of ordinary indulgence. Then he saw a sage sitting under a tree, his face radiant with the peace and joy of spiritual knowledge. The prince knew at once that he could not accept the throne of his kingdom.

The First Dalai Lama in his classical epic poem on the life of Buddha describes it as follows:[5]

> Shortly thereafter while walking in the garden
> He saw men in twisted states of weakness,
> Men tortured by sickness, old age and death.
> Disillusioned with samsara, thoughts of freedom arose.
>
> Then he saw a mendicant, peaceful and serene.
> 'A renunciate is praised by the wise,' he thought;
> 'His life is happy and he attains immortality.
> For the sake of myself and others, I should follow that way.'

Consequently the prince devised a plan to escape his father's palace. He achieved this and entered the jungle, where he took up spiritual practice. The First Dalai Lama continues:

> He walked to the banks of the Nairanjana River
> And there strove again and again to reverse confusion.
> For six years he submitted himself to every authority
> And dwelt in samadhis vast as the sky.

As we can see, from the very beginning, Buddhism has placed awareness of death as an important motivational stimulant. The theme appears again and again in Buddhist history. Lama Gungtang did not invent the theme, but replays it with a touch of irony and sarcasm, adding a flavor of comedy to an age-old adage.

A Conversation with an Old Man

by Lama Gungtang Konchok Dronme

Homage to the Buddhas, who, having
Abandoned the seeds of cyclic existence,
Are beyond the suffering nature
Of birth, sickness, age and death.[1]
May they inspire us to cut the chains
Of wandering in the samsaric realms.

Once upon a time a haggard old man lay
Exhausted by the road in a wilderness.
A haughty youth appeared
And this is the conversation that followed.

'Old man, in sitting, walking or working,
You are unlike anyone I have seen.
What is it that so afflicts you?'

To this the old man replied,
'O youth, who flies in the pride
Of having strong flesh and blood,
Listen to me, for many years ago
I was even stronger than you.

'In running I could outrun a horse,
And when I wanted to trap
I caught even the wild yak of the north.
I was as light on my feet
As the birds of the air,
And my face as handsome as that of a god.

'I wore magnificent clothing,
Adorned myself with jewels,
Ate the finest delicacies
And rode the most swift of horses.

'There was no sport I did not play
And no pleasure I did not know.
I gave not a single thought to death
Or the advent of old age.
The noise of the friends
And relatives who surrounded me
Constantly held my attention
And turned my face from everything else.

'But the stealthy suffering of age
Slowly pressed in upon me.
At first I did not notice it,
And when I did it was too late.
Now when I look in a mirror
I am repelled by what I see.

'When one receives tantric initiation
The initiation waters first touch one's head
And then descend through the body.[2]
Death comes in a similar fashion:
The crown of one's head turns white
And then the symptoms descend.

'My hair is white as a seashell.
I did not wash out the color.
The Lord of Death has spat on me
And the frost of his spittle covers my head.

'The many lines and wrinkles on my face
Are not folds in the baby fat of a youth.
They are time measurements sketched
By the hand of the Keeper of Time.

'This constant squinting of my eyes
Is not caused by smoke.
My powers of vision have diminished
And I must squint in order to see.

'When I lean forward like this
And cup my ear in order to listen,
It is not that I expect you to
Whisper me a secret message.
But to me all sounds seem remote
And I must strain in order to hear.

'Droplets fall unexpectedly from my nose.
This is the ice of my youth
Being melted by the sun of old age,
Not pearls falling from a necklace.

'My teeth have all fallen out.
This was not part of a cycle
Heralding the growth of new teeth;
The meals of this life have been eaten,
And the cutlery therefore put away.

'I do not continually drool because
I want to anoint the earth with water.
Rather, all that I once enjoyed
Now only disgusts me,
And my spittle drops of its own accord.

'My unclear conversation
Is not a dialect learned
In some cold, foreign land.
Once I indulged in meaningless talk without end,
And my tongue is now worn out.

'This ugly face that you see
Is not a monkey's mask that I wear.
It is just that my mask of youth—
Mine only on loan for a short while—
Has now been taken back, and
Only the ugly bones of death remain.

'This constant wobbling of my head
Is not a sign of my disapproval.
The Lord of Death has struck me with his club
And ever since then my brain is unsteady.

'This manner of walking that you see,
My eyes cast down at the road,
Is not in order to find
A needle that has been lost.
The jewels of my youth have fallen to earth,
And I walk in a daze,
Barely able to remember my own name.

'The way I rise on four limbs
Is not a playful imitation of an animal's ways.
My legs will no longer support me,
So I must use both arms and legs to move.

'The way I drop down when I sit is not
Intended as a display of bad manners.
The threads of my happiness have been broken
And the cords of my youth have been cut.
Hence I can no longer move with grace.

'When I walk I stagger,
Not as a way to show off
And pretend I am a big man,
But because the burden of age
Rides heavily upon me
And I cannot walk properly.

'This constant shaking of my hands
Is not because I itch for jewels.
The eye of death is upon me, waiting
To steal life's gem from my hands
And I tremble in apprehension.

'The restricted diet that I follow
Is not so fixed because I am a miser.
My digestive powers have diminished
And I fear to die of overeating.

'The light clothing that I wear
Is not planned for a fancy dress party.
My physical strength has so diminished
That even clothing is a burden to me.

'The way I breathe so heavily
Is not because I am reciting prayers
For the benefit of others.
It is a sign that soon the breath
Of my life will melt into the sky.

'My extraordinary manner of behavior
Is not an inspired artistic expression;
I am held by the demon Death
And I have no power to move as I wish.

'I continually forget what I am doing
Not in order to demonstrate
That I have no respect for endeavor,
But because my brain is worn out, and
My memory and intelligence have grown dim.

'There is no need to laugh at me,
For all receive their share of old age.
Within the span of a few years, the first
Messengers of death will come to you too.

'My words have not yet impressed you,
But soon this same condition will befall you.
These days people do not live for long,
And you have no guarantee
To see as many years as have I.[3]
Even if you reach me in years,
There is no assurance that you will have
Even the powers of body, speech and mind
Demonstrated by this feeble man before you.'

The youth was repelled
And cried out in disgust:

'O you miserable creature
Despised by men and harassed by dogs,
Your body is ugly and spent.
I would rather choose to die now than
To remain alive in your condition.'

The old man smiled.
'You want to be young forever
And you do not wish to become old.
You say you prefer death to old age,
But when the time of your death draws near
You will discover that it is not so easy
To face death willingly and with confidence.

'If one never harms the gentle,
Always guards one's spiritual precepts
And follows the threefold application
Of study, contemplation and meditation,
Perhaps it would be easy to die happily.

'But my mind did not for a moment
Give thought to spiritual values.
Even though my body is grown old,
I now cherish every day as an opportunity
To train in the principles of Dharma,
And I do not want to die so soon.'

When the old man had spoken thus
The attitude of the youth was transformed.
'Yes, aged one, it is true.
What I have seen with my eyes
And what I have heard with my ears
Indeed confirm what you have said.
Your words have moved me deeply.
The sufferings of age are indeed great.
You are old and have gained much experience,
So, tell me truly, is there no method
By which one can overcome this terror?'

The old man smiled once more.
'Yes, there are such methods,
And these are not particularly difficult.
Everything that is born must die

And not many live even to old age.
To live and not to die would require
The fabulous elixir of immortality,[4]
And that seems rather difficult to acquire.

'All great beings of the past have died:
Buddhas, bodhisattvas, saints and kings alike.
The righteous as well as the evil,
All must one day face death.
How can you be any different?

'However, if one practices the spiritual path
The mind abides in joy, regardless of one's age.
Then when death falls one is like a child
Gleefully returning to his home.
Even Buddha did not speak of
A more profound method than this.

'This is my innermost advice to you;
It is from my heart, not just my mouth:
Your fate is in your own hands
And you must follow your deeper instincts.'

To this the youth replied,
'Indeed, you are correct. But before
Devoting myself to intensive practice,
There are matters I should clear up,
Such as the needs of my family,
As well as my house and property.
When these have been accomplished
I shall return and speak with you again.'

The old man grunted,
'Your attitude is empty of reason.
Previously I also lived with the thought
To engage in practice soon.
Work is like a man's beard:
No matter how much you cut it,
The cutting never ends;
The beard just grows out stronger.
For me, years passed like this
But the work never reached an end.
Procrastination is merely self-deception.[5]

'If your idea is to procrastinate forever
You will have no hope of spiritual accomplishment
And our conversation has been in vain.
You should just return to your home
And leave this old man to meditate in peace.'

The youth cried out in shock,
'Old man, do not be so harsh with me.
It would be insane of me to simply
Abandon everything I have undertaken!'

To this the old man replied,
'Yes, you can say this to me.
But the Lord of Death who dwells in the south[6]
Does not consider the state of one's plans.
You should speak with him.
When he comes to call on you,
He will not ask if you are young or old,
High or low, rich or poor, ready or not.

'All are forced to go alone,
Leaving behind their unfinished works.
The thread of life suddenly is broken
Like a rope snapping under a heavy load.

'There is no time for plan-making.
To die without spiritual knowledge
Is to die in pathetic helplessness.
At that time one's attitude will change
Toward the importance of ephemeral works.

'Would it not be more useful
To change the mind now
While time for training remains?
But useful advice is rare in this world
And those who follow it even rarer.'

At this the youth was overcome with emotion
And prostrated to the old man, saying,
'Not the highest guru on the most ornate throne
Nor any of the greatest scholars or yogis
Has ever given me a more profound teaching.

Old man, you are a true spiritual friend
And I will follow your advice.
Please speak to me further on this matter.'

The old man answered,
'I have lived on this earth for many years
And thus have seen much of life.
Nothing is more difficult to understand
Than the principles of the spiritual path,
The way producing higher being, liberation
And omniscient enlightenment.

'It is not easy to cultivate an experience
Of the truth taught by the enlightened ones
And even more difficult to do so in old age.
Youth is the time to learn and
To become familiar with the teachings.
Then as one grows old with the passing years,
It is easy to dwell within practice.

'If one really understands
Even a single point of the teachings,
All activities are accordingly benefitted.
There is no need to intellectualize;
When spiritual experience has been generated,
All actions of body, speech and mind
Take on a spiritual perspective.

'The root of practice is to rely
Correctly upon a spiritual master,
And to guard one's trainings
As carefully as one does one's eyes.

'Turn your back on worldly works
And engage in study, contemplation and meditation
Upon all the beneficial essence teachings
Of Buddha, and of Lama Tsongkhapa, his regent in Tibet.[7]

'By applying oneself in this way
While establishing as a background
The methods for collecting merit
And purifying the mind of negative traits,

Illumination falls into one's very hand.
Then, my son, you will know joy
And all your aspirations will be fulfilled.'

The conversation proceeded in this way
And the two became spiritual friends.
They dwelled together in the forest
Free from the eight worldly concerns,
Fully absorbed in the practice of meditation.

Thus is complete my story of the old man
And the youth who met in the forest one day,
And the record of the conversation that ensued.
I have written it out to inspire
Myself and others in the practice of Dharma.

I, the author Konchok Tenpai Dronme,
Am not particularly experienced in life
But I thought that if for posterity's sake
This conversation were to be written down,
Some benefits may arise in the hearts of mankind.

Chapter Four

The Death of Gye-re Lama

There is a Reaper whose name is Death;
And with his sickle keen,
He reaps the bearded grain at a breath,
And the flowers that grow between.

—Longfellow: *The Reaper and the Flowers*

TRANSLATOR'S PREAMBLE

The material in the first chapter of this collection aimed at revealing how the practice of death meditation is performed in the Tibetan tradition and how this practice relates to the general schemata of Buddhist trainings. Chapter 2 gave us a survey of the range of Tibetan Buddhist traditions associated with death and dying from the Hinayana, Mahayana and Vajrayana branches of the tradition, covering subjects from daily meditation on death to the manner of training in consciousness transference for the moment of death, the manner of relating to a dying person, the disposal of the corpse and so forth. Finally, chapter 3 presented a dialogue on the purpose, necessity and function of death awareness as a stimulus to spiritual endeavor.

This fourth chapter looks at an entirely different aspect of the subject: the death of an accomplished yogi. This has been a popular theme with Buddhist authors over the centuries, from the very time of the Buddha himself. The biographies of most masters dedicate a considerable amount of attention to the account of the master's death.

As said above, the tradition begins right from the time of Buddha. There are a number of early Indian accounts of the life and death of the Buddha. From amongst them, two important works are the *Lalita-vistara-sutra* and the *Buddha-charita*, the latter being a short verse work from the first century that is based on the former long prose account.

In the *Buddha-charita*[2] it is related that three months prior to Buddha's death the earth was afflicted by a mighty earthquake and also a storm. His disciple Ananda inquired of him as to the meaning of these omens, whereupon he replied, 'This earthquake portends that I have sacrificed the remaining years of my life. Reckoned from today, I will sustain my life for only three more months.'

Three months later as Buddha and his disciples came to a mango grove they were approached by a householder called Chunda, who invited them to a meal. Buddha accepted, but later instructed his disciples that he alone was to eat of the food to be offered. After the meal he became ill, and insisted that they walk on to Kushinagar. Here he bathed and then asked Ananda to make him a bed. 'O Ananda,' he said to his grief-stricken disciple, 'the time has come for me to pass into peace. Go and tell the Mallas about it, for they will be upset should they not witness my passing.'

When all had gathered, the Buddha gave them a final sermon. 'It is not appropriate to grieve in an hour of joy.... You all weep, but is there any real cause for grief? We should look upon a sage as a person escaped from a burning mansion.... It does not matter whether I am here or not; salvation does not depend upon me but upon practicing the Dharma, just as a cure depends not upon seeing the doctor but upon taking his medicine.... My time has come, my work is done.... Everything eventually comes to an end, even if it should last for an aeon. The time of parting is bound to one day come. I have done what I could for myself and others, and to remain longer would be without purpose. I have trained all whom I could train. My teachings shall last for many generations, so do not be disturbed. Recognize that all that lives is subject to the laws of impermanence, and strive for eternal wisdom. When the light of knowledge dispels ignorance, when the world is seen as without substance, the end of life is seen as peace and as a cure to a disease. Everything that exists is bound to perish. Be therefore mindful of your salvation. The time of my passing has come.'[3]

Having said these words, the master entered into a profound meditation and passed away. The earth shook like a ship in a storm, and thunder and lightning filled the heavens.

Later when the Mallas attempted to cremate the body of Buddha, the pyre refused to catch fire, for the great disciple Mahakashyapa had not yet arrived. Then when Mahakashyapa arrived it spontaneously burst into flame although nobody stood near it.

Such are the stories concerning Buddha's own death, as related in the *Buddha-charita*.

Also in the *Mahaparinirvana-sutra* it is said that on numerous occasions the Buddha had hinted to Ananda that a sage has the power to live as long as he should so wish. Later, after he had announced his approaching death and Ananda began to cry, Buddha reminded him of these many occasions, saying to him, 'Verily, Ananda, the time for requests has now passed.' Until his passing he continued to remind Ananda that had he but once responded to these hints and requested him not to pass away he would have been able to live for many years more. Thus Buddha's death filled Ananda with grief and guilt.

Now, there were 499 of Buddha's disciples who had achieved nirvana, yet Ananda had not succeeded in doing so himself, and consequently there was not Buddha's desired goal of 500 Arhats to meet and compile his teachings. It is said that the 499 called Ananda to them and scolded him at length, reminding him of every occasion when he had created a fault and how he had let the Buddha die through not requesting him to live long when the opportunities for such a request had arisen. They then expelled Ananda from their midst.

Ananda was so upset that he raced into the garden and swooned. Within a moment he realized Buddha's intent and instantly achieved nirvana.

In this way the Buddha dedicated his life to teaching and even used his death in such a way as would invoke the enlightenment of one of his disciples. The full quorum of 500 Arhats was achieved, and Ananda fulfilled his purpose. The energy of the guilt that the Buddha had tricked him into feeling became the trigger for his accomplishment.

Even during Buddha's lifetime we have examples of mystical death leading to the enlightenment of others. King Bimbisara was Buddha's main patron, building many residences for the monkhood and offering himself to Buddha as a disciple. After many years of practice Bimbisara achieved Arhatship, yet his son Ajatashatru had no interest in religious ways. This disturbed the king's mind, for he feared to leave his kingdom in the hands of a prince with no love for religion. Consequently he permitted the evil Devadatta to meet his son, knowing that Devadatta, hating the Buddha and also hating the king as Buddha's patron, would put evil thoughts into Ajatashatru's mind. Accordingly it came to pass that the prince plotted the murder of his own father, but when news arrived to him that his plan had succeeded he was so overcome by remorse that he expelled Devadatta from his court and embraced the religious life, following in his father's footsteps. In this way King Bimbisara led his son to the Dharma through allowing his death to manifest in a most unusual fashion.[4]

The same theme continues throughout Buddhist literary history over the centuries. The Tibetans loved the concept, and we see it occurring in the biographies of the most famous Tibetan yogis. For example, Atisha is told in a dream that if he travels to Tibet it will be very beneficial for mankind, but will shorten his life by more than a decade.[5] Similarly, the esteemed yogi Milarepa,[6] also of the eleventh century, died by consciously accepting poisoned food that he knew would kill him, doing so and making a scene of the event in order to convert to righteousness his would-be murderer.

This is the idea behind the short text that follows, *The Death of Gye-re Lama*. The plot is simple enough: the time for the Gye-re Lama's death has come, but rather than just fade out he wishes to use his death to tame the mindstream of one more disciple, the Princess Palden Zangmo. He therefore incites her to plan his murder, which she does, but afterwards she is haunted by the knowledge of her sin and is moved to confess to her people, and to give up evil. She becomes a religious recluse, dedicating her life to meditating near the spot where she had committed the grisly murder. In the end she achieves sainthood, transcending the evil nature that had motivated her and becoming free from the guilt that had propelled her into a religious life.

What is unusual about the work is that it is the account of a yogi who lived during the twelfth century, yet it was written in the 1950s by Terton Dulzhug Lingpa, a Tibetan mystic having no access to any historical materials on the subject. Perhaps it would be useful here to explain something of the tradition of this type of literature.

The title 'Terton'[7] prefixed to the author's name means 'treasure revealer,' the treasure referred to being a mystical text of paranormal origin. These treasure texts are sometimes 'found' under rocks, in caves or inside trees, etc. *The Tibetan Book of the Dead* is one such treasure text. The finders of these texts are of different talents: some find physical texts, others dream of such texts and then write them out, still others see the text for the first time in a vision and later copy down what they saw.

The Death of Gye-re Lama belongs to the second of these three categories. As is related in the opening sections of the text, the author is walking through the Lahoul Valley of northwest India with some disciples when someone asks him to stop and examine the pilgrimage site at Gye-re Mountain. The author is a famous clairvoyant by trade, although he does not state this himself openly in the text; he agrees to examine the site and notices some unusual features about it and also about his own reaction to the location. That night he dreams that a dakini appears to him and relates the story of the death of Gye-re Lama and the enlightenment of Princess Palden Zangmo.

This comprises the first half of our text. At the time, the author does not write anything down. But some months later when he passes through the same area he stays near the site of the murder he had dreamed of. That night he is unable to sleep, and in the early morning slips into a trance in which the Gye-re Lama appears to him and tells him the remaining details of his life and death. The vision ends with the Gye-re Lama transmitting a prayer and meditation to be used by those who visit the Gye-re Mountain pilgrimage site, and an account of the various characters in the story and where they have taken rebirth in the present time. It was only after this that Terton Dulzhug Lingpa was moved to write out the full account of his experiences.

The author in fact died not that long ago—in the 1960s. His death was as strange as his life. He had a dream that he should go to Nepal in search of certain treasure texts and materials, including the relics of some of Buddha's immediate disciples. Several of his disciples from Lahoul went with him. In Nepal the party was caught in a snow avalanche and buried alive.

The mountain kingdoms that border India on the north are magical places. Most of them, like Lahoul, use Tibetan as their mystical/spiritual language, and many send their most promising young students to the Tibetan monasteries for religious education. When we read texts like that of this chapter it amazes us that such an ancient and mystical way of seeing things flourishes unselfconsciously in our present age—ancient not in the sense of primitive but of timeless. I asked the Ven. Doboom Tulku, who had once met the author of this work in Darjeeling, what had been his impression of him, 'A very ordinary type of Tibetan yogi,' he replied, 'like most of the yogis of that nature.'

During the summer of 1982 a friend of mine was planning a short trek in Lahoul, so I gave him a translation of the Gye-re Lama story and asked him to visit Gye-re Mountain. The mountain is located four days' walk off the motor road, but he diligently made his way there. He witnessed the various sites mentioned in the text, such as the cave, ruins of the hut, stupa, Pit Pasture and so forth, and spent an evening there. The place had not changed in the slightest in the years since Dulzhug Lingpa's account, and probably not even very much since the time of the Gye-re Lama himself. The roads and pathways are much the same, as are the people and their way of life.

There are thousands of treasure texts of this nature in Tibetan literature that were either 'found' or dreamed. To the Tibetans, the truth embodied in them is every bit as valid as truth known in any conventional manner. Humans are prone to failure and mistakes, but in the Buddhist way of seeing things clairvoyants are no more so than anyone else, in fact probably less so. The historian scratches through clues and hints left over from the past and from these sources draws conclusions; the clairvoyant, on the other hand, merely reads into the past or future with his/her special talents for doing so.

Dulzhug Lingpa also gives some prophecies concerning things to come. One of them is that 'in eight years blood will flow on Indian soil, and this will adversely affect our way of life.' In fact, the Chinese invasion of India occurred precisely eight years later, in 1962. Although it was but a brief conflict, it had devastating effects on the small Buddhist kingdoms of Himalayan India, all of which suddenly were flooded with army camps and military installations that have remained until the present time. The areas were all sealed off to travel and listed as restricted zones. The effects of the large numbers of soldiers in these thinly populated areas naturally played cultural havoc, causing many of the women to become married off and transported away to distant parts of India, many of the young men to be drawn into the profession of soldiery, many new diseases to be introduced and so forth. The Indian government also started taking a much stronger interest in culturally assimilating the areas, opening schools in which the young children are taught only the language and culture of mainland India and are discouraged in preserving their own cultural identity. The same is the case in Ladakh, Lahoul, Spitti, Kinnaur, and all the Buddhist kingdoms of the western frontier. Much the same is the case in the northern regions on the east, such as Assam and Mon. Consequently these regions find themselves in sad and precarious times.

The account of the death of Gye-re Lama and the traditional Buddhist theme behind it is of personal meaning to me because of the manner of death of one of my own teachers, the former abbot of the Dalai Lama's monastery in Dharamsala. This great guru had served as the abbot of the Gyu-me Tantric College for several years and then as abbot of the Dalai Lama's Namgyal Dratsang for fourteen. He then retired from monastic activity due to a heart condition, and lived quietly devoting his time to meditation and to receiving private students. It was about this time that I met him. He invited me to visit him once a week to practice my Tibetan language and share the perennial cup of butter tea with him. My spoken Tibetan was very rough at the time, and he tremendously improved it, not so much because of giving me linguistic pointers but because of the attitude he cultivated in me. After I had been going to visit him for only a month or so he offered me some advice. 'I want to set a discipline for you,' he told me. 'Never let a Tibetan pass you on the street without striking up a conversation with him/her, and once the conversation has begun don't let it stop until you have made the Tibetan laugh. Tibetans love to laugh, and if they know you are going to make them laugh they will always be willing to stop and talk to you for any length of time.' I took his advice at face value, and over the next few years slowly deciphered the Tibetan sense of humor. In the process of doing so I managed to learn the language.

Several years passed like this, and I continued to visit Rinpoche in his tiny meditation room. Occasionally he would mention to me that one day when his health had improved he would give me a short formal teaching. I rarely mentioned it to him, although every new year's day I would say that I hoped his health had sufficiently improved for him to give me my teaching in the year to come. This was more by way of a conversation piece than a serious suggestion, as I knew he had given up formal teaching. Then one day out of the blue he told me, 'For several years I have been promising to give a formal instruction to you. I think the time has now come. If you wish, you can invite some of your friends to attend as well.' Because the teaching was to be given in a group he arranged for a translator, and the day of the event drew near. When the time of the discourse arrived, Rinpoche had set up the room in a most unusually formal manner, and when the auspicious prayers began I noticed his attendant enter. I was called to Rinpoche's throne and asked to perform symbolic offerings of the objects on the attendant's tray, namely, a stupa image to represent Buddha's mind, a scripture to represent Buddha's speech and a statue to represent Buddha's body, in addition to other auspicious items. As I passed the Buddha image to him I noticed that as he placed it on the table he gave it a push with the corner of his hand, causing it to fall on its back. He quickly set it straight, but our eyes locked for a moment and he met my confusion with a wonderfully reassuring smile.

The teaching then began, but after about fifteen minutes I noticed that although he looked perfect when he himself would speak, even laughing and telling jokes, when he would stop and let the translator talk his face would change color and he would curl up slightly and close his eyes to concentrate on his mantras, turning his rosary rather more quickly than usual. After several minutes had passed I leaned over and asked him if anything was wrong.

'Well,' he replied calmly, 'I'm having a heart attack.' At that moment the translator finished speaking and Rinpoche straightened himself again and went on with the discourse as though nothing were wrong. When he had paused again to let the translator speak I leaned over and asked him, 'Goodness, shouldn't we stop the teaching immediately?' He gave me a long, penetrating look. 'As you wish,' he replied. 'We can either go on now or else finish another time.' I quickly called a halt to things and got everyone out of the room. Rinpoche moved over to his bed and sat in meditation, and several of his monks rushed in and began chanting to him in low, deep tones. He sat in meditation that evening without moving. The next day I visited his house. He was not well enough to receive me, but sent me a message. 'Rinpoche asks that you remember his teaching,' his attendant informed me. That night the lama sat in meditation and ceased breathing. His heart stopped and bodily functions failed, although he did not manifest the full signs of death. This is the practice of *tuk-dam,* when a yogi retreats to the heart in death meditation. He sat like this for three days without manifesting the signs of death. Then his head fell to one side and the death process was complete. Such is the death of an accomplished yogi.

At the time all the monks of the Gyu-me Tantric College, as well as the Namgyal Monastery were in town to receive teachings from the Dalai Lama; as Rinpoche had served as abbot of both these monasteries for years, this meant that almost all his disciples were present for his death. All were permitted into his room to witness his death meditation, a sign of his enlightenment. At three in the morning of the day of the cremation, I made my way up the mountain to the temple. The weather was most amazing—one of the strongest winds I have ever seen in Dharamsala, with thunder and lightning exploding every few moments but not a drop of rain to accompany it. All the monks of

the lama's two monasteries were there. Rinpoche's body was brought
out and placed in front of the temple, and we all offered auspicious
white scarves. The long walk up the mountain to the retreat center
began, where the cremation was to take place, with Tibetans running
out of houses as we passed and placing their white scarves on the feet
of the body.

Then the cremation rite began. The fire was lit and the flames envel-
oped everything. Then a most unusual spectacle occurred. The chest
of the body suddenly seemed to crack open and the heart popped up,
almost like a Jack-in-the-box. It seemed to pulsate several times, and
then fell over to the side like a wilted flower.

I would not relate this story, except that it had so many unusual
twists and is connected so directly with the Buddhist theme of conscious death as a means of instructing disciples.

The next day I went to visit Rinpoche's house. I was feeling somewhat confused by the whole event, overwhelmed by grief at the loss
of this wonderful spiritual friend, and somewhat guilt-ridden to have
been so closely involved in his death. I expressed my emotions to his
attendant.

'There are many details of the event that are unusual,' he told me.
'The day before Rinpoche agreed to give the teaching to you he had
called me in and told me that, watching the play of the clouds on the
horizon, he had been struck by thoughts of the impermanence of all
things, and that he wished to make out his last will and his testament
of parting advice to those of his disciples who would be in need of
guidance after his passing. It was prophesied that he would pass away
this year. Then the evening before the teaching to you he had a slight
stroke. I asked him to cancel the teaching, but he said that he wished to
go on with it as planned. Again in the morning of the teaching he had
a recurrence of the stroke, but still he would not cancel the teaching.

That morning a rainbow appeared that seemed to end at his window, and the Dalai Lama who at the time was in his temple doing
prayers with his monks, mentioned that they should all pray never to
become separated in future lifetimes from great masters like Rinpoche.
All of his disciples from the last thirty years are now in town, and it
seems he wanted them to be here for his death. He seems to have
wanted very much to give the teaching to you. He dedicated his life to
teaching; it would seem that he wished to die while teaching.'

Strangely enough, when I later listened to the tape of Rinpoche's
talk his last words before I insisted on discontinuing the discourse

had been, 'We should meditate on death constantly and realize the impermanent nature of everything. This will give us the inspiration to make every effort to cultivate goodness and avoid evil, and to accomplish the prayers and aspirations of the Buddhas and bodhisattvas of the past.' I had then asked him if, in view of his being in the middle of a heart attack, we should take a break. 'As you wish,' had been his reply. 'We can either finish now or leave it for another time.' I replied, 'Rinpoche, my nerves can't take the intensity. I think we should leave it to another time.' 'Well enough,' he said, and smiled, signalling that the discourse was over. Those were the last words he spoke to me.

Buddha himself had set the example of dying in the presence of one's students and doing so voluntarily and consciously as a skillful means of inspiring the minds of those to be trained. Many of the Dalai Lamas have also followed this tradition.

For example, when the First Dalai Lama was in his eighty-third year he called his disciples to him in an assembly hall of Tashi Lhunpo Monastery and informed them that the time of his passing had come. Some pleaded with him to use his powers to extend his life span, others asked if they could not call for a physician or do anything to prevent his passing. He replied that there was nothing to be done. They then asked if there were any special prayers they should read after his death. He answered, 'Always bear the teachings of Buddha in mind and for the sake of all living beings apply them to the cultivation of your own mindstream. Remember the doctrines of Tashi Lhunpo Monastery. Make every effort to live, meditate and teach in accordance with the true teachings of Buddha. This alone can fulfill my wishes.' He then entered into tantric meditation. His breath ceased and his heart stopped beating, but he remained in meditation for thirty days without showing any signs of death. His body transformed from that of an old man into that of a youth, and emanated lights so radiant that few could bear even to look upon him. Such is the account of the First Dalai Lama's death as related in the standard biographies.[8] His remains were thereafter mummified and placed in a golden encasement. Each of the subsequent Dalai Lamas manifested similar conscious control at the time of death, enacting the scene of passing away in such a manner as would best inspire their disciples.

THE DEATH OF GYE-RE LAMA

by Tertön Dulzhug Lingpa

The remarkable story that follows began on the twenty-fifth day of the seventh moon of the Male Wood Horse Year.[1]

I, the author Dulzhug Lingpa, was walking through Pata of the Lahoul Valley when a golden dakini appeared in the sky and spoke these words: 'Kye! O mighty yogi, you should write the story of the illustrious Kumara Sengha,[2] a mahasiddha of the past.' Having said this, she disappeared into nothingness.

We travelled on for some time, and after a while came to the pilgrimage place known as Gye-re Mountain. One of my followers, a householder by the name of Katang, a man of deep faith in the Doctrine, came up to me and said: 'According to legend this is the principal site associated with Lama Gye-re, a famous sage of days gone by, a yogi renowned for his mystical abilities. The walls of his meditational hut still stand at the peak of this mountain, and below the hut is a cave in which he is said to have dedicated many years in meditation. However, many centuries have passed since he lived, and these days very little is known of his life, other than that he dwelled on this mountain and inspired countless people in the practice of Dharma. Please examine the site and see if you are able to divine anything more on the matter by means of your psychic talents.'

Thus inspired first by the mystic emanation of the golden dakini and also moved by the words of this disciple, we walked up the mountain toward Gye-re Lama's former dwelling place. Beside one of the walls of the dilapidated meditation hut we discovered a square rock marked by the indentation of a human footprint. It would seem that no one before us had noticed this stone. Indeed the impact of observing this rock stirred deep karmic instincts within me.

A short distance down the path we also discovered a huge boulder marked by three indentations. I asked some of the men in the group to turn it over, and on the underside of the rock beheld an imprint of the entire body of a human. Several of the people present commented that the impression could clearly be none other than that of the Gye-re Lama. Lying near this boulder were two pieces of a large stone that had been broken in half. Both pieces were marked by the imprint of a human waist.

We took these boulders—that with the footprint, that with the impression of a complete body and the two pieces of the broken stone bearing the impression of a waist—and placed them respectfully beside the road. Thirteen of us performed prayers, offered a mandala and flowers, and meditated on what we had seen. I also examined the mountain and its environs, and related a few drops from the liberating deeds of the past accomplished ones. All those present were moved by profound spiritual feelings.

That evening we arrived at Kunkhen Gyer. Later on, everyone started partying and making merry. I myself fell asleep quite early. Some time near midnight a young girl appeared to me in a dream. She was wearing many ornaments, and spoke these words: 'O venerable one, today you have discovered several precious articles worthy of devotion. The impressions in these three stones are in fact imprints from the body of the holy Gye-re Lama, whose name was Kumara Sengha, a disciple of the mahasiddha Kangra Ripa, the Hermit of Kangra Mountain.[3] I would like to relate the story of this holy disciple to you. You should listen well and then reveal it to others.'

Having spoken these words, she then proceeded to relate to me the following story.

In Tashi Gang there once lived a patron of Dharma, Tashi Palden by name. The Gye-re Lama lived in the same house as this patron, and one day he confided in him. 'The time of my passing is now drawing near. Soon I shall leave this life for the Pure Land Beneath None, or the Pure Land of Joy. The Lama and his disciples shall soon part, not to meet again in this life.'

The patron Tashi Palden was exceedingly upset and pleaded, 'O venerable teacher, you must live for many more years yet. You are but forty-seven years in age and are in perfect health. Please do not even speak of such matters.'

The Lama replied, 'My dear Tashi, the words of this drunken old man are without an essence. Pay no heed to them. Rather, let us drink another bowl of wine and be happy. I have spent many years in the hermitage of Gye-re Mountain. Tomorrow I shall leave for Nepal, never to return to you again. However, after I have passed away those of you who have faith in me shall receive whatever relics of my body that you wish for.'

The patron wept with sorrow and repeatedly begged the Lama to use his mystical powers and not to pass away. But the old yogi answered, 'O my dear friend, do not be upset. I will not let you fall into the lower realms of being. But it is time for me to take my leave of you. None the less, after five lifetimes I will manifest here again and then the conditions for our reunion will once more ripen.

'Soon I leave for Nepal, never to meet with you again in this life. But do not be disturbed. This is no cause of sorrow. All that lives must face with death sooner or later. Buddha himself passed away, as did all the saints and mahasiddhas of India and Tibet in the past. From beggars to kings, saints to sinners, nothing that breathes is free from the hungry fangs of the greatest of enemies, the powerful Lord of Death.

'Bear this constantly in mind and be inspired to dedicate yourselves immediately to the holy Dharma. Do not be afraid. After I have passed away I shall continue to watch over you, and shall care for you from the Pure Land of Joy.'

The next day the Lama placed his saddle on his blue stallion and rode away.

At that time the Gye-re region was inhabited by eighteen families of nomads, with Jowo Sonam Tobten as their chieftain. Jowo Sonam Tobten had a daughter by the name of Princess Palden Zangmo who, as well as owning much wealth and land, was very powerful. Her best plot of land was the Lotus Pasture, and every year during plowing season the Lama would ride his horse across this field whenever he came and went in the service of the community. This greatly irritated the princess, who gathered together nine strong youths of the Gye-re areas, offered them food and wine, and then plotted with them a most terrible plan.

'Listen to me, O men of Gye-re. I ask of you, who is there in the Myera River Valley or in Taralokinatha or Maruta[4] with more wealth or power than my father? Yet the Gye-re Lama Kumara Sengha persists in constantly abusing his faith. Although we have given him much money to do prayers for the dead, he has no modesty, appreciation or shame. You have seen how arrogantly he rides his horse up and down our best field! Last year I confronted him on this habit of his and asked him to ride around rather than over this pasture. He haughtily replied that until his death he would continue to ride across our land, and even laughed at me and said, "Anyway, what could you do if I chose to ride my horse over your head!" He spoke to me ridiculingly in this way at length. Now he has gone to Nepal. Soon he will return this way again, so let us set a trap for him. We shall dig a pit deep enough for both horse and rider to fall in, covering it with a mat of grass and branches so that it shall not be discovered. Let us construct it in such a way that, after our prey fails in, several large boulders will be triggered to fall in upon him.'

The princess spoke like this until the youths were convinced and agreed to fulfill her wishes.

Meanwhile the Lama was making his way steadily along the road leading to his hermitage. On the way a local divinity appeared to him and warned him of the dangers that lay in wait. '*Kye!* Travelling Lama, do not travel today. If you do, the evil witch Palden Zangmo will catch you in the trap she has built for you. Do not go, I beg you, or if you must go then proceed with the utmost caution, and I will watch over you.'

To this the Lama answered, 'Ah ho! Glorious one who protects the forces of goodness, be not concerned with this matter. I know far more subtle details of this event than do you. The princess was in fact an evil witch in a previous life, and at that time I killed her by using just such a trap as she has set for me now. She fell into my pit and was crushed under falling boulders, just as I must now fall into hers. She has come uninvitedly to seek revenge, but be happy, not sad. My disciples are now well trained, and my life's work is complete.

'It is not the pit that causes my death, nor the falling boulders, for I have attained mastery over the elements. Birth and death have been purified in the sphere of knowledge. It is out of my own choice that I perform this act of accepting death, an act that I have myself contrived in order to inspire those to be trained.'

When the Lama had spoken these words he mounted his horse, crossed the river and began the journey to his hermitage. Soon he neared the approach to the Lotus Pasture, and the jangling of the bells on his horse was heard by the princess and her accomplices, who were delighted that their plot seemed to be working out so well.

As expected, the Lama fell into the trap. A large boulder fell on him but, due to his mystical powers, he was not hurt. The boulder merely broke into two pieces on impact with his body, leaving a deep imprint of his waist on the two sides. The Lama tossed these away and helped the horse out of the trap.

A second boulder, this one much larger than the first, then fell upon him, knocking him down and covering his entire body. Again he was unhurt and an imprint of his entire body, from the crown of his head to his knees, was left upon the rock, with gaping holes where his arms and legs protruded.

A third rock then fell upon his right foot. This time the Lama surrendered to the karmic nature of the event and allowed the drama of death to manifest. His blood flowed forth and covered the rocks, leaving indentations and patterns wherever it touched.

Many divine spirits and celestial beings gathered in the sky above the tragic scene, crying out with sorrow. Countless dakas and dakinis appeared and filled the entire Gye-re region with plaintive song and music that was heard by all eighteen clans.

Princess Palden Zangmo also heard these sounds and was filled with a profound dread. She thought to herself, 'Alas, the heavens are filled with the melody of countless mystical beings and the earth with limitless signs of wonder. Surely this portends the death of the Lama and his horse. But these sounds could signify that the Lama was blessed by the Buddhas, bodhisattvas, meditational deities and Dharma protectors. I hope that no great misfortune will befall the people and prosperity of our tribe as a result of my evil action.'

Indeed, this thought haunted her all that day, and that night she was unable to sleep, tossing and turning in her bed like a lunatic or like a person possessed by a ghost. Therefore in the morning she decided to collect together the eighteen families of the area and take them to the Lotus Pasture.

When the party arrived at the pasture the princess was surprised to see the Lama's horse unharmed and grazing peacefully near the mouth of the trap. Peering into the pit they beheld the body of the Lama. It lay under several large boulders that were covered in a sea of blood.

With great effort they lifted out the boulders and were able to see his feet and shoulders. Both stones bore deep impressions of the Lama's body. The young men then pulled up the large boulder covering the Lama's trunk and were amazed to discover that his body, rather than being crushed, had magically pressed itself into the rock so deeply that it seemed to be part of the stone. When they separated the two, the boulder was left with an indentation that was several hands deep and the length of the entire stone.

All present were struck with wonder and awe. Shaking their heads with sorrow, they looked up at Palden Zangmo with suspicious eyes. The princess herself was filled with horror at the terrible nature of her crime. Her body slumped over with shock and shook with deep sobs. Her mouth went dry, tears poured forth from her eyes and she spoke these words to the crowd: 'All of you, please listen to me. You know that I am the daughter of Jowo Sonam Tobten. Moved by the pride of affluence and power, and misguided by a lack of wisdom, I was propelled to commit this heinous deed. Now I fear that the protective deities of this holy man shall destroy the happiness and prosperity of our people.

'Previously I thought this Lama to be vain, irreligious, unsupported by the protective deities and, in general, lacking in all spiritual qualities. But last night when I heard the divinities cry and wail in all the four directions I realized my mistake. The heavens were filled with music, the earth shook and I clearly understood the excellence of this master. Seeing his body before me now, I can appreciate and perceive that he was a saint who had attained perfect enlightenment. Inconceivable pain and regret weigh down upon my mind. This memory shall haunt me forever.'

The princess then fell into a swoon and lost consciousness. Her attendants quickly sprinkled water upon her heart and rinsed her face. When she had revived, a friend of the family, Yeshe Zangpo by name, came forth from the crowd to console her.

'Princess Palden Zangmo, take heed of my words. I speak to you from the bottom of my heart. Please do not take offense, but listen with an open mind. Generally speaking, all aristocrats are characterized by pride, and you are no exception. Therefore it is sometimes difficult for you to appreciate the goodness in others.

'The Gye-re Lama was indeed a wonderful man. When he came here many winters ago to take up practice in the cave blessed by the Sixteen Arhats[5] that is here on Gye-re Mountain he brought with him only one sack of fuel, a cooking pot and a sack of food. With only these few provisions he lived in solitary retreat throughout the winter, from the eighth month until the fifth month of the following year. All he had to wear was a simple cotton cloth and his only real possession was his meditation mat. Yet he asked nobody for assistance and expected none.

'He lived every winter in this same fashion, and in total has now blessed our land for twenty years and five months. Merely from observing his life style we can clearly see that he was a mahasiddha with a purpose behind his every action, including driving his horse over your land in such an arrogant manner. He was a mighty bodhisattva, and he would never bear a grudge even for such an extreme deed as this.

'There is nothing that can be said or done about a past evil deed. But if you regret the mistake and feel sincere repentance, you should acknowledge your error and perform purification practices. In addition, take the Lama's body and cremate it in as honorable a manner as possible, building a special stupa over it for the cremation ceremony.

'If you can do this well, your heart will be purified of the negative karma and the divinities will be able to send their supporting waves of beneficial energy to you. Then the protective deities will not seek to avenge themselves upon you for this misfortune. Please bear this simple advice in mind.'

Princess Palden Zangmo was moved with faith and confidence by these words. She cried out, 'O Yeshe Zangpo, you are an elder who is long respected and deeply loved by my father. I myself have often relied upon you during the course of my life for advice and guidance. I would be most pleased to sponsor the procedures that you suggest. My wealth and men are at your disposal. Please help me arrange to have the correct prayers read, to have the cremation pyre constructed and to do whatever else is necessary.'

With tears flowing from their eyes the young men set about making the cremation pyre. Others went out in the various directions to collect what was required for the cremation ritual. Thirteen monks came and read the required prayers for a full seven days. All the people of the Maruta area collected together in order to receive blessings from the Lama's deceased form.

Then the time of the actual cremation ritual began. When the ritualists arrived at the section of the liturgy where the fire is to be lit, the Lama's body suddenly and spontaneously burst into flames. The fire quickly spread to the wood and the entire pyre ignited. Tongues of flame shot up the chimney of the pyre and leapt far into the sky.

Suddenly the Lama's body disappeared and a rainbowlike ball of light appeared above the pyre. In the centre of the light sat an eight-year-old child, radiant in appearance, smiling down upon the crowd and fully visible to all.

The child cried out in a gentle, compassionate voice,

> O Palden Zangmo and all those who are present,
> Please listen well to what I have to say.
>
> Avoid holding negative thoughts
> Toward the gurus and Dharma masters.
> Rely instead upon respect, and upon
> Pure perception based on a positive motivation.
>
> Abandon meaningless activity
> And exert yourself to practice the path.

Having attained a precious human incarnation,
Strive to render it spiritually meaningful.

Contemplate the reality of death
And the vicious wheel of misery
In which the beings of the six realms
Find themselves enmeshed and bound.

Become wise in the teachings
On the karmic laws of cause and effect
And develop the free spirit of non-attachment,
The very legs of the spiritual path.

Just as non-attachment is the legs,
The compassionate bodhimind is the trunk
And pure perception of all that appears is the head.
Cultivate these three essential qualities,
The body and foundation of the spiritual path.

These three fulfill the three pledges—
Those of the Hinayana, Mahayana and Vajrayana.
They are indispensable to the spiritual quest.
Strive, therefore, to accomplish them.

Joyous indeed is the mindstream
Freed from attachment.
Hence, avoid the eight worldly concerns,
Which only bind the mind in negative emotions.

The five psychic poisons that afflict the mind—
Attachment, anger, jealousy, pride and ignorance—
These are the real enemies of mankind.
It is these that we should try to slay.

Avoid works of little consequence
And seek the path to spiritual joy.
The things of this life quickly fade;
Cultivate that which benefits eternally.

Constantly be mindful of the Three Jewels of Refuge
And dwell within the compassionate bodhimind.
Face your every fault and shortcoming
And cultivate every force of goodness within.

The guru is the embodiment
Of the Buddhas of the ten directions.
Avoid cynicism and negative thoughts toward him.
Do not become separated even for a moment
From the pure attitude that sees the guru's ways
As wise means for taming the minds of trainees.

Seek initiations and blessings again and again,
Until the mind is saturated with them.

Never be influenced by prejudices and superstitions;
Keep the mind always open and clear.

This is the essence of my advice to you.
Please try to observe it.
I myself will watch over your practice
From my abode in the Pure Land of Joy.

There is no need for sadness at my death.
If you follow the ways of the divinities,
I shall indeed be filled with joy, and shall
Care for you until your enlightenment,
Offering prayers that all auspicious signs appear.

At this the child concluded his sermon, transformed into a ball of light and disappeared into the sky.

The people in the audience fell upon the earth like fish hooked from the water and tossed upon the sand. Their minds filled with devotion, they cried out plaintively in the direction of the sky from where the child had spoken and into which he had melted.

As for the Lotus Pasture, because the Lama had been killed here by means of falling into a deep pit, the land was renamed 'Pit Pasture,' the name by which it is known even today. The people filled the pit with various grains and offering substances. On top of it they placed, face down, the boulder having the imprint of the Lama's body. At the top of the mountain on the side facing Chieftain Jowo Sonam Tobten's house they built a stupa in which to place the ashes and relics from the Lama's funeral pyre. From that time on the people of the district would gather annually for three days in order to offer prayers and meditations at the foot of the stupa.

As for Princess Palden Zangmo, she fully repented of her deed. She took the rock bearing the imprint of the Lama's right foot, and as an act of penance placed it in the center of the road where all passersby would behold and revere it. Each day she returned to this rock, to sit in prayer and meditation beside it. In fact, she maintained this practice diligently until eventually she attained full spiritual realization.

Thus ends the first part of the account of Gye-re Lama, which deals with his unusual death, as related to me (Dulzhug Lingpa) by the mystical golden dakini who appeared to me in a dream. When the dakini had completed her story she melted into light and disappeared.

I (Dulzhug Lingpa) didn't write down anything of the event at the time, but continued on my journey the following day.

Some months later I again passed through the Myera district. On this occasion our party stayed on the corner of the Pit Pasture. I had to share a bed with my son Kunzang Namgyal, who at the time was nine years old. Kunzang was restless during the night and I spent the time hovering between sleep and wakefulness. I began to reflect on what I knew of the Gye-re Lama from my dreams and experiences, and I thought that perhaps it would be useful to write them down. In addition, several of my disciples had expressed the need for a biography of this excellent yogi.

I didn't write anything then, and the next day our party moved along, until we arrived at the hermitage of Patanam, where we planned to spend the night. The following morning I again experienced a vision of the Gye-re Lama. The vision came to me just after dawn as the light was changing. This time the Lama appeared to me in the form of a sixteen-year-old boy. He hovered amidst a halo of light in the space before me. His face was white with a reddish tinge, his long hair was tied on his head in a yogic knot, a meditation band was wrapped around his body and he wore only a small cotton waistcloth. He held a vajra in his right hand and a skull-cup filled with ambrosia in his left, and his feet were in the position of the vajra dance.

He looked at me and said, 'O mighty one, I will reveal to you a fragment of the life of Kumara Sengha. You should reveal it to others.'

He then proceeded to speak the following revelation to me.

'During the time when the great guru Padma Sambhava[6] was living at Samye Monastery, I, the Gye-re Lama, was incarnate as Gonlu Wang-po. In the life that followed, I took rebirth as Rashak Terton. It is in the life that followed this that I became the Gye-re Lama Kumara Sengha.

'In my life as the Gye-re Lama I was born at Dozang [Copper Rock] of Azha. The place gained its name because it was characterized by a large copper rock shaped like a drum for calling forth the dakinis.

'Dozang had eight villages. The village that I was born in was slightly poorer than the others. My father's name was Tobgyal and my mother's Palzom Kyipa. My parents had three sons, of whom I was the youngest.

'By the age of six I had learned to read and write. After that I went to study under Gyalwa Gotsang[7] and there performed the preliminary and foundation practices. I also received initiation into the four classes of tantra. As part of the training I spent five years in intensive practice on Tilbu Mountain[8] at the instruction of my teacher. I then went on pilgrimage to the holy places of India for a year.

'Having completed the pilgrimage to India, I went to the town of Kangra and upon the mountain there raised the victory banner of the three-year retreat at a quiet spot just above the place where the straw weavers work. There I met with the mahasiddha known as Kangra Ripa, or 'The Hermit of Kangra Mountain.' It was under his guidance that I accomplished the outer and inner practices of the secret Vajrayana.

'I then returned to Azha and Zangling, spending a year in each place meditating and giving teachings.

'Then one day I had a vision of a dakini, who advised me to travel to Tibet. Consequently I visited the four parts of Central Tibet for seven years and spent considerable time at Samye, Chimpu, Lhodrak, Kharchu, Olkar, Dvakpo, Tsangrong, Sakya, Mt. Kailash,[9] and so forth, raising the victory banner of practice in these places and guiding many spiritual aspirants to higher planes of realization.

'After this I spent a year inside the borders of Nepal, working for the benefit of the Doctrine and living beings.

'I then stayed on the Pangge and Kashmir side of the mountains for a year. During that time I did what I could for the Doctrine and the beings there. I also practiced *karmamudra*[10] with many celestial, naga and human females, and thus accomplished the state of a knowledge holder with power over life and death.

'The time then came to tame the peoples of the Myera River Valley. With this thought in mind I built a meditation hut upon Gye-re Mountain. A small cave was nearby in which I would live for a month every summer. Also nearby was a cave known as Brilliant Source of Truth, which was located near a small turquoise pond at the foot of the snow mountains and was said to carry the blessings of the Sixteen Arhats. Every winter I would dwell in this cave from the eighth month until halfway through the fifth month of the following year.

'In my thirty-fifth year a Nepali yogi by the name of Jigme Tseling also took up practice on Gye-re Mountain. As a consequence, one day an invitation came to me from Nepal requesting me to come there and teach. By means of magical ability I flew to Nepal and turned the Dharma Wheel for them for three months, and then flew back. Because of how I went there and returned, I became known as the "Flying Lama." The beings there were very sophisticated and quite wealthy. When I left I took several strains of grain seeds with me and later gave these to the five villages of Tashi Gang. For the five years that followed, their fields yielded three times the normal harvest.

'In the year that followed my return from Nepal I lived in a large field on Gye-re Mountain for about a year, performing incense and golden vessel offerings and satiating the eight types of local spirits.

During this time I experienced a vision of Gesar[11] and also Druk Lhamo.[12] This latter divinity, known as the Dragon Queen, offered me a skull-cup filled with the elixir of immortality. Since then the field in which I had been living has been known as the Dragoness Pasture.

'There was a cave at the head of the river that runs through this field, and in it I hid several treasure texts of instructions concerning the elixir of immortality and the yogic methods for achieving longevity.[13]

'In total I spent twenty years and five months like this in the Gye-re district working for the welfare of the people and other living beings of the area. Finally I enacted the death scene that was revealed to you earlier by the golden dakini. As this has already been described to you, there is no need for me to relate it again now.'

When the Lama of my vision had finished speaking, I placed the following question to him.

'*Kye!* O lord of mahasiddhas, how wondrous is the story of your life and liberation. But you have said that after five lifetimes you would again be seen by your disciples. As the people of those five lives are long dead and gone, how is this prophecy to be fulfilled? Please speak of these five incarnations.'

To this the Lama answered, 'These five are as follows. 'The first of the five was Kumara Sengha, the Gye-re Lama who was born at Azha. The second was as Rangrig Repa of Palding. The third was Namkha Rigzin Wangdrak of Chong-gyal. Fourthly I was reborn in Eastern Tibet as Khangdong Sonam Wangdu. My fifth incarnation was as Khajo Lingpa of Zalmo Gang-gyu.

'*Kye!* O mighty knowledge holder, heed my words. This is how my followers from so long ago will come to know my history and to see me as prophesied. The Lama Kumara Sengha is now incarnate as Samanta, who is present in this district at the moment. By the power of my prayers and because my disciples did not turn away from their tantric commitments of practice, those of them with whom I have had strong karmic connections in numerous past lives have taken rebirth in this very district at the present time.

'And just who are they? Kumara Sengha's patron Tashi Palden now bears the name Kathang. Kumara Sengha's chief disciple has taken rebirth in Azhal as Dorje Zangpo and is known by the name Jangchub.

'The elderly family advisor Yeshe Zangpo is now reborn as Purnakirti. His elder brother Tsering Pal has been reborn recently as Pema Dechen.

'The chieftain Jowo Sonam Tobten is now Tsering Namgyal. His wife Jowo Singmo now bears the name Ram.

'The Lama's blue stallion is now reborn as Kanu. The Lama's disciple from the border area between Drak and Kong is reborn as Vidyadhara Dipa.

'As for the princess Palden Zangmo, she has been reborn in the area as a girl named Chokyi, who lives near the Pit Pasture.[14]

'Furthermore, if anyone sees the stone impressions of my body, my places of meditation or this biography and if as a result they experience a sensation of intense faith, this is a sign that he/she was a disciple or patron of mine in a past life.

'In fact, most of the men and women living in the Myera River Valley at the moment were among the disciples and patrons of the Gye-re Lama Kumara Sengha. And I am still continuing to watch over them with compassion.

'Those who share a strong karmic connection with me should cultivate a strong tradition of invoking the Urgyen Norlha on the tenth day of the sixth month of each year. They should also erect a stupa of Mara's Defeat at the head of the valley, and should apply themselves to the subduing of evil.

'They should diligently practice the yogas of the *Vajrakilaya-tantra*,[15] performing these and other such methods in order to guard the land from disease, war and violence. The lay people should try to recite the Mani, Tara and Vajraguru mantras.[16]

'If this advice is followed, then for eight years there will be signs of prosperity, and both disease and the signs of disease and evil energy will be eliminated.

'Alternatively, should no efforts be made in order to turn away negative conditions, then suffering will increase every year. Contagious diseases will enter the valley and the forces of darkness shall show increasing strength in the minds of the people. Appreciation for the spiritual path will be replaced by faith in sinful ways. The people will become confused inside and will be disturbed by unhappy thoughts. Many of them will embrace the religion of the barbarians [i.e., Islam],[17] and the Buddha Doctrine shall decline. The mountains will erode and the rivers become polluted. In the end the young people will abandon our valleys and go to live in other places, leaving the villages empty.

'Although the Three Jewels of Refuge have profound compassion for living beings, when the times are filled with negative conditions there is little that the Jewels of Refuge can do; and even when the people strive in the ways of turning negativity away, they easily are distracted and lose their focus to the sceptical, faithless mind.

'It is difficult to achieve significant spiritual results when the basis of one's practice is devoid of confidence. Therefore avoid the mind of doubt and timidity. Those who wish to experience higher joy and happiness must pass beyond the double-pointed mind of hesitation and doubt, applying themselves single-pointedly to the methods that turn away negativity. Then there is no doubt that for eight years goodness, happiness and prosperity will ensue.

'After that there will come a period of difficulty for these Himalayan mountain kingdoms. In eight years [i.e., 1962] blood will flow on Indian soil, and this will adversely affect our way of life here. Fewer people will then become devoted to the Doctrine, and the forces of evil shall gain in strength.

'Therefore those with faith in Dharma should quickly apply themselves to the spiritual path. Guarding their tantric commitments as they would their heart's blood, they should follow the instructions of their spiritual guides and should abandon distorted attitudes. Without wavering, they should persevere in practice and in generating positive energy by making offerings to the Three Jewels and by being generous toward the needy. Constantly maintaining compassion and the free spirit of non-attachment, they should follow the ten paths of virtue and overcome evil by being mindful of their spiritual practices.

'The methods of producing happiness here and hereafter as well as achieving all levels of spiritual attainment depend upon not becoming separated from the holy teachers and also upon maintaining self-discipline in one's practice. Those of good fortune carefully pursue these two themes. *Samaya.*'

When the Lama of my vision had completed his prophecy and advice, I begged him to relate a prayer by which those who were devoted to him could pray to him. This is the prayer that he transmitted, explaining that it 'was a general method of praying to him as being inseparable from and in the form of Guru Padma Sambhava, and that if there were people who felt stronger karmic connections with other lineage masters they could merely change and adapt the words of the prayer accordingly.'

> O Padma Sambhava, Lotus Born Guru, precious one of Urgyen, embodiment of all saints and scholars of India and Tibet, as well as of the Tathagatas of the three times, lord of the dakas and dakinis, king of guardians and Dharma protectors, teacher more kind than all other Buddhas of this degenerate age to the peoples of the Himalayan kingdoms, to you I turn for inspiration day and night without let.

The Lama then went on to say that this was a brief prayer for praying to the Gye-re Lama as one with Guru Padma Sambhava, and that if anyone required a longer practice focusing directly on the Gye-re Lama in his own form, they could use the following liturgy:

Namo! Homage to the Three Jewels.
In order to benefit all living beings,
I give rise to the altruistic bodhimind.
In the presence of the Three Jewels,
The gurus, deities and protectors
I acknowledge all my weaknesses and failings
And face every mistaken action I have created.

I rejoice in your marvelous excellence
And request you to turn Dharma's wheel.
Do not pass out of the world,
But remain with us and teach us, I pray.

May any creative energy
Thus generated by my voicing this prayer
Be dedicated to the sublime goal
Of emptying the ocean of samsaric existence.

Ah!!! In the space before me
At the center of a vibrant rainbow
Sits the crown jewel of all Enlightened Ones,
Kumara Sengha, a protector of living beings.

He is handsome with youth
And his hair is tied up in a knot.
He is charmingly pleasant to behold,
His white skin flushed with red.

In his right hand he holds a golden vajra
And in his left a skull-cup filled with elixir.
Wearing a cotton cloth and red meditation band,
He sits in the royal posture,
The sun and moon the cushions of his seat.
In nature he is all objects of refuge.

Kye!!! O precious Lama,
Look with eyes of compassion upon
The beings of poor fate and ill karma.
Help us to gain freedom from sorrow.

Pacify the world and its beings.
Pacify illness, war, violence and weakness.
Look with love, mercy and compassion upon
The beings without refuge or protection.

Free us from the mud of suffering.
Protect us from the rivers of the eight samsaric terrors.
Lead us to the jewel isle of enlightenment.
Make our tent the awareness of deeper truth
Held firm by the strong ropes
Of love, compassion and non-attachment.

May all the living beings quickly accomplish
The great purpose of enlightenment
For the benefit of themselves and others.
Bless us to realize in this very life
The state of a master who has attained the four *kayas* of a Buddha.
O source of all hope, treasure of love and compassion,
Grant blessings that these prayers may be fulfilled.

May the Buddha-nature in living beings
And the fresh vase of higher awareness
Enter into communion with the Inner Guru
The primordial Buddha within.

May the living beings achieve perfection,
The liberation that does not cling
To either samsara or nirvana,
Magically manifesting in the world of form
As a magnificent rainbow body.

This is the prayer that the Lama conveyed to me. He then instructed that at the completion of the prayer the faithful could recite the name mantra of Kumara Sengha, maintain awareness of empowerment, make dedications and offer prayers and auspicious substances. In this way the devout could place a seal at the center of their hearts.

The name mantra that he transmitted is as follows: *OM AH HUM VAJRA MAHAGURU KUMARA SENGHA SARVA SIDDHI HUM.*

These were the words that the Lama spoke to me from the sphere of self-awareness beyond thought and expression.

The colophon: This account of the life and death of Gye-re Lama Kumara Sengha and of the pilgrimage site on Gye-re Mountain where the Lama meditated, together with the prayer to the Lama, has been written out by the treasure revealer Terton Dulzhug Lingpa, assisted by the scribe Ngawang Tubten. It was first requested by my disciples Jangchub and Sonam Drakpa, as well as several other of my disciples. In addition, my fatherly teacher advised me to write out my dreams, visions and so forth concerning the Gye-re site. Thoughts of these encouragements repeatedly entered my mind during the construction of the Ehvang Lung Stupa at Myera, and when several more disciples again pressed me to record my revelations, I felt it would be appropriate to do so. May it contribute to the goodness of the world and the spiritual unfoldment of mankind.

Chapter Five
Self-Liberation
by Knowing the Signs of Death

Behold a pale horse; and his name that sat on him was death.

—Revelations 6:8

TRANSLATOR'S PREAMBLE

The Tibetans seem to have always possessed a love for magic and mystery. Although trained in the high logic of Nagarjuna and Dharma-kirti, they none the less still hold a strong interest in the methods of natural psychic lore. This is perhaps not surprising in that the early Indian logicians, including Nagarjuna himself, wrote on the mystical sciences such as alchemy, divination and so forth, and lived dual lives of conservative monasticism and midnight tantric revelry.[1]

Numerous forms of divination flourished in the Land of Snows such as predictions by dice, reading rosary beads, observing cloud formations, dream interpretations, astrology, etc. Amongst these was the science (Tib., *rigpa*) of looking for signs or omens portending death, which ranked with special importance amongst tantric yogins and yoginis. Numerous manuals and commentaries have been written on this subject over the centuries both in India and Tibet, and these still enjoy a continuing popularity.

Three of the most popular versions of this type of text are: the brief outline of the signs of death and the longevity and consciousness transference yogas of the Milarepa lineage, as recorded by the First Dalai

Lama;[2] the Karma Lingpa *Self-Liberation by Knowing the Signs of Death*,
which is a Nyingma tradition; and Langdol Lama's *Analyzing for the
Signs of Death*.[3] These were all written in Tibet, the first in the early
fourteenth century, the second in the fifteenth century and the third
several hundred years later, in the eighteenth century. There were
numerous versions before, during and after these three, but none have
achieved a comparable level of popularity in the yogic community.

The First Dalai Lama in his work on the subject points out two of
the most important Indian Buddhist sources for the Tibetan system:
The Tantra of the Threefold Unmoving Vajra[4] and *The Tantra of the Source
of the Mystic Bond*.[5] He quotes these extensively to show how the Tibetan tradition of divination of the time of death is not an indigenous
system but in fact originates in India.

For this chapter, however, I elected to use Karma Lingpa's text on
the subject. Although he does not state his Indian sources, his work is
later than that of the First Dalai Lama and therefore we can presume it
has a common origin in Indian Buddhism, at least in those aspects
where the two scriptures give parallel explanations.

Karma Lingpa is one of Tibet's most renowned *terton*, or 'treasure
revealers' (see the preamble to chapter four). The *Karling Zhi-tro*[6] contains thirty-eight scriptures related to the mandala of peaceful and
wrathful deities that appear in *The Tibetan Book of the Dead*. Karma
Lingpa was the revealer of *The Tibetan Book of the Dead* itself and thus
is already a figure well known to the West, at least as an author. Not
much has been published in English on his life and works, other than
the *Book of the Dead*, although the materials that sprang from his pen
are both rich and extensive.

The text of this chapter, *Self-Liberation by Knowing the Signs of Death*,
is in fact a prefatorial section to the standard *Tibetan Book of the Dead*,
and is usually applied in context to a study of it. When the signs indicating certain death arise, a yogi of the tradition would begin intensely
familiarizing himself with the *Book of the Dead* and also the yogas of
consciousness transference.

The First Dalai Lama gives the reason for the tradition of observing
for death signs as follows:[7]

> To live and have a precious human life form is to have the opportu-
> nity to practice the spiritual path and consequently to accomplish
> that state which is ultimately beneficial to both oneself and others.
> Life is very precious when used in this way. This is the reason for the
> instructions on how to watch for the signs of death. The longevity

yogas are taught because when uncertain signs occur, the death that they indicate can be turned away by means of the application of these yogas. Moreover, once one comes to the end of one's life span and has to face death, one requires a method for controlling and directing the mind at death and for transferring consciousness to an appropriate rebirth. Therefore the study of the signs of death must also be accompanied by a study of the longevity yogas and of the methods of consciousness transference for when longevity cannot be achieved.

As Karma Lingpa points out in the opening verses of his text:

We humans face two kinds of death: death by untimely conditions and death by the natural exhaustion of our life span. Untimely death can be turned away through the methods taught for achieving longevity. However, when the cause of death is the exhaustion of the natural life span, these methods will be of little value. One's situation is then like that of a butter lamp empty of oil: without a hope but soon to be extinguished.

The First Dalai Lama gives us a more detailed analysis:[8]

There are three causes of death, namely, exhaustion of life span, exhaustion of positive energy, and exhaustion of karmic life supports. Each of these has its own remedy. When the death indicated has its cause in one or two of the above reasons it can be turned away by the appropriate methods. However, when it is caused by an exhaustion of all three, there is no way to deter the advent of death. All one can do then is to prepare one's mind for death by means of training in the consciousness transference yogas.

This is precisely the Buddhist view of the nature of our life span. Our life has no fixed or specific limit in the sense that we are not preordained from birth to die at some destined moment. Rather, it is more a case of having certain danger points in our lives. It is these that are indicated by the death signs, almost in the way a negative astrological aspect indicates a problematic period. It is not necessarily true that something horrible will occur at the time of this aspect, but it is wise to proceed with special care during the crucial phase. If not, unfavorable circumstances may erupt.

Karma Lingpa's text is a compendium of various systems and methods for divining the time of danger to our life span. Generally a yogi would adopt one or another of them. He presents such a variety of techniques that at some points in the chapter we can feel almost overwhelmed by the sheer number of methods, and can hardly see the forest for the trees. We must keep in mind that the text, as well as serving as a practical guide to a yogi wishing to perform a personal divination, is attempting to collect and preserve the tradition as a whole for the sake of posterity.

It should be noted that the manifestations of any of these signs are only of significance when the proper preliminary rituals for inducing prophetic abilities have been done, as is explained several times throughout the text. Should any of the signs appear to someone who has not performed these rites, it is not very probable that anything serious is indicated. Therefore the work will only be of practical value to initiates with the background enabling them to perform these rites. To anyone else it should be regarded only as food for thought.

Some sections will none the less be of interest to thanatologists, especially that on the experience of death. This portion of the text clarifies Geshe Dargye's explanation of the death process as given in chapter two earlier, throwing a deeper light on the Buddhist concept of the dying person's experience.

The Tibetan system of divination of signs indicating the time of death gives us an insight into the Buddhist view of the nature of life and the relationship between the individual and the world. Karma Lingpa's version also offers a perspective on the life-death-rebirth process, as well as making several important references to the body-mind relationship.

In his foreword to the *I Ching*,[9] a Chinese book of divination, the noted psychologist Dr. C.G. Jung offers some interesting reflections on the nature of the prophetic arts. As he puts it, whenever we perform a divination what we are doing is observing aspects of the moment that are 'acausal connecting principles' that share a 'synchronicity' with the subject at which the divination process is aimed. He is of course putting the process in context to the hexagram, the divination method of the *I Ching*, but the same reasoning and principles should theoretically also apply to other divination systems. Thus he says, 'When one throws the three coins, or counts the forty-nine yarrow sticks [used in the *I Ching* divination method], these chance details enter into the picture of the moment of observation and form a part of it—a part that is insignificant to us, yet most meaningful to the Chinese mind.'

The same holds true of the Tibetan Buddhist methods of performing observations for the signs of death. These signs manifest not because of the causal relationship between the observation and the subject being tested, but because of the synchronicity of the world and the events that link us to it, a synchronicity that is there even when we do not notice it. When we perform the rituals that invoke the divination, such as throwing the yarrow sticks or dice, or, in the case of the observation for the death signs, doing the prayers and rites mentioned by Karma Lingpa, what we are doing is, as Dr. Jung puts it, making ourselves aware of 'acausal connecting principles.'[10] We are not creating or conjuring up the signs that we observe, but are merely making ourselves aware of what normally are invisible 'qualities of the moment' that share a synchronicity with the object of the observation.

Karma Lingpa's text oscillates somewhat between imagery and ideas that fit well with the modern view of things, and a view of life that we can easily feel is part of a bygone culture, an obsolete perception. However, it is perhaps unfair of us to judge this type of book by our present standards, as there is little in our own culture to which it can be compared. Due to this rather unfamiliar nature of its contents I felt at first that it may be best to leave it out of the collection, but conscience got the better of me in the end, and I decided that it would be unfair to the Tibetan tradition and to the reader not to include it in a volume of this nature. Karma Lingpa's text is not in any way anything but mainstream in the Tibetan tradition; there are dozens of works dealing with methods of observing for signs of death. His text is in fact one of the most accessible in the genre. It is not an easy matter to jump from one culture to another, and this is one of the fields where this transition is especially difficult. But the sensitive reader will hopefully be able to glean some meaning from the text, and gain a degree of insight into the natural mysticism that is woven into the fiber of the tantric view of life and death.

SELF-LIBERATION BY KNOWING THE SIGNS OF DEATH

by Terton Karma Lingpa

From the self-liberation cycle of texts
Related to the profound doctrine
Of the peaceful and wrathful mandala deities,
Herein is revealed the self-liberation method
Of analyzing for the signs of death
As a condition for gaining spiritual freedom
By hearing when entering the bardo.
Listen to it closely, O noble ones.

Samaya!!! Kye-ma!!!
This weak illusory body of ours,

Born from causes and conditions,
Is unreliable, like a butter lamp
Left outside in a violent wind storm.[1]
It cannot endure for long.
Nowhere is there a samsaric body
That is not a vessel of death.
Moreover, the time of death is uncertain,
So we should always be mindful
Of the signs of approaching death
And should strive in the spiritual path.

We humans face two kinds of death:
Death by untimely conditions, and
Death caused by the exhaustion of natural life span.
Untimely death can be turned away through
The methods taught for achieving longevity.
However, when the cause of death is
The exhaustion of the natural life span,
These methods will be of little value.
One's situation is then like that
Of a butter lamp empty of oil;
Without a hope but soon to be extinguished.

Anyone interested in making the observations
For the signs that portend death
Should firstly perform the preliminary practices
Of offering *tsok*[2] to the visualized assembly
Of gurus, meditation deities and dakinis.
They should also make the *torma*[3] offering
To the Dharma protectors and guardians,
And should invoke the worldly divinities
And local spirits, making offerings to them.
Only when these preliminaries have been performed
Correctly and with diligence
Will the observation for the death signs
Be of any value or meaning.
The signs that are discussed in this text
Are not valid should they appear
When the preliminaries have not been performed.

As for the actual signs themselves,
They are of six principal types:
Outer, inner, secret,
Knowledge, short-termed and
The miscellaneous signs other than these.

THE OUTER SIGNS

The first of the six types of signs are the outer signs. As their appearance indicates danger to the very life force itself, they are called 'death
omens.'

After the preliminary rituals mentioned above have been completed,
observe the body in the days that follow. If it greatly changes in appearance, should the stomach shrink and sensory powers become
unclear, should the body, speech and mind be distorted by anxiety,
should the mind become hyperactive or depressed, should one be disturbed by dreams, should one's personality radically change, or should
the pallor of one's skin become indistinct: all these are signs that indicate the presence of a hindrance that could result in death.

General signs appearing on the body to indicate specific times of
death are as follows. Should the natural redness fade suddenly from
the limbs or nails of the body, this indicates death will follow in nine
months less a half day. If the whiteness of one's eyes fades, this portends death in five months. Should the hair on the nape of one's neck
curl upward, this indicates that death will follow in three months'
time. If when one goes to the toilet one simultaneously emits urine,
excrement and a sneeze, this is also a sign of approaching death.

Other general signs are as follows. Should one's flesh suddenly become loose and hang limply; if one's bodily odor suddenly changes; if
one's bodily luster changes; should one's voice suddenly lose its richness; should any of one's five senses lose their power or begin to mis-
apprehend objects: all these are signs indicating that one has fallen
into the hand of the mighty Lord of Death.

A yogic means by which to analyze for death signs is as follows.
This method is to be applied when one is healthy and free of disease.
Perform the preliminary rituals mentioned earlier. Then press the fingers lightly upon the eyelids and read the pattern of floating suns that
seem to appear. When no sun appears below the left eye, death will
follow after six months. When none appears above the left eye, this
indicates death in three months. When no sun appears in front of the
nose, this indicates death after one month. When no sun appears near
the ears, death will follow in two months. When no sun appears below the right eye, this indicates death in ten days. If none appears
above the right eye, death will come in five days.

An alternative test is as follows. One stops the ears with one's fingers and listens to the roaring sound that is normally heard. If it ceases
for a day one should know that death will follow after a period of six

years. If it ceases for two days, death will come in six years less three months. Similarly, in this way, for each day that the sound ceases, death will come three months sooner. That is, three days silence indicates death in six years less six months, four days silence indicates six years less nine months, and so on. However, it is said that the exact date of death cannot be precisely calculated in this way.

These are the external signs of death. It is said that the death they prophesy is easily turned away by the longevity meditations. As for these longevity practices, one can learn more about them from the standard manuals.

THE INNER SIGNS

The next category of signs, the inner signs, is read by two methods: observing the breath and observing one's dreams.

As before, perform the preliminary rites that cause the signs to arise.

The method of observing the breath is to be performed at dawn of the new moon. It is best done in a season when the days and months are equal in length.

Sit in the seven-point posture of Vairochana,[4] with legs crossed in the meditation posture, hands folded in the lap, etc. Then observe the flow of the breath.

Should the breath flow solely through the left nostril for three successive dawns and then on the dawn of the fourth day change and pass solely through the right nostril for three days, to change back to the left nostril again on the seventh day, and so on, changing after every third day, continuing like this for a month and a half; and should the pattern then reverse and begin with the breath passing first through the right nostril rather than the left, it is said that one will die after six months. Should the cycle change after a month rather that a month and a half, one will face many difficulties. If the pattern changes after only two weeks, a serious illness is indicated. If it reverses after only a few days, one will have social problems, such as coming under criticism, etc.

If at the time of observation the breath begins to flow through both nostrils and the mouth, or ceases passing through the nostrils and instead passes solely through the mouth, this indicates that death will follow very soon.

Secondly, now follows the tradition of observing dreams for signs of death. Here it is said that there is no significance in any dreams experienced between dusk and midnight, but if from midnight until dawn one has any of the following dreams they should be noted and analyzed for meaning.

It is a sign of death to dream of riding upon the back of a red cat or monkey, especially if one is riding in an easterly direction. It is also inauspicious to dream of being killed by a king.

If one dreams of riding toward the south on the back of a tiger, wolf corpse, buffalo, pig, camel or donkey, this is a sign of death.

Furthermore, to dream of eating excrement, running downhill while wearing black clothing, being caught and held in a stock or in chains, or of engaging in sexual play with a black demoness or animal, are all signs of impending death.

Other dreams indicating a threat to one's life are as follows. To dream that a black demoness attacks and disembowels you; or that a black humanlike demon with an iron staff comes and tells you to go away, or leads you away by means of a rope tied around your neck; or if you dream of being captured inside a fence and consumed by fire; or of having your head cut off and then carried away by others; or of being surrounded by crows or ghosts; of being a bridegroom being led away by a musical troupe; of being naked and seeing your hair or beard cut off; or dream repeatedly of walking with friends who have died, or being led away by them; or if you dream of jumping into a river and being swallowed by a fish or mud; or of sleeping in or entering into a womb; or of losing a war with others; or dream of wearing red clothing, carrying a red rosary, or plucking red flowers again and again; or dream of climbing on red hills or walking on the red plains of India; or of having your head wrapped in red silk scarves; or if you repeatedly dream of sleeping in a charnel ground; of being old and having to carry a heavy burden; or if you dream of the world becoming dark and that the sun and moon fall to earth; or if you dream that you fall upside down into a ditch; of dancing with evil spirits; or of going to a faraway place with the thought never to return: all of these are signs that indicate the approach of untimely death.

The death prophesied by these dreams is easily turned away by the longevity methods. Should one have any of the above dreams after the preparatory rituals have been done to induce prophetic signs of death, and if one does not apply the longevity methods, death will fall within a year.

Also, if after performing the preparatory rituals that induce prophetic signs one should dream of a lunar or solar eclipse, or dream that a parent or teacher dies, these also are signs of impending death, even if one is in perfect health.

These are the inner signs of impending death. It is said that the death indicated by them is more difficult to eliminate through yogic means than is the death prophesied by the outer signs described earlier.

THE SECRET SIGNS

Should the outer or inner signs appear, the death indicated by them should be counteracted and turned away by performing the longevity methods. However, should one perform these practices and the signs not be eliminated, one should make an observation for the secret signs of death.

Here the word 'secret' refers to the secret substances, that is, the male or female sexual fluids.

Begin by generating the bodhisattva spirit of enlightenment, the altruistic aspiration to highest awakening for the benefit of others. Then take refuge and offer prayers.

The time for the examination is the first day of the lunar cycle. The substance to be examined is the sexual fluids, as stated above.

When a male's sperm is black or a woman's flow white, this is said to be a sign that death will follow in two months' time. When the male's sperm is red he will die after six months. If it is the normal shade of white there is no obstacle.

Some sources also mention making an observation by smelling the fluids while they are still warm. This is sometimes performed in conjunction with the rituals for turning death away.

Furthermore, if a man's semen flows without any sensation of orgasm and seems to contain small droplets of sweatlike oil sprinkled throughout it; or if a woman's flow is unceasing and she dreams of plucking red flowers; or if a male's sperm flows continually even when he is not having sexual intercourse, these are signs that death will follow after four months.

Should a black mole appear near the orifice at the tip of the penis; or if one has a continual craving for sexual indulgence, these are also signs of death. In addition, they indicate a lower rebirth after death.

When any of these secret signs appear one should perform the necessary purification practices and should apply the most esoteric methods of longevity. However, it is more difficult to accomplish the esoteric methods than the exoteric. Consequently the appearance of the secret signs of death is not easily turned away.

THE KNOWLEDGE SIGNS

The knowledge signs are read in three ways. This is to discover the years, months and days, respectively, of the death that is indicated.

The subject of the observation is one's own sky-shadow. The method of projecting the sky-shadow will be explained in the following text. One projects the shadow and examines it for signs of death, the elimination of death and the elimination of hindrances.

Before making the observation perform the preliminaries as explained in the opening verses of this text. Generate devotion in your heart toward the Buddha, Dharma and Sangha, and perform the ritual offering to the Dharma Protectors. In this way the subject of observation is influenced by means of refuge and prayer.

The observation is to be made in an isolated place having a clear view of the sky. Begin at dawn of the new moon. The sky should be clear and without a wind.

Sit naked upon a pleasant piece of earth. Firstly offer strong prayers to the Three Jewels. Then recite the following mantra a hundred times: *OM AYU SHOSARA HAKARA ROSHAURO HUM PHAT.*

Now, still naked, stand up and prostrate seven times to each of the directional protectors. Then strongly stretch your limbs and, with the end of your rosary or any other religious implement, draw a letter *AH* at the centre of your shadow. Gaze intensely with both eyes at the letter *AH*, not permitting the eyes to wander. Concentrate firmly on this point. When the eyes have become slightly strained, toss your gaze toward the sky. If the sky is cloudless, an image or shadow of your own body will be projected into it. This is the subject to be read.

Should the sky-shadow of your body be complete with all limbs, this indicates that there is no hindrance. This is an excellent sign, revealing that there is no danger to one's life.

Should no image at all appear in the sky, perform the preliminaries again and offer further prayers. Then make another observation, beginning again as explained above.

Sit as before in the meditational posture and cast the gaze at the sky. If for a second time no image is projected, there is nothing to fear. A hindrance is indicated by an imperfect form appearing in the sky, or by the arising of a sudden wind.

Observe the sky when it is clear. Analyze the sky-shadow of yourself to check for quantity, shape and also color.

Firstly check the quantity as follows in order to test for the number of years until death will threaten.

If the hand implement is missing from the sky-shadow, this is the sign called 'devoid of divinity.' It indicates death after a period of seven years.

Should the right hand be missing, death will follow after five years. Should the left hand be missing, death after three years is indicated.

When the right leg is missing below the knee, one will die after two years. When the left leg is missing below the knee, death threatens to come after a year.

Now here are signs indicating the time of death in terms of months.

If the right portion of the hand is missing, one will die after nine months. Should the left portion be missing, one will die after seven months. When the head is missing from the top of the neck, one will die after five months. When it is missing from the bottom of the neck, death will follow after three months. Should the upper portion of the belly be missing, one will die after two months. Should the lower portion be missing, death will come in a month.

Next, here is how to read the sky-shadow to discern the number of days until the advent of death. If the right portion of the body is missing, one will die in twenty-nine days. If the left portion is missing, one will die in twenty-one days.

Here is how to examine the shadow for shape. When it is of a squarish shape, death will come in five months' time. A circular shape indicates four months, a disklike shape three months, a fingerlike shape two months.

The death prophesied by the above signs can easily be turned away by the longevity methods.

However, there are three signs indicating certain death, a death that cannot be overcome or eliminated by yogic means. These are as follows. Should the shape of the sky-shadow be triangular, spherical or coat-shaped, this indicates that death will fall after a month, half-month or ten days, respectively.

Then there are the observations of the color of the sky-shadow. Should the image be white, and the color missing at the heart, this is a sign that one has pleased the celestial beings. Otherwise, if the image is red but with the color missing from the left portion, this is a sign of impending illness. If it is yellow but missing the color from the head, this indicates a problem with the local spirits. If it is blue but missing the color from the legs, this indicates a problem with the water spirits. When the image is unstable or fluctuating, this indicates a danger from evil beings. When it is overly vibrant, this indicates problems in one's relationship with the soil. These are the observations of the color of the shadow.

Should one's observation of any of the knowledge signs indicate a hindrance, strive to perform the longevity rituals and meditations. Then once more observe the sky-shadow. If the image that then appears is complete, this indicates that the longevity practices were successful. However, if the longevity rituals are performed three times and still the image does not become complete, this is a sign indicating that one's life span has become exhausted.

At this point the most intelligent people should engage intensely in the meditations upon the ultimate reality, the highest level of truth, the emptiness nature of all things. Medium practitioners should engage in intensive practice of the generation and completion stage yogas of Highest Yoga Tantra, in accordance with the initiations they have received. Practitioners on the lower levels should strive in the ways of generating merit and virtue.

THE SHORT-TERMED SIGNS

The discussion so far has dealt with the long-termed signs of death. These are to be observed when one is in perfect health and there is no apparent problem or danger. When repeated performance of the longevity rites does not cause the arisal of the signs to cease, these can then be taken as indications of certain death. When the longevity practices cause the signs to disappear, this indicates that the threat of death has also been diverted.

The short-termed signs, on the other hand, are to be looked for in times of illness and suffering, when there is danger to one's life.

Should black tannin form at the base of the teeth, this is called 'withdrawal of the self-sustaining elements.' It indicates death in nine days.

Should the bridge of the nose sink, this is called 'the stopping of the flow of wind.' It also indicates death in nine days.

Should the tip of the nose move off center, this indicates death after seven days.

When the limbs continually yearn to stretch, this is the sign called 'the force ascending the mountain.' It portends death after five days.

Should the two eyes stare intensely without blinking, and the mother energy slip, this indicates death after three days.

If the cheeks sink and stretch, this indicates death on the dawn of the tenth day.

When tears flow uncontrollably from the eyes, this is called 'the earth hindrance.' It indicates death after five days.

Should the earlobe fall back flatly against the head, this is the sign called 'cutting the stairway of the ear.' It indicates death after half a day.

Other short-termed signs can be read as follows. Face southward at noon while holding your elbow on your knee. Lift up and retain the posture, your two eyes still staring south. If a subtleness enters the vision, this is the sign called 'the cutting off of the contact between earth and sky.' It indicates death after nineteen days.

If a mirage of the sea, or else a mist, appears in the east, check your shadow by projecting it on the western wall. If the upper portion is unclear, this signifies death in fifteen and a half days.

If you perceive any of these negative signs, avoid sexual activity and alcohol. Do not engage in lengthy conversations, but rather sit quietly at home.

Another method of analysis is to observe one's urine. At sunrise pass the first urine of the day into a vessel and then examine it. If the normal blue and red vapors do not arise, this indicates death in nine days. If the vapors are dark and wispy, death will follow after a day. If they are red and arise in a spherical pattern, death will come after nine days.

Alternatively, on a sunny day turn your back to the sun and look at the crown of the head of the shadow that appears on the ground. Should no vapors arise from the crown of the shadow, this portends death after five days. If the hair on the head of the shadow seems to flow upward instead of down, this signifies death after seven days.

Should any of these short-termed signs of death arise, a fixed time of death is indicated. Perform the longevity rituals three times. If you do so correctly, death will definitely be turned away. Engage the methods outlined in the cycle of texts called 'Liberation by Turning Death Away.'

When the longevity methods are performed yet signs of accomplishment not received, this indicates that the time of one's death is near, and one's life span has become exhausted.

THE MISCELLANEOUS SIGNS

Generally, the outer, inner, secret and knowledge signs are to be observed when one is in perfect health and there is no apparent danger to one's life; the short-termed signs are to be watched for when one is suffering from a serious illness. As for the miscellaneous signs, they are not given in reference to any specific state of health. One may make observations for them regardless of one's physical condition.

Look to the point of the nose. If it cannot be seen, this indicates that death will follow after a period of five months. Look to the tip of the tongue. If it cannot be seen, this signifies death in three days. When you look in a mirror, if you cannot see your left eye this indicates death in seven months.

Usually when one breathes on one's hand from a close distance the steam of the breath warms the hand, and when one breathes on it from far the hand feels a cold sensation. Should these sensations be reversed, death will follow after ten days.

Look at your reflection in a copper vessel filled with water. If no reflected image appears, this too is a sign of death.

When these or any other of the miscellaneous signs appear, test them for validity by means of the methods discussed earlier under the section on knowledge signs.

THE EXPERIENCE OF DEATH

These then are the six categories of signs indicating death. One should look for them only when the proper preliminary rituals have been done to induce prophetic omens. Should any of them appear to you, apply the longevity methods and attempt to turn away untimely death.

When the longevity methods are unsuccessful and one's natural life span has come to an end, the actual experience of death begins to manifest. Here are the very near signs of approaching death.

Firstly the five sensory powers begin to fail. The external sign is vomiting and a loss of appetite. The body begins to lose its heat and, because of fear, one has difficulty lifting one's head. The inner sensation is of one's head falling down.

Then the signs experienced with the withdrawal of each of the elements occurs.

The element of earth fails. Externally the flesh and bone shrinks slightly. Internally, the body feels heavy and one has the sensation of falling to earth from a height.

Earth dissolves into water. Externally, one's body loses its natural shape. Bodily strength fails, and internally one feels dull and hazy.

The internal water elements are blood and lymph. When they fail, this is a sign that the internal element of water has failed. Liquids flow from the mouth and nose, and one feels sensations of thirst. This indicates that the water element has dissolved into fire. The internal sensation is one of warmth. Sometimes here the mind is clear, sometimes unclear.

The internal fire element is bodily warmth and this is soon to dissolve. The eyes roll up in the head and one cannot recognize anyone. The power of the fire element withdraws into the element of air and therefore one's bodily heat withdraws.

The external wind element withdraws. Air is the external element here and when it dissolves into the inner air element the breath begins to pass in gasps, and one's limbs begin to quiver. As an internal sign, the mind becomes agitated. At that time one perceives a vision of a miragelike appearance and a wisp of smoke.

The red female drop from one's mother then moves up in the central channel. A color of redness fills the mind. This indicates that the mind of appearance has dissolved into the mind of increase. It is at this point that one should apply the tantric yogas to transform lust into enlightened energy, thus cutting off forty of the eighty conceptual minds.

The original white sperm from one's father moves down in the central channel. The vision of radiant whiteness arises, and an appearance of whiteness fills the mind. At this point the mind of increase has dissolved into the mind of attainment. Here the yogi can transform aversion into enlightened energy, and thus cut off thirty-three of the remaining conceptual minds.

The breath now passes in long, slow sighs. The female drop dissolves into the life-sustaining channel and comes to the heart. This is the stage called 'radiantly black' and is followed by an appearance of falling into a ditch in pitch darkness.

The mind of attainment dissolves into the mind of proximate attainment. Here the yogi should transform ignorance into enlightened energy and cut off the remaining seven conceptual minds.

At that time the mouth opens and the eyes roll into the head, fully revealing the whites of the eyes. The external appearance is like the setting of the sun. All sensory recollections and appearances cease and one has a vision that all images suddenly dissolve into darkness, into an immense pool of blackness. The breath now moves very shallowly, and, internally, one experiences a vision as of dusk and darkness.

Two of the five female drops, red in color, then fall together at the heart. The head loses its strength, one takes a few long breaths and the respiration becomes shallow.

Three more red female drops fall to the heart. The person makes the sound of *HIK* with a breath that moves a span in depth. A radiantly black appearance arises in the mind and one swoons into unconsciousness.

The breath then totally stops and the red and white drops of the female and male forces meet together at the heart. One then awakens from unconsciousness into a state of joy. This joyous awareness dissolves into the clear light, and one experiences the simultaneously born bliss.

The primordial awareness at the center of the heart now dissolves into the suchness of mother and son clear lights. At this point the internal energies cease and the subtle mind and energy enter into the innermost channel of being.

The basic clear light of death appears to all living beings. For high yogis, this time of the death experience, when the mother and son clear lights enter into symmetry, provides an excellent opportunity for the attainment of liberation and enlightenment. When a yogi applies the correct meditations, the mind here immediately transforms into the ultimate state of the unproduced, uncreated sphere of truth.

In this way the yogi attains enlightenment. Mind becomes the Dharmakaya wisdom and then manifests in the Sambhogakaya and Nirmanakaya forms in order to work for the benefit of living beings.[5] This is the attainment of full awakening possessed of the three Buddha *kayas*.

Thus not only is enlightenment in this lifetime possible; for those who do not achieve this goal, it is possible even at the moment of death. Therefore appreciate the significance of having attained a human life form and cherish the practice of the profound instructions. Without understanding the instructions in this lifetime, one will never be able to recognize the clear light at the time of death.

All beings have lived, died, and been reborn countless times. Again and again have they experienced the inexpressible, indescribable pure clear light. Yet because of the confusion created by the darkness of innate ignorance, they wander endlessly in cyclic existence. This is a very dangerous predicament. One should cherish the opportunities for enlightenment afforded by having a human body and mind.

THE SIGNS INDICATING THE PLACE OF REBIRTH

Now will follow an account of the signs indicating the place of rebirth of someone who has passed away.

If when dying one's hands shake back and forth and one babbles meaninglessly, and if the bodily warmth first withdraws from under the right armpit, this indicates rebirth as a titan. If wind and mucus move in the left nostril at the time of death and the bodily warmth first withdraws from the area of the left eye, this signifies rebirth as a human.

When animal sounds are emitted from the mouth, urine from the lower passage and the bodily heat withdraws at night, this indicates rebirth as an animal.

When the skin turns yellow and its luster fades, froth forms at the mouth, one feels sensations of hunger, and semen is emitted, this indicates rebirth as an anxious ghost.

When the right leg shakes uncontrollably, one feels anger and aggression, bodily warmth withdraws first from the sole of the right foot, and one simultaneously emits excrement, urine and saliva, this is a sign of rebirth in the hell realms.

When one dies in a state of pride, consciousness leaves the body via the ear passage and heat first withdraws from the ears, this indicates rebirth as a troublesome spirit.

If just before death one's illness subsides, the mind becomes clear, thoughts of one's guru and spiritual friends arise, and through application of the correct meditations the yellow fluid disappears from above the crown aperture, and consciousness is directed to leave via the crown of the head, this indicates either high rebirth or the attainment of full enlightenment.

Therefore it is important to know how to control the mind and focus it in meditation at the time of death, and how to maintain the spiritual attitudes that lead to positive, beneficial trends in the bardo, and thus produce high rebirth and sometimes even enlightenment.

The above discussion deals with the signs of body and mind that indicate the place of rebirth of a dead person. An alternative method of observation is to read the changing face of the sky at an astrologically appropriate time.

Should the sky become dark brown or black, breath steam is not seen, and if a strong wind or thick clouds appear, these are signs indicating a rebirth in one of the hell realms.

Should the yellow of the sun or moon fade even though the sky is free from clouds, if there is no wind and instead of sun there is a rainfall, especially if the rainfall comes at dusk, these are signs that one will take rebirth as an anxious ghost.

If the weather becomes mildly unpleasant, a mist arises and black clouds form in the sky, these are signs of rebirth as an animal.

Should the clouds turn dark maroon and vibrate with wrath, and a wind howls and rages noisily, or if thunder and lightning flash and the sun and moon are obscured, these are signs of rebirth as a titan.

If the sky is clear, the sun and moon unobscured, and if there is no wind or breeze, these are signs of rebirth as a celestial being in one of the worldly heavens.

If the sky is clear yet has wisps of clouds like thin white silk scarves, and if an orb of light forms around the sun and moon, these are signs that the person will be reborn as a human.

Whichever of these signs appear they indicate that rebirth will be taken into one of the six worldly states. The signs will occur two, three or seven days after the person has passed away, as is explained in the scriptures on caring for the dead and in *The Tantra on Cremating Corpses*.[6]

As for the signs indicating that the deceased has attained enlightenment in the bardo or has gained rebirth in a Buddha-field or in the Pure Land of the Dakinis, one can learn of these in the standard manuals on rituals for disposing of the dead and on achieving liberation through the various means of receiving instruction at the time of death.

CONCLUSION

Whenever any of the various signs of death arise one should make the ritualistic observations to test the signs for significance. Should these tests indicate a serious danger to one's life, it is extremely important to take up the practice of the longevity yogas. Not to do so is to commit the tantric downfall of causing one's body to become separated from the host of peaceful and wrathful divinities.

Neglect of the body is a heavy negative karma resulting in rebirth in hell. To permit oneself to die when the cause can be remedied is a worse karmic offense than creating any of the five inexpiable actions, especially if one holds tantric pledges.[7]

Therefore if one receives prophetic indications of one's death it is very important to apply the counteracting meditations, rituals and yogas. To permit the body to die because of ignoring the practices is the karma called 'killing a divinity.' The reason for the methods of divining death signs is not mere curiosity; it is in order to know of untimely conditions that can be turned away by yogic means, or, in the event that the conditions cannot be turned away, to give one time to prepare oneself for the death process. Not to apply the remedy when it would be effective is a form of suicide, which is equivalent to murder.

Should the rituals be correctly performed but the occurrence of the death signs not eliminated, one is then advised to immediately take up the practice of the yogas of consciousness transference. The nature of these practices is such that even if one has committed the five most grievous evils the effects can be overcome through confession, repentance and focusing the mind at the moment of death. Then, instead of lower rebirth, one can achieve a rebirth in the celestial realms, Buddha-fields or Pure Lands, or can even attain full liberation and enlightenment.

> *Eh-ma!!!* From the self-liberation cycle of texts
> Related to the profound doctrines of peaceful and wrathful deities,
> Herein is in complete a brief outline
> Of the self-liberating signs of death
> As a partial condition to the application
> Of the doctrine of Gaining Liberation
> By Hearing in the Bardo.[8]
> You, O future yogis, should learn it well.
>
> *Samaya! Gya gya gya!*
> May the fortunate beings of good karma
> Possess the mind of wisdom.
> May they meet compassionate spiritual masters
> And, until the end of the cycle of time,
> May this doctrine of the signs of death
> Not be lost to mankind.

Chapter Six

The Longevity Yogas
of the Bodhisattva of Life

Whatever crazy sorrow saith,
No life that breathes with human breath
Has ever truly longed for death.

—Tennyson: *The Two Voices*

TRANSLATOR'S PREAMBLE

The purpose of performing the divination for determining the death signs is, firstly, to see if there is an impending danger to one's life span, and, secondly, to ascertain whether the longevity methods will remove the hindrances. Therefore Karma Lingpa said in his text of the previous chapter, 'Untimely death can be turned away through the methods taught for achieving longevity.'

In the Buddhist view, our life is in our hands in the sense that, through our exercise of free will, we have the ability to shape the events that comprise our destiny. Yet there is always an element of karmic predisposition hovering over us waiting for the chance to catch us in a moment of weakness. It is in the times when the karmic elements are disposed against us that we are prone to untimely death.

However, karma by itself cannot exert its influence upon us without operating through the powers of delusion that we carry within ourselves. The Seventh Dalai Lama writes in one of his poems:[1]

Bad karma and delusion—
Evil spirits riding upon the horse of mind,
Shaking the very thread of life.
Thus helplessly directed, this life is made short
And the next destitute.
In this degenerate age, light is shrouded in darkness.

The meaning is that the negative karmic propensities create a danger point in our lives and then, by manifesting through the active delusions, bring untimely death upon us.

As we have already seen, the First Dalai Lama lists three causes of untimely death: exhaustion of life span, exhaustion of merit and exhaustion of karma.[2] He then gives the remedies to these: the first is eliminated by taking long life initiations, practicing healing meditations, etc.; the second by collecting meritorious energy through such means as performing tantric feasts, prayer, seeking the blessings of holy people, etc.; and the third negative condition is rectified by purifying the mind of negative karmic stains through consciously examining the negativity, generating a sense of distaste for negativity, meditation upon love and compassion, or upon the void nature of negativity, and so forth. He concludes by saying, 'When the death indicated has its cause in one or two of the above reasons it can be turned away by the appropriate methods. However, when it is caused by an exhaustion of all three, there is no way to deter the advent of death.'

Here the word 'exhaustion' (Tib., *zaypa*) has the implication not of depletion but of weakness or proneness to a break or lapse. The life span, creative energy or karmic power has a weak link that is manifesting. These factors are not depleted or spent; they are in a crucial phase, or suffering from a temporary lapse of sustaining energy.

This theory of untimely death, is also held by Tibetan medicine. The *Ambrosia Heart Tantra*[3] states:

> The simultaneous weakening of the three factors supporting life
> [i.e., life span, creative energy and karmic power] is a cause of
> certain death.

The belief, then, is that a break in the sustaining energy of any of these three factors can result in untimely death. The longevity yogas therefore aim at restoring and strengthening these by means of the mental/spiritual practices.

The First Dalai Lama lists three principal longevity methods:[4] the Amitayus yogas (as embodied in this chapter in the text of the Second

Dalai Lama); the methods associated with the tantric deity Tara; and the mystical yoga of taking the sky as food (in which one imagines absorbing life energy from the stars).

He goes on to break down the Amitayus system into four essential categories of techniques: the longevity initiation, the generation stage yogas, the completion stage yogas, and the practice of fasting and living only on mystic essence pills instead of ordinary food.

The Second Dalai Lama's text, which I have used in this chapter to show how the longevity yogas operate, does not go into such lengths of detail. Instead it gives us a twofold breakdown: the way of using the Amitayus yogas in order to extend our own life span, and the way of using them to extend the life span of someone else. To illustrate the former phase it presents the steps of a *sadhana*, a meditation manual which is to be read as a descriptive liturgy. The material dealt with here is essentially the generation stage practice or the phase of creative imagination (Tib., *kye-rim*). As the Seventh Dalai Lama points out in his work on this same system,[5] there is a period in this visualization process wherein one can pause and perform the completion stage yogas; in our text, however, the Second Dalai Lama does not bring this to our attention. In fact the completion stage yogas of this tantra are rarely practiced. Most trainees work with the generation stage yogas as in our text. Should they choose to take up completion stage meditations, they switch to the Six Yogas of Naropa, or the Yamantaka, Guhyasamaja or Heruka Chakrasamvara yoga systems.

As for the manner of using the system to benefit others, it is here that the Second Dalai Lama introduces us to the longevity initiation.

Anyone who has spent time in Tibetan Buddhist communities will be familiar with the festive atmosphere that surrounds the long life initiation. When I was in Bodh Gaya in 1972 the present Dalai Lama gave one such initiation to several thousand Central Asians. Again in Dharamsala he gave the Amitayus longevity initiation to more than 5,000 devotees. I was also present in New Delhi in 1981 when Sakya Trizin Rinpoche, the head of the Sakya sect, performed the ceremony for some 2,000 people. At each of these occasions one experienced the blend of religious devotion and festive jubilation that so often accompanies the 'initiation of life.' One is reminded of the ancient fertility rites wherein spirituality and merriment meet in midstream.

The main portion of the Second Dalai Lama's text, however, is given to the practice of the Amitayus yogas as a daily meditation, or the generation stage yoga. It is for this reason that I have included the work in this volume. Although brief, the Second Dalai Lama's analysis of the system is comprehensive, and it illustrates the exact manner in which a trainee wishing to achieve the fruits of longevity practice should proceed.

In keeping with tradition, the text opens with a verse of homage to the tantric deity symbolizing the yogic system, Amitayus, Bodhisattva of Boundless Life and Wisdom. The teachers of the lineage are then referred to, in order to inform us to which of the numerous transmissions the tradition belongs. In this case it is the lineage of the esteemed yogi Milarepa, whose name rose to great fame in the Land of Snows during the late eleventh and early twelfth centuries, and who is now well known in the West due to the popularity of *The Hundred Thousand Songs of Milarepa*[6] and also the various editions of his biography that have appeared.[7] The lineage was brought to Tibet by Milarepa's own disciple Rechungpa at Milarepa's behest. Rechungpa then gave the lineage of transmission to his teacher, and the line was passed on accordingly throughout the succeeding generations. Its Indian source is given in the text as Tipupa,[8] famous disciple of Naropa; mention is also made of Siddharani, a female student of Naropa who achieved enlightenment and then taught extensively in Nepal.

The meditations of the Vajrayana generation stage are based on the transformation of symbols and images, on the theory that a picture can tell a thousand stories. The meditation process opens with the standard verses of refuge, generation of the Mahayana attitude and recitation of the four altruistic aspirations. The sphere of perception is then dissolved into clear light emptiness by means of the *svabhava* mantra, and we are ready to begin.

In the beginning there appears the word *PAM*, symbol of pure awareness. This transforms into a lotus, symbol of pure activity, which bears the symbol *AH*, symbol of the highest wisdom; *AH* transforms into *HRIH*, symbol of the compassionate aspect of wisdom. This transforms into oneself as Amitayus, the Bodhisattva of Boundless Life and Wisdom.

These steps may seem simple enough, but they represent the essential unfoldment process of enlightenment. The old sense of self is dissolved and we arise on the basis of higher awareness, pure action, perfect wisdom and compassionate energy. It is through these underlying forces that we are able to generate the new identity of Amitayus, Bodhisattva of Life and Wisdom, and to practice the longevity meditations. We then call forth the blessings of all practitioners of the past in the form of the Wisdom Beings, and then refresh the tantric initiations by means of the Initiation Deities, confirming our own perception of ourself as Amitayus by means of these two processes.

This is the preliminary phase of generating oneself as a tantric divinity. One is now ready to undertake the actual longevity meditation, which is performed in conjunction with the mantric recitation.

The Second Dalai Lama now gives a brief form of the absorption of the 'essences' by which longevity is produced. This is done in two phases: firstly by summoning back whatever of one's life span has been 'stolen, captured or lost,' and secondly by summoning forth the essence of the four great elements (earth, air, fire and water), as well as of all good things that exist in the world, the life energy of all that lives and finally the blessings of the enlightened beings.

This all comes and absorbs into the mantras at one's heart. The mantras emanate longevity nectars, which fill the vase in Amitayus' hands, who is seated upon one's head. The nectars overflow and fill one's body, granting the powers of life and wisdom.

The Second Dalai Lama then expands on the absorption process and describes how, if one wishes to perform a more detailed meditation, each stage of essence absorption is to be conducted. In general, the brief form of the meditation is used as a daily practice, and the extended version would be used during retreats, when more time is available for each sitting.

The text thus presents us with a picture of the practice a yogi of the system would apply. It does not go into the theory of how the longevity process works, or the philosophy of the body-mind relationship held by the tantric Buddhists which enable them to believe that a mental exercise can have beneficial physical effects.

We have already seen how the Buddhists perceive life span and its relationship to karma and delusion. The fundamental principle at work in the longevity yogas is that the basis of all that happens to us has to come into focus or contact with us through our own mindstream. Therefore in Tibetan medicine, which is based largely on Indian Buddhist medical practices, it is said that all diseases have their root in the mind and its delusions.

Conversely, just as the negative factors must approach us through the mind, the process can be reversed: the mind can cut off the approach of the negativities, and in addition can act as a source to generate positive energies. Therefore when we meditate that we are absorbing into our body the essential qualities of the world that sustain and nourish life, this will have a beneficial effect on our physical well-being.

The power of the mind to influence the body was studied in 1982 by a group of doctors from Harvard and the University of Virginia, who had gained permission from the Dalai Lama to come to Dharamsala and observe the physical transformations of the local practitioners of the much discussed mystic heat yoga, in which bodily temperatures are said to be controllable in meditation. The Dalai Lama chose a number of his students for their study. The yogis raised their temperatures to between 112 and 115 degrees in a matter of minutes.[9]

This type of mental control is the primary ingredient in the longevity trainings. There is also a considerable level of positive thinking involved. By means of these two, mind over matter proves the mechanics of the system.

The Amitayus longevity practice was very popular in Tibet. The First Dalai Lama, whose commentary I have quoted quite extensively above, widely propagated the lineage, and is said to have extended his own life span by several decades by means of it. The First Panchen Lama, guru of the Fifth Dalai Lama, also widely taught it. Thus although originally an exclusively Kargyu tradition, over the centuries it spread to all sects of Tibetan Buddhism. Today it is common amongst lamas of all Central Asian lineages.

In closing it should perhaps be noted that the usage of Amitayus in Tibetan Vajrayana Buddhism for the purpose of longevity meditation and Amitabha Buddha in western China in the Pure Land sects are not disconnected, although the lineages have no historical link. Both have separate lines of transmission from India. But Amitabha and Amitayus are in fact identical Buddha figures; the difference is that the former, whose name means Boundless Light, symbolizes the final wisdom form of the Buddha, and the latter, whose name means Boundless Life, symbolizes the active bodhisattva aspect. In addition, there is a difference in that the Pure Land sect does not practice the Vajrayana lineage of Amitabha, but is a Sutrayana school based upon the *Amitabha-sutra*. The Amitayus longevity yogas, on the other hand, are not connected with Amitayus as a Sutrayana figure but as a symbol of the Vajrayana path. Consequently there is a connection between the two in that both are aspects of the same Buddha essence, but there is a difference in that one is utilizing the Sutrayana form and the other that of the esoteric Vajrayana. This reflects in the final practice; in the exoteric system Amitabha is seen as an external figure to be prayed to for blessings, whereas in the esoteric Vajrayana one transforms into Amitayus and meditates from within the sphere of actually being the

Bodhisattva of Life and Wisdom. The former is a passive method, the latter active. This is the essential difference between the sutra and tantra attitudes toward the Buddha forms. One sees them as external figures; the other sees them as symbols of meditative principles.

THE LONGEVITY YOGAS
OF THE BODHISATTVA OF LIFE

by Gyalwa Gendun Gyatso, the Second Dalai Lama

> Homage to the bodhisattva Amitayus,
> Embodiment of life and wisdom,
> The mere thought of whom bestows
> Longevity and profound knowledge.
> Now herein is explained the yoga
> Of meditation in accordance with this tradition.

Herein lies the method of extending the life spans of both oneself and others through meditation upon the tantric deity Amitayus in accordance with the transmission from the Indian female Buddhist saint Siddharani. The tradition was brought to Tibet by the yogi Rechungpa and transmitted through the renowned meditator Milarepa, most famous of Tibetan ascetics. From Milarepa it has been passed in an unbroken line until today.

There are two parts to this commentary on the Amitayus tradition: how to use the method as a personal practice in order to extend one's own life span; and, secondly, how to perform the long life initiation in order to extend the life span of others.

PART ONE: A METHOD TO EXTEND ONE'S OWN LIFE SPAN: A BRIEF PRACTICE

To take up the meditation practice of the Amitayus yoga, begin by arranging a comfortable seat in front of a small altar. On the altar place an image of Amitayus, together with the standard water and sensory offerings. Consecrate these in accordance with the standard Highest Yoga Tantra method.

The meditation opens with the process of generating the vision of oneself as Amitayus, invoking the lineage of gurus and meditation deities, and then, by the following liturgy, taking refuge and generating the bodhimind.

> I turn for refuge to the Buddhas, the Dharma and Sangha
> Until full enlightenment is attained.
> Through the energy of my engaging in this practice,
> May Buddhahood be gained for the sake of all.
>
> May all beings have happiness and its causes.
> May they be separated from suffering and its causes.
> May they abide in the joy beyond suffering.
> May they abide in equanimity that sees all beings as
>   equal, be they friend or enemy.

When these preliminaries have been completed, one purifies the meditation by means of the *svabhava* mantra.[1] Then follows the generation of the mystic form of Amitayus.

All is seen as emptiness. From within the sphere of emptiness there appears the syllable *PAM*. This transforms into a lotus marked by the syllable *AH*. The syllable *AH* becomes a moon disc upon which is my own mind in the form of a red letter *HRIH*.

This completely transforms and I appear as the transcendental Amitayus, embodiment of undying life and wisdom. My body is red in color and my two hands are folded in the meditation posture at my lap. In my hands is the mystic vase, which is filled with the nectars of immortality. My feet are folded in the vajra position and my body is embellished with the 112 marks and signs of perfection. The jeweled ornaments and the bodhisattva silks adorn me. The syllable *OM* marks my crown, *AH* my throat and *HUM* my heart.[2]

Lights radiate from the *HUM* at my heart, summoning forth the Wisdom Beings from Sukhavati, the Pure Land of Joy of the Western Realm. These Wisdom Beings, who resemble the Amitayus described above, come and merge into me, the Symbolic Being. *JAH HUM BAM HOH.*

Lights once again emanate forth from the *HUM* at my heart. This time they summon forth the Initiation Deities. I request them to bestow initiation upon me. They hold up their vases and pour their initiating nectars onto me, while reciting the mantra of initiation: *OM SARVA TATHAGATA ABHISHEKATA SAMAYE SHRI YE AH HUM.*

Saying this, they bestow initiation upon me. My body becomes filled with nectars, which cleanse me of all stains of negative karma collected by means of body, speech and mind.

The nectars fill my body and then overflow via my crown aperture.

The overflow transforms into Guru Amitayus, who is in actuality my own personal initiating teacher.

One then makes the visualized water and sensory offerings, and recites the verse of praise:

> Homage to the transcended Amitayus,
> He free from negativity and from karmic stains,
> Whose form is vast as the sky
> And whose mind dwells in the one taste of suchness.

Upon a moon disc inside the vase of the Guru Amitayus above my head is a syllable *HRIH*, with both the essence mantra and long *dharani* mantra circling it in a clockwise direction.[3] Lights emanate from these, summoning forth whatever of one's life span has been stolen, harmed or degenerated by the forces of negativity. This life energy comes in the form of skull-cups and vases filled with the nectars of immortality, and is absorbed into the mantra chains.

Similarly, lights once more emanate forth from the seed syllable, mantra and *dharani* at Amitayus' heart. They summon forth the essence of space and then of the four great elements—earth, air, fire and water—together with the essence of the life energy and merits of all the living beings, all perfect things of the three worlds, and also the inspiring powers of the body, speech and mind of all the Buddhas and bodhisattvas. These come and dissolve into the mantra chains.

There then issues forth a stream of nectars from the syllable *HRIH* and from the mantras at Guru Amitayus' heart. These fill the vase in his hands, causing the nectars of longevity to froth up and overflow. They pour down the crown of my head and enter my body via my Brahma aperture. My body becomes filled with nectars, which purify me of all stains and faults, and infuse me with the power of healing and wisdom.

Contemplating in this way, one recites the essence mantra [*OM AMARANI JIVANTA YE SVAHA*] as many times as possible.

Thus is the power of longevity attained. One then dissolves the images meditated upon into emptiness, and dwells in absorption upon this sphere of the unformed for some time.

To conclude the practice, arise from emptiness in the form of Amitayus. Offer a prayer for accomplishment of the path, the benefit of all living beings and the manifestation of every auspicious sign.

This is a brief method of performing the longevity meditation upon

Amitayus. It includes the [eight] stages of taking the essence of what has been stolen and harmed, extracting the essences of the four elements, absorbing all worldly excellences, absorbing all spiritual qualities, and absorbing the blessings of the lineage masters.

A METHOD TO EXTEND ONE'S OWN LIFE SPAN: A MORE EXTENSIVE PRACTICE

To expand the meditation, each of the essences is taken individually and the mantra and *dharani* recited with each individual phase.

When this is done one begins the meditation in the same manner as above in the short process, and performs the generation of oneself as Amitayus with Guru Amitayus on one's head in the same way as described above. Then, when one comes to the emanation of the lights and the absorption of the essences, one does this for each essence individually instead of doing so collectively.

The process has three phases: summoning back whatever life span has been stolen; reviving whatever has been harmed or weakened; and, thirdly, absorbing the blessings of the transmission of Amitayus, the Bodhisattva of Boundless Life.

Summoning Back What Has Been Stolen

Inside the vase in the hands of Guru Amitayus above my head is a lotus and moon, and upon this is the seed syllable *HRIH*, surrounded by the essence mantras and long *dharani*.

Lights go out from these, summoning back whatever of one's life span has been stolen, captured or harmed by the Lord of Death, as well as by evil spirits, harmful beings, and so forth. This is drawn back into the vase, coming in the form of skull-cups and monk bowls filled with the longevity nectars, which dissolve into the mantric syllables in Guru Amitayus' vase.

This causes a stream of nectars to issue forth, completely filling the vase with longevity fluids. These overflow and come to the crown of my head, entering my body and cleansing it inside and out of all faults and stains. My body becomes covered with a fine vajra cloth able to destroy all harmful elements. Whatever life span has been stolen is returned, and I attain the state of an immortal vajra holder. The regained life span is thus retrieved, never to be lost again to the forces of negativity.

As one meditates in this way one recites the essence mantra, known as the Amarani mantra:[4] *OM AMARANI JIVANTA YE SVAHA.*

At the conclusion of the mantric recitation, one recites the prayer: 'May I gain the power of longevity. May I become a swaotika of undying life. May I become an indestructible vajra, an unsetting victory banner. May I gain the state of an immortal knowledge holder.' One concludes with a verse of prayer for auspicious signs to arise.

Rejuvenating Whatever Has Been Harmed or Weakened

This includes three topics: rejuvenating degenerated life energy, rejuvenating degenerated life span by absorbing the essence of power and merits, and, thirdly, rejuvenating weakened spiritual precepts and commitments.

Rejuvenating degenerated life energy. As before one turns one's attention to Guru Amitayus, and to the seed syllable and mantras at the center of his vase. Lights emanate from these, summoning forth in the form of blue lights and nectars the essence of space, such as the sky and all hollow places. These nectars dissolve into the mantras, causing the mantric syllables to issue forth a stream of nectars of immortality that fill the vase, overflow and come to my crown, entering via my Brahma aperture, washing me inside and out, purifying me of all diseases, negative instincts and mental obscurations. Especially I am purified of any degeneration of mind and awareness, and gain the state of an immortal knowledge holder of healthy body and mind with the life basis made firm. The mantra is recited throughout the meditation.

To conclude, recite the prayer and auspicious verses as before.

Lights again emanate forth from the mantras, summoning in the form of green lights and nectars the essence of the airs and winds of the ten directions. These dissolve into the mantric syllables. A stream of nectars of immortality are released. They fill the vase and then overflow, coming to my head, entering via the Brahma aperture, and cleansing me inside and out of all negative traits and mental obscurations. Especially, any degenerated life span caused by a misbalance in the windlike energies of the body is restored. One gains the strength and agility of an immortal knowledge holder. The mantra is recited throughout the process. To conclude, the words of truth are spoken as before, and also a verse of auspiciousness.

Once more lights emanate from the mantra chain. They summon forth in the form of red lights and nectars the essence of the fire element, which is drawn forth from all fires, fire crystal, the fire of meditation, etc. This dissolves into the mantra chain, which releases a stream of nectars that fills the vase, overflows and comes to my head. The nectars fill my body, cleansing me inside and out of all faults, and especially they restore any degenerated life span caused by misbalance in the bodily heating system. The body thus becomes wonderfully radiant and as vibrant as the essence of the sun, or like the brilliance of the wish-fulfilling gem. The mantra is recited throughout. One concludes with the prayer and auspicious verses.

Again lights shine forth, drawing back in the form of white lights and nectars the essence of the water element, such as the seas and rivers, the internal bodily fluids, etc. These enter the mantra chains, causing a stream of nectars to be released. These fill the vase, overflow and come to the crown of my head. They fill my body, cleansing me inside and out of all negativities and obscurations. Especially, they restore any degeneration in life span caused by problems in the bodily fluids, such as blood, lymph, etc. The body becomes as lustrous as the root of a lotus, and I gain the state of an immortal knowledge holder. The mantra is recited, and one concludes with the prayer and auspicious verses.

Once more lights radiate forth, drawing back in the form of yellow lights and nectars the essence of the earth element, such as the essences of Mt. Meru, the golden mountains, the jewel mountains, the snow mountains, mountains of medicinal herbs, fields of food crops, etc. These lights and nectars dissolve into the mantra chains, causing a stream of longevity nectars to be released. These fill the vase, overflow, come to my head and enter my body and purify me of all negativities and obscurations. Especially, any degeneration of life span caused by problems of the internal earth element, such as defects in flesh tissue, bone tissue, etc., is restored. Thus I gain the state of an immortal knowledge holder with a body as strong and firm as the very King of Mountains.

This is the method of restoring degenerated life span by means of summoning forth the essence of the five great elements: space, wind, fire, water and earth. It is the meditation known as 'rejuvenating degenerated life energy.'

Rejuvenating degenerated life span by means of absorbing the essence of power and merits. Lights emanate forth from the mantra chains, summoning forth the essence of the power and merits of everything in the world and beyond. The power of the worldly gods such as Brahma and Vishnu, the worldly spirits such as the naga Ananda, the world rulers such as the four kingly protectors, etc. all comes forth. The merits of the spiritual friends and learned gurus, the practitioners accomplished in the mind of love, compassion, the bodihimind, insight into suchness, and the leaders of men and gods all come forth. Also, the worldly merits of kings, leaders, those with long life, health and prosperity, etc., all come forth. In brief, the power and merits that sustain all beings in the world and beyond is summoned forth, together with the splendor and excellence of everything in existence. This all comes in the form of the eight auspicious emblems, the seven kingly jewels, the seven precious stones, the eight auspicious substances, and so forth. These dissolve into the mantra chains, causing a stream of nectars to be released. These fill the vase and overflow, coming to the crown of my head, entering my body via my Brahma aperture. My body is filled, and I am cleansed inside and out of all stains and faults of body and mind. Especially, any degeneration of life span caused by a lack of power or merits is restored, and I gain the state of an immortal knowledge holder equal in fortune to the mightiest of gods.

Meditating in this way, one recites the mantra, concluding with the prayer and auspicious verses as before.

Restoring weakened life span by rejuvenating and correcting any failures in one's spiritual precepts and commitments. Lights emanate forth from the mantra chains. They summon forth the blessings of all the gurus in the lineage of transmission of this longevity tradition, as well as all Buddhas, bodhisattvas, dakas, dakinis, and Dharma protectors, etc., as well as all the human and transcended knowledge holders. These come in the form of the Buddhas and bodhisattvas, the vowels and consonants of the alphabet, mystic implements such as vajras and bells, and so forth. They dissolve into the mantra chains, causing a stream of longevity nectars to be released. These fill the vase and then overflow, coming to my head and entering my body via the Brahma aperture. My body is filled with the longevity nectars, and I am cleansed inside and out of all stains of negative karma and of all mental obscurations. Especially, any breaches in my spiritual commitments and vows are restored, and I am placed in the state of an immortal knowledge holder.

As this meditation is done, one recites the mantra and then concludes with prayer and auspicious verses.

This is the long form of performing the meditation on the restoration of life span degenerated by any of the three means of reviving degenerated life energy, absorbing the essence of power and merits, and restoring degenerated vows and commitments.

Absorbing the Blessing Powers of the Bodhisattva of Life

Lights emanate from the heart of Guru Amitayus, summoning the bodhisattva Amitayus from Sukhavati, the Pure Land of Joy, who comes from the western heavens. He is surrounded by all the gurus in the lineage of transmission, together with all the Buddhas and bodhisattvas of the ten directions. These dissolve into Guru Amitayus, who melts into light and dissolves into me. Thus my body, speech and mind become of one taste with the body, speech and mind of Guru Amitayus, and I attain the state of an immortal knowledge holder.

One then calls out the names of the gurus in the lineage of transmission.

> O Buddha Amitayus, accomplished bodhisattva
> Who embodies boundless life and wisdom;
> O Siddharani, queen of the mahasiddhas;
> And Tipupa, the Pigeon Mahasiddha[5]
> Who attained every tantric power;
> And exalted Rechungpa, a yogi who
> Passed beyond birth and death;
> Milarepa, most accomplished of meditators,
> Gampopa, the great Kargyu forefather;
> Tatsepa, kingly yogi from Kham
> Who embodies the spirit of all Buddhas;
> And Drikungpa, master yogi known
> To all as the Kyura Rinpoche;
> O Chen-ngawa, lord of spiritual knowledge;
> Gyalwa Yang-gonpa, he of sublime insight;
> Chen-nga, heart son of the master [above];
> And Zurpukpa, a truly omniscient yogi;
> Barawa Gyaltsen Palzangpo, transcended lord;
> Supreme yogi Ahnan Choje, he who attained knowledge;
> Lord of Dharma Paljor Gyaltsen;
> Kunga Gyaltsen, embodiment of Buddha Vajradhara;
> And all the gurus in the line of transmission;
> Down to my own kind initiating master,
> I make this request to you.
> Holy lineage and foundation teachers,
> I offer you this prayer.
> Bestow your blessings and inspiring powers.
> Grant me your merciful guidance.

Whatever diseases afflict the body,
Whatever sufferings afflict the mind,
Whatever obstacles and hindrances cause stagnation,
Whatever astrological conflicts come from above,
Whatever naga spirits cause harm from below,
Whatever evil beings bring trouble in between,
And whatever else may occur to create problems
Or bring untimely death to this practitioner,
May the lineage and foundation gurus
Grant their protective blessings
To turn these negative conditions away.

One then recites the Amarani mantra and long *dharani*, meditating that one becomes imbued with a stream of blessings and transforming powers from the gurus, and gains every freedom from negative karma, obscuration, disease, conflict and obstacles to life and wisdom.

This process of absorbing the powers of life by means of receiving the blessings of the past and present gurus of the lineage can be repeated three or seven times. Also, if one has the time it is best to repeat the complete prayer after the name of each guru in the lineage of transmission, or at least after calling the names of every three gurus. Otherwise, if one does not have much time it is permissible to recite all the names first and then to read the prayer at the end as written out above.

At the conclusion of the practice one recites the mantra again, dissolves the visualization into emptiness, and then arises from emptiness in the form of Amitayus, to dedicate the merit and offer a prayer for the attainment of enlightenment and the happiness of the world.

This then is the practice of the Amitayus longevity yoga as a means to extend one's own life span. It can be performed either as a daily meditation practice or else as a method for making intense retreat. The details of how to perform the retreat should be learned from one's own teacher.

PART TWO: THE LONGEVITY INITIATION AS A METHOD TO BENEFIT OTHERS

There are a number of ways in which the Amitayus yogas can be used for the benefit of others. One of the most effective of these is the longevity initiation, which one can perform for either another person or for a group.

Begin by arranging the altar with the image of Amitayus, the water and sensory offerings, etc., as before. In addition, place the longevity vase, longevity wine and longevity pills as stated in the standard manuals. The vase goes in the center, with the wine to its right and the pills to its left. The water and sensory offerings are arranged around these, as are the ritual cakes, etc. These are all consecrated in accordance with Highest Yoga Tantra methods.

One begins by consecrating the vase. Firstly it is purified in emptiness by means of the *svabhava* mantra. The vase is visualized as dissolving into the sphere of emptiness beyond all grasping.

All is seen as emptiness. From within the sphere of emptiness appears the syllable *BHRUM*. This syllable then transforms into the jeweled vase, red in color, having a wide belly, long neck and wide lip at the top. It is draped in celestial silks and its mouth is adorned with a branch from the wish-fulfilling tree. By nature this vase is immaterial and insubstantial, as though made of light, like a rainbow. It is in the form of a vase, but its real nature is the Inconceivable Mansion, the divine palace of Amitayus, having four entranceways, four archways and all the features of a divine, mystical abode.

At the center of the vase is a lotus bearing a moon, and upon this is the syllable *HRIH*. This syllable then transforms into Amitayus, Bodhisattva of Life and Wisdom. His appearance is as described earlier.

Inside the vase in his hands is another vase, and inside this is the syllable *HRIH* upon a lotus and moon disc. This is encircled by the essence mantra and long *dharani*.

One recites these, and lights emanate forth and summon back any of the life span that has been lost, stolen, degenerated and so forth.

This is drawn back into the vase in the form of longevity nectars, until the vase is completely full. Meditating in this way one recites the essence mantra and long *dharani* as many times as possible.

This is the method of consecrating the initiation vase. One then consecrates the longevity wine in the same manner as the inner offering is consecrated, using the syllables *HUM* to purify it, *AH* to perceive it as transcendental and *OM* to cause it to become infinitely vast. As for the longevity pills, which are ambrosial substances produced from the various prescribed medicines and medicinal herbs, one visualizes drawing the essence of all things in samsara and nirvana into them, thus imbuing them with the essence of the ambrosia of immortality.

In the process of these consecrating meditations on both longevity wine and pills one recites as many of the essence mantra and long *dharani* as possible. The ritual cakes are also consecrated in the manner of the inner offering. It is then offered to the Amitayus of the vase.

One concludes the section by offering prayers for the fulfillment of the rites.

The recipient or recipients of the ritual then wash, prostrate, offer the mandala and make the threefold request to be given the longevity initiation. The ritualist agrees, delivers a brief discourse on the general and specific sufferings of cyclic existence as well as the benefits of the holy Dharma, gives a brief account of the lineage of the transmission to be given, as well as some stories of the beneficial effects of the longevity initiation in order to encourage the recipients and put them in positive frames of mind, and then imparts refuge and the bodhisattva pledge. The recipients are advised to envision the initiating ritualist as having the form of and being one with Guru Amitayus, and to see the vase as having the ideal form but being in nature the divine abode of Amitayus, with a tiny Amitayus seated at its center. The recipients are then dissolved into emptiness, purified by means of the *svabhava* mantra and generated from emptiness in the form of Amitayus. Seeing themselves as Amitayus seated upon a lotus and moon disc, the three syllables of *OM, AH,* and *HUM* mark them at the crown, throat and heart.

This concludes the preliminary rites of the initiation. One can then proceed with the actual initiation.

The actual initiation is given in four ways: by relying upon the initiation vase, by means of the initiation wine, through the initiation pills, and by means of calling upon the words of truth.

Initiation by Means of the Longevity Vase

As in the actual practice for personal meditation described earlier, this has three phases: absorbing back whatever life span has been stolen, rejuvenating whatever has been weakened, and absorbing the powers of the Bodhisattva of Life.

Each of these three processes is conducted with much the same visualization pattern as was used in the stages of the practice for one's personal longevity accomplishment as described earlier. The main difference is that earlier the emanation of lights and so forth was from the heart of Guru Amitayus on one's head, and the object of purification was one's own body and mind. Here in the initiation by means of the longevity vase the lights emanate forth from the Amitayus who sits at the center of the initiation vase. Also after the essences have been drawn back and the vase overflows, the nectars of longevity emanate to the heads of the recipients, not only purifying them and so forth as was done in the personal practice, but also granting the initiation of life. But with these exceptions, the steps and processes of the meditations proceed as described earlier and one can refer back in the text to the according section to see precisely how this is done.

In the first of the three phases, lights emanate from the Amitayus in the vase, bringing back any of the recipients' life span that has been lost to or stolen by the Lord of Death, etc., and bring this back in the form of skull-cups, monk bowls, etc. This causes nectars to emanate forth, fill the vase, overflow, come to the heads of the recipients, fill their bodies, purify them inside and out, and restore any lost or wasted life span, etc., as before [in the personal practice]. The nectars bestow the longevity initiation and the powers of immortality.

The ritual master recites the essence mantra while this is being done, and concludes by pronouncing the words of truth and offering a prayer of auspiciousness.

In the second phase, rejuvenating whatever has been degenerated, there are three steps, namely, restoring weakened life energy by means of absorbing the essence of the five elements of space, air, fire, water and earth; rejuvenating weakened life span by means of absorbing the essence of power and merits; and rejuvenating weakened life span by means of restoring broken vows and spiritual commitments.

In each of these processes the visualization is much the same as in the similar stages of the personal practice, with the exception that the emanation and absorption happens from the Amitayus in the initiation vase, and the ritualist meditates that the nectars from the vase enter the recipient of the initiation, purifying him/her and granting the according initiation of immortality. In this way the life spans, elements, precepts and commitments of the recipient are restored as a condition to promoting health, well-being and long life.

At the conclusion of each phase the initiating ritualist recites the mantra, words of truth and auspicious prayer, and touches the vase to the crown of the head of the recipient(s).

In the third phase, that of absorbing the blessing powers of the lineage masters, one meditates that Amitayus, together with the lineage of transmission gurus, and all the Buddhas and bodhisattvas, are absorbed into the initiation vase. They melt into light, which is absorbed into the recipient, causing his/her body, speech and mind to become one with those of Amitayus. As in the personal practice, the names of the lineage masters are then called out, and the prayer offered to them in request of their blessings.

In this way the recipient of the rite is purified of all obstacles to health and long life, and attains the power of longevity by means of the vase initiation.

Initiation by Means of the Longevity Wine

The skull-cup in which the initiation wine is held is visualized as being white outside and red inside, and as being vast and deep in size. The substance inside is imagined to be the five meats and five liquids.

Above the skull-cup are the three syllables *OM, AH* and *HUM,* one above the other. Lights emanate from these, summoning back the abiding nectars, such as those found in the great oceans, and summoning also the nectars of the wisdom of non-duality, such as is possessed by the Buddhas of the ten directions. The lights also summon forth wisdom nectars from the syllables at the hearts of the dakas and dakinis of the twenty-four places. The lights then place all sentient beings in the state of Amitayus, and draw them all forth into the nectars of immortality in the skull-cup.

The recipients of the longevity initiation now take a drink of the wine/nectars, visualizing that the 72,000 energy channels of the body are filled and saturated with the nectars of immortality, and that the eighty conceptual mind patterns are arrested in the *dharmadhatu* wisdom. The recipients become adorned with the *samadhi* that directly experiences clarity and emptiness, or, alternatively, directly experiences the wisdom inseparable from great bliss. All degenerations to the energy channels, mystic drops and vital energies are restored to full vitality and the state of an immortal vajra holder is attained. In particular, one gains the fortune to be able to engage successfully in the longevity practices that rely upon the completion stage yogas.

The longevity wine is then given out to the recipients of the initiation.

Initiation by Means of the Longevity Pills

The initiation pills are to be visualized as being made of ambrosial substances produced from the various medicinal herbs and so forth, and have the potency to eliminate all 404 fundamental categories of disease.

Lights emanate forth from the pills, drawing back all the transcendental and worldly qualities of mystic pill ingredients. These are absorbed into the initiation pills, and one imagines that the pills become mystic ambrosial medicines with the power to provide the body with all nutrients and essential substances,[6] and with every healing power and potency to bestow longevity.

The recipients of the initiation then eat the longevity pills, imagining that in this way they are freed from and purified of all 404 types of disease, the 84,000 kinds of hindrances, and all forms of interferences and obstructions, and that they thus gain the state of an immortal knowledge holder. In particular, the recipients attain the good fortune to be able to practice the longevity methods of living solely on mystic essence pills without having to rely on coarse food at all.

The master of the initiation rite reads the verse:

> Mystical food to support auspicious life,
> Mystic essence containing every essence:
> By partaking of this essence food
> May you taste the ambrosial food of Buddha Amitayus,
> And by relying on this mystical ambrosia
> May you be freed from all disease
> And gain the powers of longevity.

Having chanted this verse, the remaining pills are distributed.

Initiation by Means of Calling Upon the Words of Truth

One visualizes that in the sky above there appears the victorious Amitayus, surrounded by the lineage gurus, the Buddhas and bodhisattvas of the ten directions, all dakas and dakinis, all Dharma protectors and guardians of truth, and all human and celestial knowledge holders. They release a rainfall of flowers and an ocean of auspicious music and song.

In their presence one recites the following words of truth, concludes with a prayer for auspicious signs to arise, and tosses a handful of flowers to the visualized assembly.

> By the power of the words of truth
> Of the vows made by the Buddhas and bodhisattvas,
> The strength of the spiritual path,
> The purity of the Sangha who dwell in practice,
> The power of the laws of cause and effect,
> The nature of appearance and emptiness,
> And by the limitless merits that exist
> In both the world and beyond,
> May this son/daughter of good fortune
> Gain the power of a strong life force.
> May he/she become an undying swastika of immortal life.
> May he/she become an indestructible vajra,
> An unsetting victory banner
> Of power over the forces of death.
> May he/she be granted

The initiation of long life
That washes away all causes of death.
May he/she gain the glorious state
Of an immortal knowledge holder.

May there be auspicious signs of the deeds
Of the Buddhas and the bodhisattvas;
May there be the auspicious signs
Of happiness, peace and creative energy
Filling the world and its inhabitants;
And by the power of Amitayus, Bodhisattva of Life,
May there be signs of accomplishment
Of the sublime longevity yogas.

THE CONCLUSION

By the virtue of whatever merits there may be
In this brief elucidation of the longevity methods
For benefitting both oneself and others
In accordance with the wondrous yogas
Of the Amitayus tradition of practice
As transmitted through the female mystic Siddharani,
Tipupa, Rechungpa and Milarepa,
May countless sentient beings be led to the state
Of a knowledge holder with the powers of immortality.

Thus is complete my explanation of the method of practicing the Amitayus yogas as a method to benefit both oneself and others. The composition was inspired by the persistent requests of the Dharma master Gelek Namgyal, a lord of truth who serves as the very root and limbs of the Buddhadharma in this degenerate age. I, the Buddhist monk Gendun Gyatso, wrote it while residing in the Ganden Podrang residence at Drepung Monastery. May it be of some small benefit to the preservation of the longevity methods and the well-being of all that lives.

Chapter Seven

The Yoga of Consciousness Transference

Fear death?—to feel the fog in my throat,
  The mist in my face,
When the snows begin, and the blasts denote
  I am nearing the place,
The post of the night, the press of the storm,
  The power of the foe;
Where he stands, the Arch Fear in a visible form,
  Yet the strong man must go.

—Robert Browning: *Prospice*

TRANSLATOR'S PREAMBLE

The author of the material in the chapter that follows is the eighteenth-century mystic Tsechokling Yeshe Gyaltsen, who was the guru of the Eighth Dalai Lama and also a prolific commentator on various aspects of the Tibetan tradition on death and dying.

The subject to be dealt with now is the yoga of consciousness transference. Karma Lingpa has already advised us, in the conclusion of chapter five:

> If one receives prophetic indications of one's death it is very important to apply the counteracting meditations, rituals and yogas.... Not to apply the remedy when it would be effective to do so is a form of suicide, which is equivalent to murder.... However, should the rituals be correctly performed but the occurrence of the death

signs not be eliminated, one is then advised to immediately take up the practice of the yogas of consciousness transference. The nature of these practices is such that even if one has committed the five most grievous evils the effects can be overcome through confession, repentance and focusing the mind at the moment of death, and instead of lower rebirth one can achieve a rebirth in the celestial realms, Buddha-fields or Pure Lands, or can even attain full liberation and enlightenment.

The First Dalai Lama says much the same thing in his commentary to the system:[1]

> Should it happen that one's application of the longevity yogas is unable to turn away the signs of death, one should take up training in the yogas that prepare the mind for consciousness transference. It is said that one should enter this training at least six months prior to one's death.

The Second Dalai Lama gives similar advice in his *Tantric Yogas of Sister Niguma*[2]:

> One should make observations for the signs of death and, when they occur, apply the longevity methods. When these fail and the signs of death continue to appear, the time has come to utilize the actual transference yogas.

He then continues,

> It is best to apply the training techniques before becoming too weak with illness. Once severe illness has set in, one will not be able to master the trainings no matter how hard one tries, or how strong one's wish may be.

In other words, the training in consciousness transference must be accomplished while our body and mind are still strong and clear. The main function of this training is to familiarize ourselves with the practice, so that at the crucial moment of death we are able to execute the steps of transference effectively.

The first Western study of the transference yogas was made by Dr. Evans-Wentz, in *Tibetan Yoga and Secret Doctrines* (Oxford, 1935), in the section on the Six Yogas of Naropa. Since then a great deal on the Six Yogas has appeared in English, Professor Guenther's *The Life and Teachings of Naropa* (Oxford, 1963) being perhaps the best. Garma C. Chang has also brought out several works on the Six Yogas, although these have been neither as accurate nor as informative as either of the above two works.

My own *Selected Works of the Dalai Lama II: The Tantric Yogas of Sister Niguma* (Ithaca. Snow Lion, 1984), which contains sixteen texts by the Second Dalai Lama, has two sections on the subject: chapter three, part B, 'A Meditation upon the Guru as a Method to Prepare the Mind for Death'; and chapter six, 'The Tantric Yogas of Sister Niguma.'[3]

The Six Yogas of Naropa as transmitted through Marpa and Milarepa, and the Six Yogas of Sister Niguma, which Naropa transmitted to his sister/consort Vimala and were subsequently brought to Tibet by Khyungpo Naljor, are in fact the same six yogic practices. There is a slight difference in the order, however, and in which aspects of each yoga are stressed. In the Marpa/Milarepa transmission one begins with the mystic heat yoga, then goes on to the illusory body, dream yoga, clear light, transference and finally the bardo. The Niguma transmission has the order of the last two yogas reversed. In addition, the Marpa lineage places special emphasis upon the illusory body and bardo trainings, whereas the Niguma tradition emphasizes the dream yogas and clear light trainings. Both systems, however, have their consciousness transference yogas from the lineage originally stemming from the *Vajrayogini-tantra*. As we will see later, Tsechokling points out that most Highest Yoga Tantra systems of transference trace back to either the *Vajrayogini-tantra* or the *Guhyasamaja-tantra*.

The First Dalai Lama's commentary on the death signs, the longevity yogas and the transference methods gives us a more complete picture of the Tibetan traditions.[4] He writes:

> Various methods of preparing the mind for death and consciousness transference have been taught in both the sutras and tantras. To list but a few of the Sutrayana techniques: there is the instruction called 'Transference by Means of the Thatness of Being,' which is the practice of *vipashyana* meditation or insight into the profound emptiness nature at the moment of death; the *lo-jong* method of meditating on the conventional altruistic bodhimind of love and compassion at the time of death, of which there are many variations; and so forth. Then there is the famous method uniting both Sutrayana and Vajrayana techniques, known as 'Instruction on the Three Essential Moments,' wherein it is said, 'Abandon all attachment and offer your body as a gift to living beings. Unite with the seed of light and transfer to the Tushita Pure land.'
>
> To list but a few of the numerous Vajrayana methods for transference of consciousness: the Transference of the Three *Kayas*; the Avalokiteshvara transference instruction; the transference methods of the *Vajrayogini-tantra*; the *Lam-dre* [Path and Fruit][5] transference

by means of the four initiations, such as transforming appearances of mind by means of the vase initiation, and so forth; transference by means of mantric syllables; transference by means of the orb of light; and so forth. One should train in whichever of these is most suitable to one's own abilities, background, karmic propensities and subconscious inclinations, to be determined in consultation with one's guru. Then when death does fall one can easily engage the technique and make the desired transference.

Tsechokling's text, which I have used as the basis of this chapter, focuses on the Maitreya lineage. In accordance with the above analysis by the First Dalai Lama, it would thus be connected with the lineage of the instructions on the Three Essential Moments,[6] which aims at effecting transference to the Tushita Pure Land.

The author gives us an excellent picture of the general nature of the Buddhist attitude on how to meditate and behave at the moments leading up to death. He then introduces us to the Sutrayana concept of Tushita, and explains the difference between this and the tantric view in the Vajrayana practice we are about to undertake. He leads us first through the Sutrayana preliminaries that are used as the foundation of the practice, and then guides us through the actual stages of training.

The training in consciousness transference, then, has many styles, methods and levels. In the beginning it is the act of taking refuge in the Buddha, Dharma and Sangha as an expression of spiritual sentiment and trust. After this it is the process of developing the inherent goodness and wisdom of the mind and of gaining experience in the general spiritual trainings, which guard and protect the mind from degeneration. In terms of the three *yanas*: as a Hinayana training it is the practice of eliminating attachment and aversion; as a general Mahayana training it is the cultivation of the conventional bodhimind of love and compassion as causes of lasting happiness here and hereafter, and also the cultivation of the ultimate bodhimind of awareness of the profound emptiness nature, as explained by the First Dalai Lama; finally, as a Vajrayana training it is the generation of divine view and transcendental identity at the time of death, and the focusing of the mind in accordance with the instructions on whichever of the four divisions of the tantras one is engaging in. In particular, it is the control of the subtle energies and the elimination of coarse awareness during the period of the dynamic psychic evolution that immediately precedes and follows the death experience.

The practice of consciousness transference on at least one of these levels is found in every form and lineage of Buddhism. In Tsecholding's summary and guide we can see the underlying Buddhist sentiment and rationale to death and dying, and the Buddhist theory of the inner dynamics that lead to a meaningful conclusion to the life cycle.

THE YOGA OF CONSCIOUSNESS TRANSFERENCE

by Lama Tsechokling Yeshe Gyaltsen

NAMO ARYA MAITREYA.
Homage to Maitreya Buddha,
A bodhisattva long familiar with compassion,
Who reaches out to the helpless beings
Fallen over the precipice of cyclic existence
And guides them to the lotus garden
Of goodness, well-being and joy.

Herein lies an explanation of the consciousness transference yoga focusing upon Maitreya Buddha.

There are in Tibet many different Buddhist lineages of consciousness transference yoga. The most popular is perhaps that connected with the female tantras, namely the *Vajrayogini-tantra*. However, of almost equal renown is the male tantra method associated with the *Guhyasamaja-tantra*, which was propagated in Tibet by Marpa the Translator, and is known as 'the interwoven transference yoga.'

Yet no matter what specific tradition of the transference yoga we train in, the ultimate and highest form of the practice depends upon the completion stage yoga of mind refinement,[1] wherein all energies of the body are withdrawn just as at the time of death and a meditational experience equivalent to death is aroused. This is clearly stated by Khedrub Choje in his *Ocean of Mystic Attainments*,[2] as well as in numerous other reliable sources. But this yoga of mind refinement is a topic solely of Highest Yoga Tantra, and is not dealt with in the lower tantras.

There are limitless stories of illustrious Buddhist masters in both India and Tibet who have accomplished the yoga of consciousness transference in accordance with the various systems, such as those of Guhyasamaja, Vajrayogini, the Six Yogas of Naropa, Amitabha, Maitreya and so forth. Their excellent oral traditions still exist today, as do many of the scriptures they wrote on how to control and focus the mind at the time of death, the stages of training in the transference methods, and so forth. These are all available to us, and we should not just leave them on the shelves of libraries.

My treatise will deal with the system of training in consciousness transference associated with Maitreya Buddha. The practice involves two trainings: the preliminaries and the actual yoga. I will firstly deal with the preliminaries.

THE PRELIMINARIES

The preliminaries mainly aim at overcoming attachment. This is because the mind of attachment is the principal obstacle to high rebirth. It is due to attachment to our body, possessions, involvements, friends, relatives and the other pleasurable objects of the samsaric world that the transference yogas are difficult to actually accomplish. How we evolve after death very much depends upon the inner freedom or inner attachment of the mind. Therefore it is important to eliminate the habit of grasping at the transient, ephemeral things of worldly existence. When our mind is bound by attachment there is nothing that the compassion of the Buddhas and bodhisattvas can do for us.

This is illustrated by the story of the group of merchants living on an endangered island. Avalokiteshvara, the Bodhisattva of Compassion, manifested as a navigator of a boat and came to them, offering to carry them to safety. But most of the merchants, attached to their possessions, chose to stay behind in the vain hope of protecting their material investments. In the end they died on the island. Had they been without attachment, the compassion of Avalokiteshvara could have saved them, but due to their greed there was nothing that he could do for them.

To eliminate attachment we should contemplate the value and rarity of the human life form, and also its impermanent, transient nature. Avoid indulgence in the illusory drama of constantly struggling to overcome enemies and pamper friends, a meaningless drunken dance that never ends and that leads only to fatigue. Contemplate the nature of karmic law and strive to live in the ways that close the gates to lower rebirth. Remember that, should you take rebirth in the lower realms, a great deal of suffering will have to be experienced, and it will not be easy to find your way back to the higher realms.

Even if we are not reborn in the lower realms but instead manage to achieve a rebirth in the higher samsaric worlds, such as the human or celestial realms, this will be of no significant benefit unless accomplished on the basis of wisdom giving liberation from the cyclic process. Without the basis of wisdom, the subtle traces of latent karmic instincts will one day emerge, to overpower us and cause our downfall. The highest divinity in the highest samsaric heaven one day will fall back to the lower realms and will then have to face confusion, pain and sorrow.

We should contemplate the nature of karmic law and the shortcomings of samsaric existence in this way, and cut off attachment to thoughts of achieving higher samsaric pleasures. What one needs is an attitude that regards the entirety of samsara as a prison filled with misery. This eliminates attachment at the time of death, the most powerful hindrance to a happy rebirth.

As well as avoiding negative mental traits at the time of death, one must cultivate positive thoughts and conditions. This is accomplished by means of the Mahayana oral tradition of consciousness transference[3] by means of relying upon the five powers: intention, the white seed, familiarity, destruction of negativity, and aspiration, or prayer. The basis of this general transference method is meditation upon the bodhimind, the altruistic bodhisattva spirit of love and compassion that aspires to enlightenment as the best means to benefit the world. During one's life one develops these five powers as a practice: the intention and determination to generate realization of the bodhimind; the consistent accumulation of goodness as a condition to generating the bodhimind; familiarity with the bodhimind through constant meditation upon it; destruction of the inner forces of darkness, such as anger, aversion and self-cherishing, that hinder the growth of the bodhimind; and the aspiration to realize the bodhimind for the benefit of the world.

Then at the time of death the five powers are adjusted to perform as a consciousness transference method. The white seed becomes accumulation of merit by leaving all one's possessions to worthy causes. One recollects any negative karma collected during one's life, confesses it to the visualized Buddhas and bodhisattvas, takes refuge in the Three Jewels, generates thoughts of the bodhimind, and purifies any breaches of one's spiritual precepts and commitments. Aspiration becomes the strong prayer not to become separated from the bodhi-mind during death, the bardo, rebirth or in any future lives.

Destruction becomes the determination to avoid self-cherishing and to remember the bodhimind at all times during the death experience. Intention becomes the thought to practice meditation upon the ultimate and conventional bodhiminds, come what may. Finally, familiarity becomes the practice of lying in the position that Buddha died in, that is, on one's right side with one's right arm folded under the body and the ring finger of the right hand closing the right nostril. Meditating on the bodhimind while lying in this, 'the lion posture,' one breathes in and visualizes that while doing so one is inhaling the sufferings of all living beings; and then breathes out with the visualization of giving living beings all causes of happiness.

In this way one cuts off all attraction to the things of this life and becomes familiar with the five powers as a method of consciousness transference over a long period of time, so that at the moment of death one can apply the powers effectively. Thus at the time of death one dedicates all possessions to good causes, makes the prayer of dedication of merits to a pure rebirth as a means to fulfill the bodhisattva spirit and, by means of action and attitude, directs all energies at maintaining clarity and control.

The most important factor at the time of death is a strong, clear meditation. This gives us the advantage of facing the death experience with full awareness.

In his *Encyclopedia of Buddhist Metaphysics*[4] the Indian sage Vasubandhu says:

> Just as beings can transmigrate
> From a high realm to a low one,
> So also can they transmigrate
> From low to high.

In the Maitreya system of consciousness transference, the Pure Land to which the transference of consciousness is made is the Tushita Pure Land, the quiet, gentle paradise presided over by Maitreya, the Buddha of Love. It is said that Shakyamuni Buddha, who was our historical Buddha Gautama, was the fourth Buddha of this age to perform the function of a universal teacher, and that Maitreya is prophesied to be the fifth. Our age, it is said, will have 1,000 such Buddhas who act as universal teachers. All of these 1,000 are said to emanate from Tushita in order to manifest the act of enlightenment to mankind and perform the deeds of a universal teacher.

There are many stories in the scriptures of how Maitreya practiced on the path with Buddha Shakyamuni when in earlier lives they were still both mere bodhisattvas in training. Thus we who practice the teachings of Buddha Shakyamuni, which are so in accord with the future teachings of Maitreya, have a very special karmic connection with Maitreya. Especially, in this age when he sits absorbed in meditation in Tushita awaiting the time to fulfill prophecy and manifest in the world, the powers of his prayers are particularly strong. Any meditations upon him at this time will be most effective.

There are said to have been numerous scriptures in India dealing with the nature of the Tushita Pure Land, although these have not appeared in Tibet. There are of course many references, such as those in the *Sutra Like a Cluster of Jewels*.[5]

In the practice of the transference yoga, Tushita is visualized as being joyously radiant. At its center is the wisdom palace of Maitreya Buddha, the victory banners of truth shining above it more radiantly than 1,000 suns. It is embellished with jewels, bells and so forth, and surpasses the most splendid celestial mansion in beauty. In front of this divine palace is a ring of trees resembling that under which Maitreya will manifest his enlightenment when he takes birth as a universal teacher and fulfills his prophecy. The earth of Tushita is made of gold and is studded with lapis lazuli, yet it is soft and supple on the feet as one walks. In the courtyard in front of the palace sits Maitreya Buddha upon a Dharma throne upheld by eight lions of enlightenment. He is adorned by the 112 marks and signs of perfection, and is expounding the theory of transcendental wisdom. To his right sits the bodhisattva Namkha Trimame and to his left the bodhisattva Jampel Nyingpo.[6] Countless bodhisattvas sit around them in a circle, listening in rapture to Maitreya's discourse. One visualizes this image and generates a strong aspiration to achieve a pure rebirth in this realm.

When engaging in this training it is useful to arrange an altar with an image of Maitreya in the center. He is in the half-seated posture, as though about to stand up. If such an image cannot be acquired, then any form of Maitreya will do, and even if this is impossible, any representation of the body, speech and mind of the enlightened ones will suffice. In front of this image or images place the standard water and sensory offerings. Then arrange a comfortable meditation seat and sit on it in either the full or half lotus posture. Take refuge in the Buddha, Dharma and Sangha, and generate the altruistic thought of highest enlightenment.

Establishing the correct attitude and motivation in this way prepares the basis for entering into the actual yoga of training in consciousness transference. To meditate merely because of the physical or mental pleasure experienced in serene meditation is not a pure motive. Should one die with an impure motivation or thought such as this, the result would be impure rebirth and continued existence amidst inauspicious conditions.

Therefore when we engage in the training of consciousness transference in order to achieve a pure rebirth, the basic motivation should be pure. One's thought should be, 'I wish to attain a high rebirth in order to continue along the path to enlightenment in as quick and efficient a way as possible, in order to benefit the limitless number of living beings who are lost in confusion and suffering.' The mental foundation must be this essential bodhisattva aspiration to attain greatness in order to be able to perform great deeds for the benefit of others.

This is the pure motivation to be generated at the beginning of every practice session, and to be maintained throughout with strength and clarity. We who have fortunately been born in this world cycle have a special karmic connection with Maitreya, and thus can easily achieve a pure rebirth in Tushita. But our motivation should be to do so in order to hear his pure teachings and to practice their essence as a method to gain enlightenment in order to benefit all living beings, not merely to benefit ourselves by escaping the ordinary world.

Thus the preliminaries to the training in consciousness transference are nothing other than the general Mahayana practices, such as the methods of generating the conventional bodhimind of love, compassion and the altruistic aspiration to highest enlightenment, and the methods of generating the ultimate bodhimind of *vipashyana*, or insight into the deeper nature of reality, the panoramic view of emptiness. In turn, the basis for these Mahayana techniques is the Hinayana training in the mind of non-attachment. If we can lay the basis of our training in this way, we will be accomplishing the preparations in the manner shown by the great masters of the past.

Of all Mahayana practices, the two most essential are those of cultivating the conventional and ultimate bodhiminds mentioned above. As for the order of these trainings, it is said in *The Essence of the Middle Way:*[7]

> Those of sharpest capacity
> First train in the view of emptiness
> And then cultivate great compassion
> For the living beings of samsara.

Thus as is said here we can see that the order for those of highest potential is to first gain experience in the methods for understanding the emptiness nature of phenomena. They are then directed to enter the trainings of the conventional bodhimind, such as cultivating love, compassion, the sense of universal responsibility, and so forth. This is the procedure for those of highest karmic background.

For ordinary beings, however, the approach is reversed. As Chandrakirti states in his *Entering into the Middle View*:[8]

> First they train in great compassion;
> Then they train in the wisdom of non-duality.

That is, lesser beings must first gain stability in the method side of practice, such as the cultivation of great compassion and the conventional bodhimind. Only when an inner experience of the conventional aspect has been gained are they able to engage successfully in the ultimate bodhimind, the wisdom training.

To summarize the discussion so far, the supreme preparation for the yoga of consciousness transference is the cultivation of a correct mental basis, a basis founded on the above trainings of conventional and ultimate aspects of the bodhimind, coupled with a strong aspiration to achieve rebirth in the Pure Land of Maitreya. As stated earlier, this must be applied in context to an overall understanding of the essential teachings of Buddha and the wish to accomplish the training for the benefit of all living beings.

When we have gained experience in these preliminaries, we are then ready to proceed with the actual training in the transference yoga.

THE ACTUAL TRAINING

The actual session begins by taking refuge, generating the bodhimind and visualizing the Tushita Pure Land as described earlier. One then invokes Maitreya to come forth from Tushita and manifest in one's place of practice. This is done by means of a verse:

> O Maitreya, Lord of Tushita, the Pure Land of Happiness,
> Bodhisattva of Love, a treasury of great compassion,
> I send this request to you.
> Emanate forth from Tushita to this place of practice.
> Come with your retinue of bodhisattvas
> And manifest in the space before me.

As this verse is recited one meditates that Maitreya comes from Tushita like a bird soaring in the sky. He descends to the space a cubit in front of one's face, where he sits on a throne supported by eight lions and gazes on one with joy, smiling with delight.

One then chants a version of the seven-limbed prayer, such as the opening verses of *The King of Mahayana Prayers*,[9] in order to purify the mind and generate positive energy.

The above-mentioned liturgy of these seven limbs is somewhat lengthy, and when time is short the following brief version may be used:

> I prostrate and make offerings to the Aryas,
> In their presence I face all my shortcomings
> And rejoice in the goodness of the world and beyond.
> O wondrous masters, I beseech you,
> Do not pass beyond the world
> But remain and turn the Wheel of Dharma.
> All creative energy I dedicate
> To the peerless cause of enlightenment.

This is a general verse for purification and generation of goodness. After it has been chanted one recites the following homage to Maitreya, either 7, 21 or 108 times:

> O teacher, transcended warrior, thus gone one, in whom sorrow is eliminated, the perfect Buddha Maitreya, together with your retinue of bodhisattvas, to you I prostrate and make offerings, and in you I take refuge.

When this has been called out, a stream of nectar emanates from Maitreya's body. It comes to the crown of one's head, entering one's body via the Brahma aperture. One's body becomes filled, and one is purified of all negative karmic instincts and obscurations collected since time immemorial. All obstacles to accomplishment of the transference yoga, such as thoughts of attachment to the things of this life, are washed away. One's mindstream becomes imbued with the blessings of the body, speech and mind of the Aryas.

One then constructs the visualization in accordance with the following verses:

> Visualizing my body as being transparent
> And as clear as a crystal vase,
> The central energy channel runs
> Through the center of the trunk
> From the aperture at my crown
> To a point just below the navel.
> This channel is wide at the top
> And becomes increasingly more narrow below.
>
> At the center of the channel
> As it passes through the heart area

Is the mystic drop made of light,
Which is inseparable from the most subtle
Bodily energies and levels of consciousness.
It is as though weightless and immaterial.

As said above, one visualizes one's body as being as clear and transparent as crystal. The central energy channel is seen as running up the middle of the trunk just in front of the backbone. It is narrow at the bottom and, coming to the Brahma aperture at the crown, opens wide like the mouth of a long horn. Its bottom terminal is the point three finger-widths below the navel. At the mouth of the upper aperture stands the mystic syllable *HAM.*

Inside the channel at the heart energy-center is the most subtle energy and consciousness in the form of the mystic drop, white tinged with red. It is as though made of light, and is weightless and insubstantial, as though able to be blown away by the slightest breeze.

Here it should be noted that the central energy channel is visualized as standing straight in the center of the body, like a tree of life. One does not visualize the three channels, four energy centers, and so forth as is done in the completion stage yogas of Highest Yoga Tantra. In this context it would seem that the system here unites practices from the higher with methods from the lower tantras.

The oral tradition relates:

A sublime path and a positive mind:
These protect against negative karmic impulses.

That is to say, it is very important in the transference yoga to cut off all negative thoughts and to generate clear, conducive attitudes.

The method of cutting off the negative energy flows is not done as in the general Highest Yoga Tantra systems, which rely upon projecting mantric syllables to the various places. Rather, the following process is used.

After the purification by the showering of the wisdom nectars (as above), the places for the exit of the vital energies and, at the time of death, consciousness itself, are closed off by a coating of light and nectar, golden in color. One meditates that, because of this golden sheath, consciousness is no longer able to leave via the subsidiary pathways.

One then invites Maitreya to come to the crown of one's head. This is done by means of the following verse:

O kind foundation guru, embodiment of the Three Jewels,
Holy one uniting the blessings of Maitreya and Lama Tsongkhapa,

Treasury of compassion, I offer this prayer to you:
Send forth your transforming blessings.

Thus requested, the visualized assembly
Begins to dissolve into light,
And all dissolve into Maitreya Buddha.
He comes to the crown of my head,
Where he rests in the manner
Of a Dhyani Buddha, a Lord of the Family.

His central energy channel resembles mine,
But is inverted in shape, being wide below
And narrow at the top.

At his heart is the syllable *MEEM*,
Yellow in color, in nature great bliss
Conjoined with the five transcendental wisdoms.
It is radiant with light and
Strongly attracts one's attention.
The thought to move upward to it
Arises with tremendous force.

Thus the upper aperture of one's central energy channel and the lower aperture of Maitreya's energy channel come into inseparable contact.

One concentrates on the mystic drop of light, in nature one's own mind, which is located at the middle of the central channel at the level of one's heart. The drop looks up and becomes aware of the mantric syllable at Maitreya's heart, which has the nature of great bliss conjoined with the wisdom of non-duality.

On perceiving the brilliance of the syllable *MEEM*, the drop at one's heart becomes overwhelmed with awe, and the thought arises, 'I must lift myself up to that radiant light.'

One then recites the following prayer three or seven times:

O Maitreya Buddha, peerless refuge
You who see every opportunity to benefit living beings,
You free from partiality toward friends and enemies,
Who never stir from the sphere of working for others,
Please heed this prayer of mine.

Grant your inspiring blessings to help me
Cut the chains of attachment to the transient.
Bless me to purify my mindstream
Of negative karmic instincts and obscurations.
Protect me from the agents of darkness.

Guide me to freedom when
Visions of the bardo arise.
Help me to close the doors
To rebirth in the lower realms.

Bless me to apply successfully
The yoga of consciousness transference.
Ripen the seeds of realization within me
And guide my spirit to the Tushita Pure Land.

Maitreya hears this prayer. Rays of light emanate from his heart and shine forth. They radiate down his central channel, entering my central channel and flooding it with brilliance.

These lights then touch against the mystic drop at my heart. The drop instantly shoots upward, like an iron filing caught up in the strength of a powerful magnet, or like a fish hooked out of the water on a strong rod.

One utters the syllable *HIK* while restraining the downward-moving energies. The drop jumps up slightly and then falls back to its natural place at the heart. Again one calls *HIK*. This time the drop shoots up to the throat, and then falls back to the heart. A third time one calls *HIK*. The drop shoots up to the crown of one's head, and then falls back to the heart. Each time the drop shoots up on the sound of *HI* and falls back on the *K*.

This process is repeated a minimum of three, seven or twenty-one times.

Here it is important to take the drop only to the mouth of the channel and not to project it outside of the aperture. It is said that to project it outside of the body causes one's life span to be diminished. Nonetheless, it is permissible once each day to bring the drop up to the mantric syllable at Maitreya's heart, letting it fall back on the *K* sound as before. It travels up via the interconnecting channels, touches again the syllable *MEEM* and then falls back to its natural site.

Some traditions of training in the yoga of consciousness transference speak of using two syllables, *PHAT* and *HIK*, in the manipulation of the drop. Although this is also valid, the principal later masters in the tradition have expressed the opinion that the mantric syllable *HIK* is best for trying to direct the vital energies and consciousness upward.

Moreover, it is not enough just to recite the mantric sound *HIK* from the mouth alone; it must be made in conjunction with the yogic exercise of directing the vital energies upward.

Through application of the above yogic method to the meditation of moving the drop of subtle energy and consciousness, one may receive the signs of accomplishment, such as a small blister appearing on the crown of one's head and so forth. But if the practice is not done within the framework of an understanding of the nature of the conventional self and its relationship with the body and mind, as well as a general understanding of the illusory nature of the three circles of the transference yoga—the object transferred, the process of transference and the observer of the transference—one misses a most essential ingredient of the tradition. My own guru, the master Jamyang Shepai Dorje,[10] personally stressed this point very strongly in his treatise on the consciousness transference yogas.

The nature of the relationship between the 'I' and the body-mind complex is the subject of the Madhyamaka studies. It is important to have a grounding in these as a basis for the transference yogas. It is important in all practices to understand the nature of the self. Otherwise, when one visualizes the drop as being an embodiment of one's mind and the subtle energies, there is a question of who is visualizing and what is the relationship between the person visualizing and the object being visualized. Sometimes the 'I' appears as though one with the body, sometimes as though one with the mind, sometimes as though one with the body-mind complex and sometimes as though separate from the body and mind. It is important to understand the relationship between the 'I' and the body-mind complex when performing the yoga of transference. Otherwise, at the time of death it will not be possible to cut off attachment from within the mind, and one will grasp at the body and at the images that arise within the stream of consciousness. This undermines the effectiveness of the training.

THE CONCLUSION

At the conclusion of each session Maitreya melts into light above one's head. He then descends into one's body via one's Brahma aperture. The aperture becomes closed as though with a nectar of refined gold.

This is the method of stabilizing the blessings of the practice and thus extending one's life span.

In conjunction with this practice of training in the yoga of consciousness transference, one should study the various writings on the nature of the death experience. It is also good to learn how to make the observation for determining the outer, inner and secret signs that indicate a danger that could result in untimely death, and also to learn the methods for turning untimely death away and accomplishing longevity.

Should omens of death appear and should applications of the longevity techniques fail to produce signs of success, one should take up the methods of training in the consciousness transference yogas before one's health has degenerated too far.

Thus is complete my treatise on the consciousness transference tradition in accordance with the Maitreya system. I, Tsechokling Yeshe Gyaltsen, wrote it at the repeated request of a student, the meditator and monk Lozang Konchok of Kyagegon.

May it cause the tradition to thrive until time's end, bringing benefits to limitless beings. May countless living beings take rebirth in Tushita to hear the sublime teachings of Buddha Maitreya. And when Maitreya takes birth and manifests the deeds of a universal teacher, may all his devotees then be reborn in his presence and help him to fulfill his wondrous prayers.

Chapter Eight
A Ritual for Caring for the Dead

I travel the roads of nature until the hour when I shall lie down and be at rest; yielding back my last breath into the air from which I have drawn it daily, and sinking down upon the earth from which my father derived the seed, my mother the blood, and my nurse the milk of my being.

—Emperor Marcus Aurelius: *Meditations*

TRANSLATOR'S PREAMBLE

According to the Buddhist teaching, after the body and mind separate, the mind experiences a brief flash of clear light consciousness and then enters the bardo, or state between death and rebirth. As the present Dalai Lama explains, the state of mind of the person in the moments preceding death is very important, for this sets the tone of the mindstream experienced in the bardo.[1] This bardo state is likened to the world of a dream, and the body one has at that time to the body possessed in a dream.

In the bardo section of his commentary to the Six Yogas of Naropa, Lama Tsongkhapa explains:[2]

> The lifetime of the bardo person usually lasts for seven days, although in some cases it is even shorter than this. If in this time he/she has not found a suitable place of rebirth, he/she experiences a "small" death and is reborn in the bardo again. This may occur for as many as seven cycles, making a total of forty-nine days in the

bardo, until the person is ready to take rebirth. Then, when the time and conditions are ripe, and when the karmic conditions have accumulated, the rebirth will occur.

The methods of caring for the dead (Tib., *jezin*) work on the principle that during the period the person is wandering in the bardo he/she is in a state of transition and is sensitive to both positive and negative input. Although the state of the person's mind at the time of death affects the degree of this sensitivity, there is nonetheless always room for improvement and assistance when provided by a skilled ritualist and given a powerful method. In particular, the Buddhist belief is that any person who has been close to the deceased will be able to provide the vital link of communication between the ritualist, the ritual and the person in the bardo who is to be benefitted.

The practitioner who is adept in the high tantric yogas is in a very different position here than is the ordinary person. For him/her there is no need for conventional rituals or 'books of the dead'; theirs is a unique and self-controlled path. We saw this earlier in chapters two, four and also five, in the explanation of how at the time of death the yogi transforms the clear light mind of death into the clear light of Dharmakaya, and from this then manifests the bardo body as the illusory body of the Sambhogakaya.

The Second Dalai Lama gives a succinct explanation of this process in his *Tantric Yogas of Sister Niguma:*[3]

When an ordinary person dies, the elements of his/her continuum dissolve into one another and the clear light of mind temporarily appears. The trainee of highest capacity takes this clear light of death and applies the yoga of final mind refinement from a Highest Yoga Tantra system such as the *Guhyasamaja-tantra*. Then, instead of entering the bardo, he/she arises in the actual form of a tantric deity such as Heruka, embellished by all the signs of perfection. This is accomplished by means of the illusory body yoga. Here, mind becomes clear light and the vital energies that act as a vehicle of the clear light consciousness become the illusory body.... As for the mediocre practitioners, who through the strength of having meditated in their lifetime and having gained the ability to bring the vital energies into the central energy channel and experience the signs of entering, abiding and dissolving, the practice is as follows. At the time of death, when the twenty-five coarse elements dissolve and the clear light of death arises, which is the mother clear light, he/she blends this with the son clear light, which is the clear light experienced in meditation.... In this training there are numerous levels of application in accordance with the level of realization of the trainee.... Then there are the trainees of least capacity. Firstly they should gain familiarity with the means of recognizing the bardo experience. Then when the clear light of death arises they should visualize that it is transformed into the clear light of the path. Consequently, when the bardo body arises they are able to apply the bardo techniques to it.

Lama Tsongkhapa explains the importance of recognizing the stages of dying in order to be able to retain control in the bardo:[4]

If one can recognize the clear light of death and merge with it, one will be able to recognize the subsequent emergence of the bardo. This recognition of the stages of dying and the clear light that arises at the moment of death is the only way to be sure of recognizing the bardo once one enters it.

In the ritual that follows in this chapter, then, the first objective of the ritualist is to gain the attention of the deceased and to make him/her aware of the fact of being dead and in the bardo. The ritual begins with the summoning of the deceased, a ritual burning of his/her negative forces, the washing away of the obstacles to awareness of the six bodhisattva perfections (generosity, discipline, patience, enthusiastic energy, meditation and wisdom), which respectively are obstructed by the six delusions: selfishness, carelessness, anger, apathy, mental wandering and ignorance. After each cycle of purification, the 100-syllable mantra of Yamantaka is repeated, which is a variant of the mantra of Vajrasattva, the tantric meditation deity associated with purification.[5] The mystical powers of the Buddha, Dharma and Sangha are then called upon to pacify the three root delusions—attachment, aversion and ignorance—of the deceased. It is presumed that the dead person is a Buddhist, so calling upon these Three Jewels would have a profound subconscious effect on his/her psyche, giving rise to deeply held religious feelings.

Next is the process of the injunction to the five root delusions to return to the five elements. These five delusions are the negative poles of the five *skandhas* or faculties of a person, symbolized by the elements. The five dakinis into which they are ordered to transform are the five positive poles of the *skandhas*. The section is concluded by verses of auspiciousness, which are intended to call forth all forces of goodness and prepare the deceased for the next crucial stage, that of recognizing the bardo and focusing the mind so as to transfer consciousness out of it to an auspicious rebirth. This is the *bardo ngo-tro*, or, as Dr. Evans-Wentz translates it in *The Tibetan Book of the Dead*, 'the setting face to face with the nature of the bardo.'

By this point in the rite it is presumed that the attention of the deceased has been attracted and that he/she is now able to participate in the meditation process. The nature of the bardo is explained, as are the signs by which one can know one is definitely in the bardo. The consciousness of the deceased is coaxed into increasing levels of clarity, until the time comes when this is sufficient for the transference out of the bardo to a new rebirth, a pure rebirth in Sukhavati, the Pure Land of Joy.

At this point in the ritual, the fire is lit and the corpse or effigy cremated. The deceased is admonished to contemplate the ephemeral nature of the body and not to be attached to it or upset by its disintegration, but rather to attempt to transform his/her body, speech and mind into the three *kayas* of a Buddha, and also to transform his/her five *skandhas* into the five Dhyani Buddhas and the transcendental wisdoms associated with them.

Over the years in Dharamsala I witnessed this ritual several times. The particular text translated here is one of the most popular in use by Tibetans today, at least within the Yellow Hat order.

When reading this type of literature it is important, I think, to sit back from it and, rather than getting too involved in the form of the text, attempt to follow the mood and sentiment that is being projected. For it is this that represents the heart of the matter.

A RITUAL FOR CARING FOR THE DEAD

by Lama Mahasukha

> Lamas and masses of peaceful and wrathful deities,
> Dharma protectors who watch over goodness,
> I offer this prayer to you:
> Spontaneously fulfill and pacify all obstacles
> To every aspiration conventional and supreme.
>
> The precious human form so rare to attain
> Is quickly crushed by terrifying death.
> When death strikes it is useful if the living
> Do what they can to help the deceased.
> Therefore I write this ritual which produces
> Positive attitudes conducive to pure rebirth
> Through the whispered methods of the secret Vajrayana.

Herein, arranged in a format easy to practice, is contained a wondrous method, a yogic technique for taking proper care of a dead person. It is from the cycle of texts belonging to the *Vajrabhairava-tantra*, 'The Diamond Destroyer of the Lord of Death.' This is the Bodhisattva of Wisdom, Arya Manjushri, manifest in his most wrathful aspect.[1]

The ritualist should be an initiate of the system and should have previously completed the retreat and fire rite. Only then is he/she able to utilize this profound method.

The master commences by consecrating the implements to be used in the rite. He then generates himself as the deity [Vajrabhairava] and also generates the vision of the external deity.[2] When this has been accomplished he summons the deceased to come and listen. This is done in accordance with the following liturgy:

> All implements of the rite become seen as being empty of having an essence at which to grasp.
>
> From the sphere of emptiness appears the first letter of the deceased's name, marked above by a mystic drop and a zig-zag of flame. It completely transforms, and in its place appears the complete form of the deceased, with all aggregates, elements and sensory gates. *OM VAJRASATTVA HUM JAH!!!*
>
> By the power of the truth of the Buddha, Dharma and Sangha, and the power of the truth of the Buddha-families called Tathagata, Vajra, Ratna, Padma and Karma, and by the hearts, *mudras* and mantras of the myriad of meditation deities, and especially by the truth of the Diamond Destroyer of Death and the masses of deities associated with his mandala, and by the blessings of truth itself, may the consciousness of Such-and-such [deceased's name] come here right now, in one moment, in the time it takes for a single thought to arise, in one instant, from wherever it may be wandering in the bardo of becoming, in any of the three realms of the world, in the six realms of existence, in the ocean of living beings born in any of the four ways.

At this point the master takes up the vajra in his right hand and the bell in his left. The index and little fingers of the right hand are extended straight as pillars, and the vajra is held by the thumb and two middle fingers, which are formed into hooks. Thus showing this *mudra*, the right hand is placed over the corpse or the effigy being used. The liturgy reads:

> Lights in the form of hooks emanate from my heart. They hook the consciousness of the deceased, which is in the form of a radiant letter *AH*, pulling it into the body (or effigy) of the deceased via the crown of his/her head. It comes to rest at the deceased's heart.

The ritualist recites the appropriate mantras. He then continues:

May all misery be locked outside the mandala. May the enlightened beings of the mandala protect those in the lower realms from
the agitation of pain.

To Buddha, Dharma and Sangha I turn for refuge. *OM VAJRA-
PANI....*[3]

May the evils and karmic stains of those living in miserable
realms be destroyed. When those unfortunate beings die, may they
be reborn before the feet of the enlightened ones.

The evils, karmic stains and mental obscurations, together with their
instincts, are completely washed away, and the area of the rite is
freed from them.

A white *OM* appears at the crown of the head of the deceased, a
red *AH* at the throat and a blue *HUM* at the heart.

The master now performs the offering to the hindering spirits, ask-
ing them not to disturb the ritual being performed for the dead person.

This is followed by the prayer to Vajradaka, the Vajra Warrior, in which
the deceased's negative karmic instincts are purified by means of fire.

The meditation is first cleansed in emptiness by means of the
Svabhava mantra. Then follows the liturgy of the Vajradaka purification method:

Everything becomes seen as emptiness. From the sphere of emptiness appears the syllable *RAM*. This becomes a raging fire of wisdom. Suddenly the wrathful Vajra Warrior appears at its center.
His body is dark blue in color, his hands hold a vajra and a bell,
and his mouth is stretched open fiercely.

Turning attention to the deceased, I [the ritualist] visualize that on
the soles of his/her feet there appear air mandalas, shaped like half
moons. At his/her navel is a raging fire of wisdom. At his/her heart
stands the syllable symbolizing negative karma, the black syllable
PAM, embodiment of all evil traits and karmic traits of body, speech
and mind, and of all obscurations to liberation and omniscience.

Lights from the wisdom fire at the deceased's navel envelop the
black syllable *PAM* at the heart and force it to leave the body via
the nostrils. It transforms into the sesame seeds to be burned in the
fire rite. *OM VAJRA DAKA....*

Thus the negative karma of the deceased is visualized as leaving
the body and transforming into the sesame seeds that are to be burned.
The master, reciting the Vajradaka mantra, then takes the plate of
sesame seeds and pushes an appropriate quantity into the fire pot. As
it burns, he meditates that all the deceased's negativities are consumed.
He then recites the action and 100-syllable mantras and offers the following prayer:

I command the negative karmic stains and obscurations to the liberation and enlightenment of this deceased person, who is called Such-and-such, to be pacified, be pacified, be pacified!!! *OM SARVA PADAM....*

May this deceased person, who is called Such-and-such, be instantly freed from evil tendencies, obscurations to liberation and enlightenment, and karmic propensities for rebirth in any of the three lower realms. May he/she quickly attain clear, ultimate enlightenment. *OM SARVA....*

The master then takes a strand of *kusha* grass in his right hand and, reciting the appropriate mantra, dips the stem into the vase and sprinkles a little water:

This water, in nature generosity itself,
Cleanses away stains of selfishness and
Bestows a special excellence.
Thus do I wash him/her visualized before me.
OM YAMANTAKA SAMAYA... [the 100-syllable mantra].

May the evil actions, negative karmas and mental obscurations that this person called Such-and-such, who has passed beyond life and gone to the other side of the world, has collected over the countless previous lives since beginningless time, and especially all stains of the afflicted emotion selfishness, be cleansed and purified, and may he/she fully accomplish the perfection of generosity and quickly attain clear, highest enlightenment.

This water, in nature discipline itself,
Cleanses away stains of carelessness
And bestows a special excellence.
Thus do I wash him/her visualized before me.
OM YAMANTAKA SAMAYA....

May the evil actions, negative karmas and mental obscurations that this person called Such-and-such, who has passed beyond life and gone to the other side of the world, has collected over the countless previous lives since beginningless time, and especially all stains of the mental distortion of carelessness, be cleansed and purified, and may he/she fully accomplish the perfection of discipline and quickly attain clear, highest enlightenment.

This water, in nature patience itself,
Cleanses away stains of anger and
Bestows a special excellence.
Thus do I wash him/her visualized before me.
OM YAMANTAKA SAMAYA....

May the evil actions, negative karmas and mental obscurations that this person called Such-and-such, who has passed beyond life and gone to the other side of the world, and especially all stains of the mental distortion anger, be cleansed and purified, and may he/she fully accomplish the perfection of patience and quickly attain clear, highest enlightenment.

> This water, in nature enthusiastic energy,
> Cleanses away all stains of apathy and
> Bestows a special excellence.
> Thus do I wash him/her visualized before me.
> *OM YAMANTAKA SAMAYA....*

May the evil actions, negative karmas and mental obscurations that this person called Such-and-such, who has passed beyond life and gone to the other side of the world, and especially all stains of the mental distortion apathy, be cleansed and purified, and may he/she fully accomplish the perfection of enthusiastic energy and quickly attain clear, highest enlightenment.

> This water, in nature meditative concentration,
> Cleanses stains of mental wandering
> And bestows a special excellence.
> Thus do I wash him/her visualized before me.
> *OM YAMANTAKA SAMAYA....*

May the evil actions, negative karmas and mental obscurations that this person called Such-and-such, who has passed beyond life and gone to the other side of the world, and especially all stains of the distorting factors of mental wandering and dullness, be cleansed and purified, and may he/she fully accomplish the perfection of meditative concentration and quickly attain clear, highest enlightenment.

> This water, in nature wisdom,
> Cleanses stains of all ignorance
> And bestows a special excellence.
> Thus do I wash him/her visualized before me.
> *OM YAMANTAKA SAMAYA....*

May the evil actions, negative karmas and mental obscurations that this person called Such-and-such, who has passed beyond life and gone to the other side of the world, and especially all stains of the mental distortion ignorance, be cleansed and purified, and may he/she fully accomplish the perfection of wisdom and quickly attain clear, highest enlightenment.

By washing with these six waters,
The six stains of the mind are washed away
And the six bodhisattva perfections gained.
To him/her thus cleansed of failings I pay homage.
OM YAMANTAKA SAMAYA....

With faith in making devotions to the Enlightened Ones
Who possess the six excellent perfections
And are fully purified of the six stains,
I perform this cleansing ritual.
OM YAMANTAKA SAMAYA....

May the evil actions, negative karmas and mental obscurations that this person called Such-and-such, who has passed beyond life and gone to the other side of the world, and especially all stains of acting in contradiction to the six bodhisattva perfections, be cleansed and purified, and may he/she fully accomplish the six perfections and quickly attain clear, highest enlightenment.

Attachment, aversion and ignorance:
These are the worldly poisons.
May the Enlightened Ones, who possess no poisons,
Crush all poisons by the force of Buddha light.
OM YAMANTAKA SAMAYA....

May the evil actions, negative karmas and mental obscurations that this person called Such-and-such, who has passed beyond life and gone to the other side of the world, and especially all stains of the psychic poisons that arise from the forces of mental distortion and afflicted emotions, be cleansed and purified, and may he/she quickly attain clear, highest enlightenment.

Attachment, aversion and ignorance:
These are the worldly poisons.
May the Dharma, which possesses no poisons,
Crush all poisons by the force of Dharma light.
OM YAMANTAKA SAMAYA....

May the evil actions, negative karmas and mental obscurations that this person called Such-and-such, who has passed beyond life and gone to the other side of the world, and especially all stains of the psychic poisons that arise from the forces of mental distortion, be cleansed and purified, and may he/she quickly attain clear, ultimate enlightenment.

Attachment, aversion and ignorance:
These are the worldly poisons.
May the Sangha, who possess no poisons,

> Crush all poisons by the force of Sangha light.
> *OM YAMANTAKA SAMAYA....*

May the evil actions, negative karmas and mental obscurations that this person called Such-and-such, who has passed beyond life and gone to the other side of the world, and especially all stains of the psychic poisons that arise from the forces of mental distortion, be cleansed and purified, and may he/she quickly attain clear, highest enlightenment.

> Earth is the mother of the psychic poisons;
> Earth is the father of psychic poisons too.
> By the power of these words of truth,
> May the deceased's psychic poisons become nothing.
> Poisons, return to earth.
> Poisons, go into the vessel of hardness. *SVAHA!!!*
> Poisonous elements and poisons which arise
> From the elements, separate from the element earth.
>
> Dissolve into the element earth.
> May the element earth of the deceased
> Be purified, and may it manifest
> In the pure nature of the dakini Lochana.
>
> Water is the mother of the psychic poisons;
> Water is the father of the psychic poisons too;
> By the power of these words of truth,
> May the deceased's poisons become nothing.
> Poisons, return to water.
> Poisons, go into the vessel of fluidity. *SVAHA!!!*
> May the water element of the deceased
> Be purified and may it manifest
> In the pure nature of the dakini Mamaki.
>
> Fire is the mother of the psychic poisons;
> Fire is the father of psychic poisons too.
> By the power of these words of truth,
> May the deceased's poisons become nothing.
> Poisons, return to fire.
> Poisons, go into the vessel of heat. *SVAHA!!!*
> May the element fire of the deceased
> Be purified, and may it manifest
> In the pure nature of the dakini Pandara.
>
> Air is the mother of the psychic poisons;
> Air is the father of the psychic poisons too.
> By the power of these words of truth

May the deceased's poisons become nothing.
Poisons, return to the air.
Poisons, go into the vessel of motility. *SVAHA!!!*
May the air element of the deceased
Be purified, and may it manifest
In the pure nature of the dakini Tara.

The master then chants the following auspicious verses, tossing a flower at the conclusion of each:

The saints and holy ones, having peaceful minds
That have passed beyond harmful thoughts, and
Who have totally crushed stains of attachment,
Will bring but goodness and joy to you.

The spiritual masters who direct beings
To the path of ultimate freedom
And reveal every truth
Will bring but goodness and joy to you.

The teachers, supports of living beings,
Who for the sake of the world
Guide seekers to the land of bliss,
Will bring but goodness and joy to you.

The saints, with hearts of love,
Regard each and every living being
As a mother does her only child;
They will bring but goodness and joy to you.

The bodhisattvas, who act as a home and a friend
To help and support every living being
Circling in the sea of becoming,
Will bring but goodness and joy to you.

They who appear as spiritual heroes
To bestow everything sublime
And to fulfill all hopes of the world
Will bring but goodness and joy to you.

Those whose very birth caused
The earth and its forests to quiver in awe
And living beings to weep in bliss
Will bring but goodness and joy to you.

They who when they passed to enlightenment
Caused the six worlds to shake
And evil people to be filled with anxiety
Will bring but goodness and joy to you.

They who turn the Wheel of Dharma
And speak the four truths seen by the Aryas
By manifesting as a Muni, a sage,
Will bring but goodness and joy to you.

They who with the power of beauty
Tumble the wrong views of sophists
And tame the wild minds of barbarians
Will bring but goodness and joy to you.

May the Enlightened Ones bring you every joy
And every goodness of men and gods.
May they bring you happiness surpassing
That of the most powerful divinity.

May the Enlightened Ones, who have merits
And thoughts more sublime than all the gods,
Fulfill for you this very day
Your each and every hope for goodness.

May the Enlightened Ones bring joy to mankind,
May they bring harmony to the animal kingdom,
May they bring the world to the way of truth
And in future may they hold us in happiness.

May they bring joy day and night
And during dawn and dusk as well.
May they encourage every happiness
By imparting the joy of spiritual knowledge.

May they bring joy day and night
And at noon and midnight as well.
May they give us every happiness
By showing the ways through which evil is cleansed.

May this person called Such-and-such, who has passed beyond life and gone to the other side of the world, be freed from rebirth in the lower realms of samsara. May he/she take rebirth in a happy place. May all interferences to this be overcome and may every auspicious sign manifest.

At this point in the ritual the master reads a version of a scripture in the cycle known as 'pointing out the nature of the bardo.'[4] There are many varieties of texts in this genre. A brief version is as follows:

Ah! So be it!
   O you who are called Such-and-such, who have died and gone to the other side of the world, listen to me now. You are dead. Your old body has been left behind, but a new one has not yet been found. This is the state of existence called 'the bardo of becoming.' You

must understand that this is precisely the situation you are in.

How can you know that you are in the bardo? Many strange and fearful sights unlike anything you have beheld before are occurring. This is a sign that you are in the bardo.

Also, the powers of the bodily energies of the earth element have failed, and therefore you are experiencing sounds of mountains cracking open and the earth trembling; and, above the earth, everything seems to be disintegrating and falling, and a rain of stones is pelting down.

The energy of the water element has failed, and consequently the terrifying sensations of sinking in the middle of a huge ocean are occurring.

The energy of the fire element has failed, and therefore it seems that fire is blazing everywhere, and terrifying sounds as of crackling and the rushing of flames are exploding in your ears and pounding in your heart.

Finally, because the energy of wind is reversed, you feel as though you are standing in the midst of the great windstorm that marks the end of an age, and you are overcome by terror.

These various terrifying events are all signs that you have died and are now in the bardo.

As well, there are also the six distant signs. Previously, things like mountains and walls would obstruct your free movement, but now nothing does and you can go anywhere you wish merely by thinking about it. Previously you would have had to make an effort to accomplish anything, but now everything is effortless. Also, before when you would speak to friends or relatives an answer would be forthcoming, but now nobody answers anything you say. As for mental indications, no light comes from the sun and moon, and your bardo body casts no shadow. These are six sure signs that you have died and are now in the bardo.

There are also the six signs of unstable behavior, which indicate a lack of security and continuity. These are as follows: continually moving through places known and unknown, sometimes in beautiful places and sometimes in ugly, frightening ones; being inside many environments in rapid succession, such as forests, then temples and so forth; one moment walking and the next eating, sleeping or sitting; changing reactions to food, which sometimes will seem good and the next will seem putrid; the uncertainty of companionship, which one moment will seem friendly and the next seem strange or intimidating; and, lastly, the instability of thought patterns, which oscillate from one subject to another. The appearance of these six signs of unstable behavior indicate that you have died and are now in the bardo.

Furthermore, the Lord of Death will appear to you with eyes blazing like fire. His agents, huge and fierce, will throw their sharp weapons at you. Many people of the opposite sex, some beautiful and some ugly, will appear to you and try to allure your mind.

And you will meet with great spirits of judgment who will count your life deeds with black and white pebbles, tallying up the bad and good. Your mind will be difficult to control and will stray wheresoever fancy takes it.

These are sure signs that you have died and are now in the bardo. Notice them and recognize your predicament.

If you are headed for rebirth in the lower realms, you will see burned forests, smoke and the like. Alternatively, if you are headed for rebirth in the higher realms you will behold signs such as gold and/or white virgin wool. Of course it is wonderful if the signs of a high rebirth appear; but even if negative signs arise do not become upset. A sentient being in the bardo is like a small boat on a large river, and its direction is easily changed. The power of the blessings of the gurus and the Three Jewels of Refuge are inconceivable, and the strength of mantra and meditation is great. Therefore have no fear. No matter what terrifying visions appear to you, understand them to be mere hallucinations. In fact nothing whatsoever is really there to harm you, not even the tiniest speck of dust.

You are dead now. And just as you have left all friends and relatives behind, so also have they left you. Regard friends, relatives and possessions like objects experienced in a dream, and be not attached to them. If you entertain attachment at this time, you will not be able to gain freedom from the terrors of the Lord of Death nor from the lower realms.

You should make every effort now to remain free from fear. If you can single-pointedly abide in refuge in your spiritual guide and the Three Jewels, you will he able to escape rebirth in the lower realms. Therefore make your thoughts firm and fix them on these subjects, not letting them degenerate.

Meditate that a channel, straight as an arrow, runs down the center of your body, from the crown of your head to your navel. At the heart is your mind in the form of a white drop formed from light. It is the size of a pea, but buoyant and immaterial, like fluff. The top of the channel stands open at the crown, like a gaping mouth. As the following verses are chanted, visualize that Buddha Amitabha is summoned from Sukhavati, the Pure Land of Joy. He is in nature your own principal teacher. Coming from Sukhavati in a single moment, he rests above the aperture at your crown.

O Guru inseparable from Buddha Amitabha,
Together with your mystic entourage,
Come from the divine abode of the Pure Land of Joy.
Out of great compassion come forth, I pray.
Rest with pleasure above the crown of the deceased.

I bow to you and make you every offering,
I acknowledge my failings and rejoice in all goodness.
Please turn the vast and profound wheel of Dharma;
Remain in the world, never leaving us behind.
All meritorious energy I dedicate
To the cause of peerless enlightenment.

The master then performs a mandala offering and recites the verses of prostration to Amitabha, Buddha of Boundless Light, as was done before. Then:

O fortunate child of noble character,
The end of life is always death,
And death divides not between young and old.
Be aware of the significance of death
And pay heed to these words.

Let not your mind wander
But hold it tightly at the heart.
O child, have no attachment to your corpse,
Nor for the wealth and property left behind,
Nor for former friends and relatives.

Should attachment arise at this moment,
There is the danger of rebirth as a ghost;
But if you can stay free from attachment,
You will attain the Pure Land of Joy.

O child, the end of collecting is dispersal,
The end of building is disintegration,
The end of meeting is separation
And the end of birth is death.

The time of your death has arrived,
But in this you are not unique.
Death is the fate of all that lives.
Know that you are now dead,
But do not be disturbed by this knowledge.

O child, no one is more fortunate than you,
No one need be happier than you.
For on a lotus and moon above your head
Sits the all-kind root guru
Inseparable in nature from Buddha Amitabha.

Pray to him now to clear and open for you
The pathway of the consciousness transference.
Meditate with all your strength
As you offer this prayer to him.

Lord Amitabha, Buddha of Boundless Light,
Embodiment of the perfect objects of refuge,
Hero who saves living beings from lower rebirth,
Navigator who leads beings to the Pure Land of Joy,
To you I turn in prayer.

Protect the living beings from evil,
Free them from the dangerous passes
Hold them back from the lower realms.
Guide them to Sukhavati, the supreme abode.

These last two verses are each repeated three times. The master of the ritual visualizes that light rays in the form of hooks emanate from Amitabha's heart and enter the crown aperture of the deceased, coming to his/her navel. In the process the lights strike against the drop at the deceased's heart, which in nature is his/her mind. All the energies of the body respond as do iron filings to a magnet, and a fierce wind of energies arises from the navel below the drop.

The master calls out the syllable *HIK*, and the drop at the deceased's heart jumps to the throat. A second time *HIK* is called, and the drop of consciousness jumps from the throat to the forehead. A third time the master calls *HIK*, and the drop comes to the crown.

The master then shouts *PHAT*, and the drop of consciousness shoots out the crown aperture, coming to the heart of Amitabha Buddha, to become of one nature with him.

Amitabha, the Buddha of Boundless light, instantly returns to Sukhavati, taking the consciousness of the deceased with him, where it takes rebirth in a celestial form inside a lotus flower. From his heart Amitabha emanates lights, which strike the lotus, causing its petals to open. The deceased thus beholds the glorious face of Amitabha Buddha for the first time and has the excellent fortune to listen to his nectarlike voice. There he/she shall dwell in meditation until the state of perfect enlightenment has been attained.

The master should rest in meditation upon this thought for a few moments and then conclude by offering prayers and auspicious verses.

This then is the process of pointing out the nature of the bardo to the deceased and of guiding the consciousness to a pure rebirth.

The master of the ritual then invokes the image of Vajrasattva, the Diamond Hero embodying the purification yogas, and in his presence offers this prayer:

May this person called Such-and-such, who has passed beyond life and gone to the other side of the world, be free of attachment to the beautiful forms of the world that are seen by the eye. May he/she have the good fortune to enjoy the objects of sight, but to do so in such a way as to attain clear, highest enlightenment.

May he/she have no attachment to the melodious sounds heard by the ear, but have the good fortune to enjoy the objects of hearing in such a way as to attain clear, perfect enlightenment.

May he/she have no attachment to the sweet fragrances perceived by the nose, but have the good fortune to enjoy objects of smell in such a way as to attain clear, highest enlightenment.

May he/she have no attachment to the many tastes of the world, but have the good fortune to enjoy the various foods in such a way as to attain clear, highest enlightenment.

May he/she have no attachment to sensual contact produced by touch, but have the good fortune to enjoy the objects of the body in such a way as to quickly attain clear, highest enlightenment.

In brief, may he/she have no attachment to any of the objects of sensory experience, but have the good fortune to enjoy the objects of the five senses in such a way as to quickly attain clear, highest enlightenment.

O child who has passed from life,
You must leave behind all relatives and friends.
Have no attachment for them, but make ready
To meet now with endless goodness.

Have no attachment to the five sensory spheres,
But may you have the good fortune
To enjoy the objects of the senses
As a means to attain highest enlightenment.

May you be purified in body, speech and mind
By the most precious jewel light
Arising from the supreme field of gems,
The Buddha, the Dharma and the Sangha.

May you quickly traverse the five paths
Leading to highest enlightenment:
The paths of accumulation of goodness,
Preparation, vision, meditation and
The peerless path beyond training.

May you gain this fifth path
Which is beyond all obscuration,
The path of final liberation.
May you purify every negative tendency
And reach the stage of every perfection.

At this point in the ritual the master of the rite should generate conviction that the deceased has definitely taken rebirth in Sukhavati, the Pure Land of Joy.

Earlier in the ritual the corpse was made into a repository of all negative karmas, evil tendencies and spiritual obscurations possessed by the deceased, and in this way the mind of the deceased was separated from all shortcomings and negative traits. Thus it is the corpse as a repository of the deceased's negativities that is the substance to be consumed by the fires of wisdom. With this as the meditation the master calls out:

Child of noble family, grant me your attention.
You who have died and passed away, hear me now.
The blazing fire of the five Buddha wisdoms
Is consuming as fuel your five contaminated aggregates.

Child of noble family, grant me your attention.
You who have died and passed away, hear me now.
The blazing fire of the four mindfulnesses
Is consuming as fuel your four contaminated elements.

Child of noble family, grant me your attention.
You who have died and passed away, hear me now.
The blazing fire of the altruistic bodhimind
Is consuming as fuel your six contaminated sensory powers.

Child of noble family, grant me your attention.
You who have died and passed away, hear me now.
The blazing fire of the six wisdom dakinis
Is consuming as fuel the six contaminated objects of perception.

Child of noble family, grant me your attention.
You who have died and passed away, hear me now.
The blazing fire of the three Buddha *kayas*
Is consuming as fuel your body, speech and mind.

In order to benefit all living beings,
May the deceased attain this instant
The three perfect Buddha *kayas*
And the five transcendental wisdoms.

Homage to Vairochana, the Buddha of Radiant Form,
He who shows the *mudra* of supreme enlightenment,
Whose vajra body is the *dharmadhatu* wisdom,
The space of ignorance transformed into the wisdom of
    radiant emptiness.

Homage to Vajra Akshobya, the Unmoving Buddha,
He who shows the *mudra* of subduing evil,
Whose vajra body is the mirrorlike wisdom,
The earth of attachment transformed into vajra stability.

Homage to Ratnasambhava, the Self-born Jewel,
He who shows the *mudra* of supreme generosity,
Whose vajra body is the wisdom of equality,
The fires of anger transformed into blazing vajra gems.

Homage to Amitabha, Buddha of Boundless Light,
He who holds the *mudra* of perfect meditation,
Whose vajra body is the all-distinguishing wisdom,
The water of lust transformed into diamond knowledge.

Homage to Amoghasiddhi, Buddha of Activity,
He who holds the *mudra* of giving refuge,
Whose vajra body is the all-accomplishing wisdom,
The winds of jealousy transformed into vajra action.

Thus is complete the ritual for caring for the dead. The master should conclude by reciting the 100-syllable mantra, and offering prayers for the long life of the gurus. He/she should also adorn the end with a few verses of dedication of merit and prayers for auspicious conditions to fill the world with happiness, peace and joy.

May any benefits in my having written this text cause numberless beings to find their way to happiness and liberation. I, the lama called Mahasukha, wrote it at the request of several disciples who wished for a ritual text on caring for the dead that could be easily performed and, in addition, would be in accord with the tradition of the mighty *Vajrabhairava-tantra*, the Diamond Destroyer of Death. I penned the present work by drawing from the teachings of my numerous gurus and spiritual guides. May it be a wish-fulfilling gem to those who would assist living beings who have come to the end of their lives, and by means of it may countless beings find their way to an auspicious rebirth.

Chapter Nine

Meditations on the Ways of Impermanence

I have a rendezvous with death
At some disputed barricade,
When Spring comes back with rustling shade
And apple-blossoms fill the air.

—Alan Seegar: *I Have a Rendezvous with Death*

TRANSLATOR'S PREAMBLE

The last item in this collection is a short inspirational poem written by the Seventh Dalai Lama. The Seventh is my own favorite of all the early Dalai Lamas; his life exemplifies the simplicity and beauty of the perfect sage,[1] and his writings are among the best to appear in the Land of Snows from the time it acquired the art of literature until the present day.

All the early Dalai Lamas were great in their own ways, and most were prolific with the pen,[2] but the Seventh was so in the face of tremendous internal difficulties in Tibet. His was a life and times fraught with intrigue, conflict, war and violent change, with Mongolia playing havoc from the north,[3] China spinning cunning plots from the east, and the various factions of his own people caught in between. Somehow he lived through it all without succumbing to any of the corruptions of the period, and when he died in 1757 Tibet mourned the passing of one of the most beloved saints to have appeared in its long and mystical history.

Thoughts of death remained close to the Seventh Dalai Lama throughout his life, and reflections on it appear repeatedly in his writings. This no doubt is partially because he practiced and widely taught the Atisha[4] lineages, in which meditation upon death and dying play an important role. But one gets the feeling from his writings that somehow it is more than this, that he is expressing the constant danger he senses surrounding his life.

The poem I have selected from amongst the many that he wrote is called simply 'Meditations on the Ways of Impermanence.' It is perhaps the best known of his poems to Tibetans, being loved for the typically Tibetan images it calls forth. One can almost taste the butter tea and barley porridge in it, and smell the yaks. It speaks of death and impermanence, but draws its inspirations from golden mountains, rings of mist, turquoise crops, and a sun that rises 'like an umbrella' into the sky.

We can sense his awareness of the Tibetan devotion toward his own personage and his perplexity at the naivete of their faith when he writes:

> They die old, they die young, day upon day.
> I am asked to throw their souls to a Pure Land
> Or to prophesy their conditions of rebirth.

We can almost see him looking out the window of the Potala in the verse:

> In the belly of the vast plateau below me
> The campfires of visiting traders glow like stars.
> But tomorrow they depart, leaving only refuse.

The Fifth Dalai Lama wrote more cleverly than this, but not more movingly nor with as simple a grace. The Sixth Dalai Lama composed more cryptically in verse, but not with such vivid sensuality. And then there is the constantly repeated refrain, 'My mind turns to thoughts of my death,' like the steady drone of a Tibetan monastic chant.

The omnipresence of death is at once the simplest fact of life and also the most immediately powerful. It has the ability simultaneously to terrify and to console. In one light it gives our life ultimate meaning and urgency, and in another seems to rob us of all purpose and significance. The Seventh Dalai Lama deeply feels these two implications, and creates an exquisite tension in his verses through his balance of the two.

MEDITATIONS ON THE WAYS OF IMPERMANENCE

by Gyalwa Kalzang Gyatso, the Seventh Dalai Lama

To the Lama-lha,[1] my refuge and father,
The recollection of whom dispels all sadness,
I turn for spiritual guidance;
Bless my mind with your transforming powers,
That the thought of death may never evade me,
That I may practice the holy Dharma perfectly.

On the golden mountains far in the distance
Rings of mist hang like belts on the meadows.
Now seemingly solid, so soon they dissolve.
My mind turns to thoughts of my death.

In spring, the season of warmth and growth,
The stalks of the crops were turquoise green.
Now, autumn's end, the fields lie naked and parched.
My mind turns to thoughts of my death.

On each branch of the trees in my garden
Hang clusters of fruit, swelling and ripe.
In the end, not one piece will remain.
My mind turns to thoughts of my death.

From behind the peaks of Mount Potala
The sun rose like an umbrella into the sky.
Now it has gone, fallen behind the western ranges.
My mind turns to thoughts of my death.

They die old, they die young, day upon day.
I am asked to throw their souls to a Pure Land
Or to prophesy their conditions of rebirth.
My mind turns to thoughts of my death.

Gray clouds cover the sky, obscuring it;
The first drops of rain are about to fall,
To be scattered everywhere by the dark, red wind.
My mind turns to thoughts of my death.

In the belly of the vast plateau below me
The campfires of visiting traders glow like stars,

But tomorrow they depart, leaving only refuse.
My mind turns to thoughts of my death.

Warm summer days, the earth thronging with life;
The minds of the people are lost in gaiety.
Suddenly the cold winter wind crashes them down.
My mind turns to thoughts of my death.

High above, turquoise dragons roared in harmony;
Around me, cuckoo birds chattered sweetly.
But times have changed; where are they now?
My mind turns to thoughts of my death.

Dharma, the precious teachings of the Awakened Ones,
Is a medicine supreme, curing all the mind's ills.
These days many saints of old look down from Pure Lands.
My mind turns to thoughts of my death.

Hard it is to leave the mother who carried us,
And hard to part from relatives and friends.
Yet, as the years pass, our links with them corrode.
My mind turns to thoughts of my death.

A young man, with teeth for the future,
With plans for months and years ahead, died,
Leaving but scant traces. Where is he now? Gone!
My mind turns to thoughts of my death.

Buddha attained the glorious immortal vajra body,[2]
Yet he still enacted a death scene.
This body of flesh, blood and bone, covered in skin,
Like a bubble of water is bound to perish.

From its very birth a child sees his parents slowly age,
Sees them each day come closer to the grave.
How can you say to me, 'But I am still young'?
I warn you, there is no hope of hiding from death.

Spirits were high with expectations this morning
As the men discussed subduing enemies and protecting the land.
Now, with night's coming, birds and dogs chew their corpses.
Who believed that they themselves would die today?[3]

Look and ask among the people of your land
For anyone even a hundred years old.

You will be lucky to find even one.
Do you not think your own death certain?

If you look closely at and contemplate deeply
The people and things that appear around you,
You can see that everything is in constant flux.
All becomes the teacher of impermanence.

I remember this body when it was a child's,
As it gradually took the form of a youth.
Now its every limb is twisted and worn.
It is my own body, yet it delights not even my own eyes.

The mind itself is impermanent, constantly oscillating
Between feelings of pleasure, pain and indifference,
The respective fruits of positive,
Negative and neutral karmas.[4]

Look where you will at yourself or others,
Life passes like a flash of lightning.
When death's agents surround you, intent on murder,
What do you think will happen to you?

Relatives, friends, wealth and property
Shine with splendor in the eyes of worldly people;
Thus they bind themselves in shackles of attachment.
This pathos, how will it end?

Body lying flat on a last bed,
Voices whispering a few last words,
Mind watching a final memory glide past:
When will that drama come for you?

If you create nothing but negative karma,
You will stand naked of instincts to benefit the hereafter.
Where will you go after death?
The mere thought of it makes you tremble.

Therefore I myself and beings like me
Should leave behind meaningless ways
And entrust ourselves to the gurus, mandala deities and dakinis,
Requesting them to prepare us for death's road.

In order to die well, with the joy and confidence
Of being within the white rays of spiritual awareness,

It is essential to begin readying yourself now.
Familiarize yourself with the profound methods
Of the sutra and tantra lineages of transmission.

By this song may those like me,
Irreligious people little better than savages,
Be caught in the flames of spiritual inspiration.
May we evolve in spirit
And attain knowledge and liberation.

The colophon: Verses for meditation on the ways of death and impermanence, to inspire the minds of myself and others.

Epilogue

Let the mind be enlarged, according to its capacity, to
the grandeur of the mysteries, and not the mysteries
contracted to the narrowness of the mind.

—Sir Francis Bacon: *Advancement of Knowledge*

As we have seen, the Tibetan tradition on death and dying is a construct of numerous elements, a house built of various materials. Some of this is straightforwardly rational, such as the meditative systems illustrated by the first two chapters of this collection. Other aspects are mystical in the yogic sense, as exemplified by chapters six and seven. There is also a wealth of occult materials, such as the text of chapter five, and a veritable ocean of ritual manuals associated with the afterlife, like that of chapter eight. Then there are poems, prayers, songs of realization, clairvoyant accounts, and a seemingly endless variety of subsidiary branches of literature dealing with other facets of the tradition. Each of these topics could easily receive a study in itself, and indeed each could fill several volumes without the source materials becoming exhausted.

In fact, all previous studies of the Tibetan tradition on death and dying have concentrated on one or another of these subjects. Such an approach has the advantage of being able to go into far more detail on specific points, but it also has the disadvantage of presenting a partial view of the overall system and runs the risk of creating the according distorted perception in the reader's mind. *The Tibetan Book of the Dead* was graced with this advantage but also created something of a distorted image of the overall Tibetan tradition. The work is marvelous both in the original and in translation, but it created a generation of western Tibetology hobbyists with a concept of the Tibetan lamas as magical ritualists whose main preoccupation is sitting around reading occult texts into the deaf ears of corpses. I suppose Dr. Timothy Leary's *Psychedelic Experiences Based on the Tibetan Book of the Dead* did not contribute to a correct understanding (although no doubt it did help sell a few more copies). How many times in the East did I see the lamas roll their eyes in amusement at Westerners whose total conception of Tibetan Buddhism was based on either of the above works!

This volume is an attempt to look at the Tibetan system on death and dying as a living, organic entity. It is not in any way intended as a replacement or alternative to *The Tibetan Book of the Dead*, but rather as a supplement to it and the other works on the subject that have previously appeared. It aims at giving a survey of the system as a holistic approach to life and death, and thus aspires to contribute to the territory carved out by earlier works in this area. My motive in writing it was to render the earlier studies more useful to serious students by bringing to them a perspective of the total tradition. In doing so I have brought forth a number of translations to illustrate my themes. These are intended to represent genres of literature, and each piece is chosen for being exemplary of its class.

The Tibetans have a saying, 'The teaching of Buddha is like a cushion; no matter from which corner you grab on to it, you get a handle on the whole thing.' Perhaps nowhere is this so true as with the teaching on death and impermanence, which pervades the Buddhist doctrine at every level. As Geshe Dargye points out in chapter two, it was included in Buddha's first teaching at Deer Park near Varanasi, when he spoke of the four truths seen by the Aryas, and it was his final teaching, when he passed away in front of his disciples and with his last breath pronounced, 'All things are impermanent. Work out your own salvation with diligence.'

Buddha taught for forty-five years, and his doctrines, scattered between the Hinayana, Mahayana and Vajrayana vehicles, were indeed rich and vast. The Tibetans dedicated themselves to the absorption of these doctrines from India with a devotion, intensity, sincerity and zeal that is nothing short of remarkable. Unlike other Buddhist countries, which acquired their Buddhism from one part or another of India during one specific time or another, the Tibetans systematically imported their Buddhism from wherever in India it could be found over a period of almost 1,000 years. In this sense Tibetan Buddhism is somewhat special, representing the complete Indian Buddhist tradition in all its aspects of Hinayana, Mahayana and Vajrayana.

In terms of the Buddhist legacy on death and dying, the Tibetan tradition is therefore uniquely rich in lineages from these three *yanas*. In Tibet the lamas were not content to leave these concepts as dry words in translated books; consequently Tibetan literature abounds with indigenous writings on the various lineages. These commentarial writings quote abundantly from the Indian Buddhist scriptures in order to show the source of each individual teaching. This serves to illustrate their intention to preserve and develop the pure Buddhist faith not in the sense of parroting the past masters but rather, out of respect for the ageless wisdom expressed by the accomplished teachers of the lineage, to use the knowledge of the past as a springboard into the present and future.

In my collection I have not used Tibetan books that were translated from Sanskrit, but instead chose indigenous materials; these represent the Tibetan tradition as a living system much better than would the translations from India. I have, however, selected Tibetan materials that quote extensively from the early Indian sources in order to demonstrate that the Tibetan tradition is without a doubt based firmly on the groundwork laid by Buddha and the Indian masters. Lamaism,[1] as Tibetan culture is so often termed, is merely Indian Buddhism as preserved and developed by the scholars and yogis of the Land of Snows. The 'degenerated Tibetan Buddhism' that is 'corrupted by shamanic remnants from old Tibet' that we read about in so many Western books is actually a degenerate, corrupt figment of Western imagination born from a lack of true study of the tradition. Tibet went to great pains to acquire pure lineages of Buddhism from India and to preserve these without letting them degenerate with the ravages of time. Any objective observer who examines the historical accounts of the lines of transmission and the content of the numerous Tibetan commentaries will easily see that this is fact and not a mere whitewashing of history. The large number of Buddhist Sanskrit texts that have been discovered in Nepal and elsewhere reinforce this view.[2]

The mystery of death is an enigma that perhaps can never be solved in a scientific, conclusive sense. It may always remain within the sphere of personal spiritual knowledge, part of the mystical perception that has separated saints from ordinary people since the beginning of time.

It is a reality we can see every day around us, but never really apply to ourselves on anything but the most superficial, intellectual dimension. To all but a few, even though knowing of death from childhood, in the end death comes as a shock, a terrible threat and a tragedy.

Our Western society has gone to tremendous lengths to forget death and to hide it from the public eye. As Dr. Kubler-Ross[3] has put it:

> The more we are making advancements in science, the more we seem to fear and deny the reality of death. We use euphemisms, we make the dead look as if they were asleep, we ship the children off to protect them from the anxiety and turmoil around the house, we don't allow the children to visit their dying parents in the hospitals, we have long and controversial discussions about whether or not dying patients should be told the truth. Maybe the question has to be raised: Are we becoming less human or more human?

Buddhism takes precisely the opposite approach to death. Our impermanent nature is to be kept at the forefront of our awareness at all times if we are to live happy, healthy, wholesome lives. To repeat a quotation given by Geshe Dargye in chapter two:

> If on waking up in the morning one does not meditate on death, the entire morning will be wasted. If we don't meditate on it at noon, the afternoon will be wasted. Similarly, if we don't meditate on death in the evening, the night will be lost to meaningless pursuits.

This in a nutshell is the Buddhist feeling on the subject.

Western society has come a long way over the last few millenniums, but somehow, although we have achieved material progress, there does not seem to be any significant increase in the inner peace and happiness of individual people. The average person on the streets of New York or London, on close examination, seems to come up with as many if not more signs of anxiety and inner suffering than does the person from a primitive yet spiritually advanced village in Asia or Africa. Nor does mankind as a collective unit seem to be any closer to the ideal of world peace. Something in the wheel of progress seems to have been overlooked.

The Buddhist answer is awareness of impermanence and death. Through this awareness we lose attachments to meaningless endeavors and gain a deeper sense of our humanity. Understanding our own humanity we are able to see the humanity in others. Thus this awareness firstly cuts our attachments to self-destructive aims, and secondly increases our tolerance toward and understanding of others.

By mitigating our attachment and intolerance, we weaken the chain of negative patterns that causes us to harm ourselves and others out of ignorance of our mutual humanity. Then, through understanding death we transcend its negative effects, gaining the deathless state.

This is the reason that Buddha Shakyamuni made the subject of death and dying both his first and then his last teaching.

Notes

Introduction

1. The importance of death in the Egyptian religious attitude is exemplified in *The Egyptian Book of the Dead*, first published in translation in 1895 by order of the Trustees of the British Museum, translated and edited by E.A. Wallis Budge (rpt. New York: Dover Press, 1967).

2. See Jacques Choron, *Death and Western Thought* (New York: Collier Books, 1963).

3. See Norman L. Farberow, ed., *Taboo Topics* (New York: Atherton Press, 1963).

4. See Elizabeth Kübler-Ross, *On Death and Dying* (New York: Macmillan, 1969).

5. Dr. Geoffrey Gorer, *Death, Grief and Mourning* (New York: Doubleday, 1965).

6. Dr. Arnold Toynbee, et al., *Man's Concern with Death* (New York: McGraw-Hill, 1969).

7. Dr. Richard Kalish, 'Some Varieties in Death Attitudes,' in *Death and Identity*, ed. Robert Fulton (New York: Wiley, 1965).

8. This saying is from Shantideva's *Bodhisattvacaryāvatāra*, an English translation by Stephen Batchelor being available under the title *A Guide to the Bodhisattva's Way of Life* (Dharamsala: LTWA, 1979). A less accurate though more poetic translation had been made earlier by Marion L. Matics under the title *Entering the Path of Enlightenment* (London: Allen & Unwin, 1971).

9. Kübler-Ross, *On Death and Dying* (New York: Macmillan, 1969).

10. This verse is quoted by Geshe Ngawang Dargye later in chapter two. It is originally drawn from *The Sutra of Buddha's Entering into Parinirvana* (Skt., *Mahā-parinirvāṇa-sūtra*; Tib., *mDo-sde-mya-ngan-las-'das-pa*). This scripture is the source of numerous popular quotations of Buddha's sayings.

11. Gendun Chopel, *The White Annals* (Tib., *Deb-ther-dkar-po*), trans. Samten Norboo (Dharamsala: LTWA, 1978).

12. This new script was modelled after a Kashmiri variation of Sanskrit. Hence it is a phonetic script like that of India and Europe, and not pictorial like that of China and Japan. Being based on Sanskrit, it was tailor-made for translating Buddhist texts into Tibetan accurately.

13. This period of Tibetan history is wonderfully told by Lady Yeshe Tsogyal, *The Life and Liberation of Padma Sambhava* (Tib., *Gu-ru-rnam-thar*), trans. Kenneth Douglas and Gwendolyn Bays (Emeryville: Dharma Publishing, 1978).

14. The danger of their extinction came not from physical intimidation but from conversion. Buddhism is a non-violent religion and does not believe in forceful action. But the temptation for the Bön to convert must have been strong, for Buddhism certainly possessed a sophistication lacking in their own faith.

15. Tib., *bKa-'gyur,* or 'Translated Word [of Buddha].'

16. Tib., *bsTan-'gyur,* or 'Translated Treatises.'

17. For a full discussion of the distinction between these three vehicles, see H.H. the Dalai Lama, Tsong-ka-pa and Jeffrey Hopkins, *Tantra in Tibet* (Ithaca: Snow Lion Publications, 1987).

18. See 'The History of the Advancement of the Buddhadharma in Tibet' in the 14th Dalai Lama's *The Opening of the Wisdom Eye* (Wheaton: Quest Books, 1966).

19. D.L. Snellgrove and H. Richardson, *A Cultural History of Tibet* (London: Weidenfeld & Nicolson, 1968).

20. See Prof. Robert Thurman, ed., *The Life and Teachings of Tsong Khapa* (Dharamsala: LTWA, 1982). Also my own *Four Songs to Je Rinpocbe* (Dharamsala: LTWA, 1978).

21. This legend is related by Geshe Rabten in *The Life and Teachings of Geshe Rabten,* trans. Alan Wallace (London: Allen & Unwin, 1980).

22. Thurman, *The Life and Teachings of Tsong Khapa.*

23. Sir Charles Bell, *The Religion of Tibet* (Oxford: Collins Books, 1931).

24. Ibid.

25. Ibid. After being placed in power, the Fifth Dalai Lama established laws certifying religious freedom. These were later further clarified by the Seventh and then the Thirteenth Dalai Lamas. See the Tsepon W.D. Shakabpa, *Tibet: A Political History* (New Haven: Yale University Press, 1967).

26. When the present Dalai Lama arrived in New York in 1979 on his first U.S. tour he gave a press conference. One reporter asked what he missed most about life in Tibet. His Holiness replied, 'The yak.' This simple answer struck a warm chord in the hearts of the press people. The following day the newspapers carried very positive articles on the Dalai Lama, quoting the yak reference to illustrate how he had lived up to their romantic expectations of the stuff of which Tibet was made. In the West, the dog is our best friend; to the Tibetan, this function was served by the yak.

27. The rigors of this study period are described by Khyongla Rato Rinpoche in his book *My Life and Lives* (New York: Dutton Press, 1977).

28. *The Tibetan Book of the Dead* (Oxford: Oxford University Press, 1927), Introduction.

29. *Foundations of Tibetan Mysticism* (London: Rider & Co., 1960).

30. Lama Chimpa and A. Chattopadhyaya, *Atiśa in Tibet* (Calcutta: Indian Studies Institute, 1967).

31. My analysis here is based on Tsongkhapa's *Lam-rim-chen-mo*, and also upon the Third Dalai Lama's *Essence of Refined Gold*, this latter work being my own translation (Ithaca: Snow Lion Publications, 1982).

32. *Udāna-varga*, 'The Chapter on Discipline.'

33. Plato, *Phaedo*.

34. Dr. Evans-Wentz discusses this in his introduction to *The Tibetan Book of the Dead*.

35. This is clearly stated by Tsongkhapa in the section on dream yoga in his *Six Yogas of Naropa*. See my translation *Tsongkhapa's Six Yogas of Naropa* (Ithaca: Snow Lion Publications, 1996).

36. *Udāna-varga*, op. cit.

37. Tib., *Bar-do-thos-grol-chen-mo*.

38. E.A. Wallis Budge, op. cit.

39. Tib., *Bar-do-ngo-sprod*.

40. This is a specifically Nyingma arrangement of the tantric deities. It should be remembered that these are just meditational symbols and do not literally appear in the bardo visions. The point is only that the aspects of consciousness that these deities symbolize unfold in stages corresponding to the meditation upon the deities as laid out in the mandala. A person who had meditated upon the mandala of the 110 Peaceful and Wrathful Deities during his/her lifetime would therefore meditate upon their appearance at the time of death. To anyone who had not meditated upon them, however, they would be irrelevant.

41. I included a Tara longevity meditation by the Seventh Dalai Lama in my collection *Meditations on the Lower Tantras* (from the works of the Early Dalai Lamas) (Dharamsala: LTWA, 1983).

42. A brief account of some of the more popular *day-lok* (Tib., *'das-lok*) material is given by Lawrence Epstein in 'On the History and Psychology of the Das-log,' *The Tibet Journal* vol. VII, no.4 (Dharamsala: LTWA, 1982).

43. I must admit that I was tempted to include something on mummification in this volume. In Tibet the bodies of numerous high teachers were mummified, including those of most Dalai and Panchen Lamas. Accounts of the mummification procedures of most of these still exist in the reserves of historical materials, and I saw an account of the mummification of the Fifth Dalai Lama, which quite caught my fancy. There also exist 'how to' manuals on mummification, and these

are of considerable interest. But in the end I decided against including anything of this nature here due to the number of technical problems involved in such a translation, and for fear that eccentrics would be moved to mummify anything they could get their hands on.

In Tibet, only holy personages were mummified. These mummys were later encased in either gold or silver shrines to protect them from the elements. It is said that when the Chinese communists broke open the shrine encasing the mummy of Tsongkhapa, his body was still warm and fresh, with no signs of disintegration, and the hair and nails had continued to grow. The Chinese then threw it in the river, but it hovered above the water. They then set fire to it after dousing it in gasoline. Some Tibetans, however, managed to take some relics from this holy body from the fire and carry them to India, where they are presently enshrined in the temple of the Dalai Lama's monastery at Dharamsala.

44. This question arose during an interview I did for the AP News Service, New York. The interview was released by them in March of 1976, although this material was not included in my write-up of the meeting.

45. Kyabje Ling Rinpoche, the Senior Tutor; Kyabje Trijang Rinpoche, the Junior Tutor; Kyabje Serkong Rinpoche, the Spiritual Advisor; and the bodhisattva Tenzin Gyaltsen, the Personal Advisor. All four of these masters died in the 1980s. A very sad aspect of life with the Tibetan refugees was witnessing the steady demise of the old lamas. These senior-most teachers embodied the spiritual culture of Tibet and were learned to an astounding degree. The new generation who have grown up as refugees in India have studied hard and learned well, but it is difficult to say if they have managed to achieve the levels of greatness of the last generation. The demands of the harsh refugee life, the terrible Indian climate and the high level of disease and stress have placed them at a definite handicap.

In particular, the Dalai Lama's Senior and Junior Tutors were exceptionally remarkable men. People would come from all over Central Asia to ask advice on everything from personal matters to the most obtruse philosophical point, and for hours each day they would satisfy all who would come to them. When the Senior Tutor was in his eightieth year he gave a sermon in South India to all the most learned scholars of Central Asia. The sermon lasted for six or seven hours a day for over a month, and he never showed the slightest signs of fatigue. Similarly, a year before the Junior Tutor passed away he gave extensive sermons without showing any signs of his advanced years. Both of these masters seemed able to remember anything they had ever seen, heard or read, and there didn't seem to be much outside of their realm of knowledge. The new generation will certainly have their work cut out for them to equal either of these two.

Chapter One

Translator's Preamble

1. This group of sermons is the first item in vol. 2 of the Thirteenth Dalai Lama's *Collected Works* (Tib., *gSung-'bum*). The full title of the collection is 'Sermons and Talks together with Jataka Readings, from [the Thirteenth Dalai Lama's] Visits to

Kum-bum Monastery, from Other Monastic Visits, and at the Great Prayer Festival of Lhasa.' The reference to the Jataka readings is because the full moon oor mon at the Great Prayer Festival would always include a partial transmission of Arya Asurya's *Jātaka-mala*, a set of thirty-four stories from the previous lives of Buddha.

2. In fact, the festival would last for a complete month, but only the first two weeks of it were a national holiday.

3. Tib., *Rin-po-che'i-thar-rgyan*. An excellent translation of this work is by Professor H.V. Guenther (London: Rider, 1959; rpt. Boulder: Shambhala).

4. Tib., *Zhen-pa-bzhi-'bral*. No major translation of the several dozen manuals in this genre have been published.

5. Tib., *rDzogs-chen-kun-bzang-bla-ma'i-zhal-lung*.

6. Tib., *Byang-chub-lam-rim-chen-mo*.

7. An excellent account of this is given by Peter Fleming in *Bayonets to Lhasa* (New York: Harper & Brothers, 1961).

8. Sir Charles Bell, *Portrait of a Dalai Lama* (Oxford: Collins Books, 1946).

Death and the Bodhisattva Trainings

1. This verse is taken from Atisha's *A Summary of the Means for Accomplishing the Mahayana Path* (Skt., *Mahāyāna-patha-sādhana-varna-saṃgraha*; Tib., *Theg-chen-lam-gyi-sgrub-thubs-yi-ger-bsdus-pa*), a short work on Mahayana practice. A translation of this text appears in *Atisha and Buddhism in Tibet*, which I co-authored with Ven. Doboom Tulku (New Delhi: Tibet House, 1983).

2. These eight freedoms and ten endowments are the eighteen conditions whereby Dharma practice and therefore enlightenment become possible.

3. Tib., gSer-gling-pa, 'The Man from the Golden Islands.' Serlingpa possibly came from Borobudur. At least, this is the implication of several Tibetan scriptures on the subject which I have encountered. However, further research remains to be done on the subject. At the moment, most scholars place him in Sumatra rather than Java, but this is more due to habit than evidence. His ordination name was Dharmakirti, though he is not to be confused with the earlier Indian logician of the same name.

4. *Seven Points for Training the Mind* (Tib., *bLo-sbyong-don-bdun-ma*), written out by Geshe Chekhawa, is one of the most essential practice manuals in Tibetan Buddhism. I included a translation of the First Dalai Lama's commentary to it in my *Selected Works of the Dalai Lama I: Bridging the Sutras and Tantras* (Ithaca: Snow Lion Publications, 1982).

5. These are the two types of accomplished Hinayanists.

6. See note 4 above.

7. Skt., *Ratna-gūna-saṃgraha*, Tib., *dKon-mchog-yon-tan-bsdus-pa*.

8. Both this and the following verses are taken from Nagarjuna's *Friendly Letter* (Skt., *Suhṛlleka*; Tib., *bShes-pa'i-spring-yig*).

9. Skt., *Udāna-varga*; Tib., *Ched-du-brjod-pa'i-tshoms*. The name literally means 'Selected Sayings (of the Buddha).' I have used the name *Tibetan Dhammapada* because an English translation by Ven. Gareth Sparham has been published with this title (New Delhi: Mahayana Publications, 1982; rpt. London: Wisdom Publications, 1986). The text is the Mahayana equivalent of the *Dhammapada*, although it is much longer.

10. Skt., *Rājā-vavā-daka-sūtra*; Tib., *rGyal-po-la-gdams-pa*.

11. This verse is taken from the poem 'Melancholy Visions of Imperfection,' one of the forty-one poems in my Seventh Dalai Lama collection, *Songs of Spiritual Change* (Ithaca: Snow Lion Publications, 1982).

12. Skt., *Garbha-vakrānti-sūtra*; Tib., *mNgal-'jug-gi-mdo*.

13. Skt., *Śisya-lekha*; Tib., *Ka-ni-ka'i-slob-yig*.

14. Skt., *Abhidharma-kośa*; Tib., *Chos-mngon-par-mdzod*.

15. See note 9 above.

16. Skt., *Ratnāvalī*, Tib., *Rin-po-che'i-phreng-ba*.

17. See note 8 above.

18. See note 13 above.

19. See note 13 above.

20. See note 4 above.

21. Tib., *Blo-sbyong-tshig-brgyad-ma*, another important pith work often used even today as the basis of discourse. The present Dalai Lama has given several discourses on it in the West. One of these is included in his *Four Essential Buddhist Commentaries*, trans. Tsepak Rigzin and Jeremy Russell (Dharamsala: LTWA, 1982).

22. Skt., *Śrāvaka-bhūmi*; Tib., *Nyan-thos-kyi-sa*.

23. A well-known teacher of the First Dalai Lama.

24. This is the author of *An Encyclopedia of Buddhist Metaphysics*. See note 14 above.

25. A twelfth-century Kadampa teacher.

26. See note 24 above.

27. This is from the Great Fifth's verse work on how to combine worldly and religious life. Entitled *Srid-zhi-zung-'brel-gyi-slab-bya*, it came to be used as a guide by monks working in the government services, and later also was used by lay officials.

28. Skt., *Ārya-dāka-jñāna-sūtra*; Tib., *'Phags-pa-da-ka-ye-shes-kyi-mdo*.

29. This verse is from Tsongkhapa's *Song of the Stages in Spiritual Practice*. A translation with commentary of this work is included in my Third Dalai Lama collection, *Essence of Refined Gold* (Ithaca: Snow Lion Publications, 1983).

Chapter Two

Translator's Preamble

1. Tib., *rNam-grol-lag-bcangs*.

2. As Dr. Evans-Wentz points out in the introduction to *The Tibetan Book of the Dead* (Oxford: Oxford University Press, 1927), the Tibetans practiced four methods of disposal of corpses in accordance with the four elements of the body—earth, fire, water and air. The most appropriate manner for the specific individual would usually be determined by astrological observation. Earth refers to burial, fire to cremation, water to immersion in a river or at sea, and air to being fed to the birds. In pre-Buddhist Tibet, only burial was practiced. The latter three methods were inherited from India. In the case of a high lama, a special encased funeral pyre shaped like a stupa would be constructed. I witnessed this in the cremation of the Dalai Lama's late Junior Tutor. When the Dalai Lama's Senior Tutor passed away a year later, however, he was mummified—the first to receive this tribute in India.

Tibetan Traditions of Death Meditation

1. This saying is from the *bKa'-gdams-gsung-'bum-thor-bu*.

2. Also from *bKa'-gdams-gsung-'bum-thor-bu*.

3. Skt., *Bodhisattvacaryāvatāra*; Tib., *Byang-chub-sems-dpa'i-spyod-pa-la-'jug-pa*.

4. See Introduction, note 10.

5. This is the death meditation technique elucidated by the Thirteenth Dalai Lama in chapter one. Therefore I have largely edited out Geshe Dargye's commentary here.

6. Tib., *Rin-po-che'i-thar-rgyan*.

7. Tib., *Lam-rim-chen-mo*.

8. This method will be discussed in chapter eight.

9. Dr. Evans-Wentz gives a lengthy commentary to the meaning of the three *kayas* in his introduction to *The Tibetan Book of the Dead*. We will also hear more of them later in this volume, in chapters five and eight.

10. Skt., *Udāna-varga*; Tib., *Tshoms*.

11. Chapter seven is dedicated to this subject, so we will hear more detail then.

12. These five are taken from *Seven Points for Training the Mind*, referred to earlier in chapter one, being the fourth of the seven points. This theme is elaborated upon later in chapter eight.

13. This theme is elaborated upon later in chapter eight.

14. Skt., *Abhidharma-kośa*; Tib., *Chos-mngon-par-mdzod*.

15. Tib., *mCod*, or 'cutting ritual.' A translation of a text of this nature was included by Dr. Evans-Wentz in his *Tibetan Yoga and Secret Doctrines* (Oxford: Oxford University Press, 1935).

Chapter Three

Translator's Preamble

1. The full title of this text is actually *A Conversation between an Old Man and a Youth on the Nature of Death and Impermanence.* See the bibliography at the end of this volume.

2. Skt., *Ratnāvali*; Tib., *Rin-po-che'i-phreng-ba*.

3. Tib., *rNam-grol-lag-bcangs*.

4. Geshe Tubten Wanggyal, *A Guide to the Treasure Island* (Rikon: Tibetan Studies Institute, 1974).

5. This is my own translation. I had included this biographical poem in my First Dalai Lama collection, *Bridging the Sutras and Tantras* (Ithaca: Snow Lion Publications, 1982).

A Conversation with an Old Man

1. In Buddhism these are called the four great sufferings of unenlightened existence.

2. We will see how the initiation process works later in chapter six.

3. In Buddhist metaphysics it is believed that the human life span is decreasing by one year every century. This is speaking only of natural life span, and not of the lives of those who extend their life span by medical or other means.

4. The elixir of immortality is the subject of many ancient legends. Like the alchemists' magical potion, it is said to give eternal life. This elixir as a spiritual metaphor appears repeatedly in chapter seven of our present work.

5. This may perhaps he compared to Christ's teaching, 'Let the dead bury their dead.'

6. Buddhists traditionally associate death with the south. We will see this later in chapter five. For this reason Tibetans will never sleep with their heads pointed south and feet north, believing that the earth's energy flows will drain off one's life-sustaining power and thus shorten one's life.

7. This reference to Tsongkhapa, founder of the Yellow Hat order, indicates the author to belong to the Geluk order.

Chapter Four

Translator's Preamble

1. An entire sutra is dedicated to Buddha's passing, namely the *Mahā-parinirvāṇa-sūtra* (Tib., *mDo-sde-mya-ngan-las-'das-pa*).

2. An excellent translation of this work by H.E. Johnson appeared in 1936 under the title *Acts of the Buddha*. However, this book contained only the extant Sanskrit portion of Ashvagosha's text. The same translator later brought out the remaining portion, based on Tibetan sources, which he published in the Danish periodical *Acta Orientalia* XV, in 1937. A second translation based on Johnson's was published by Edward Conze in his *Buddhist Scriptures* (London: Penguin Books, 1959).

3. Buddha's last words, it will be noted from the two differing quotations in this book (one earlier in chapter two, and the other above), are recorded in two fashions. They do not match perfectly in the two accounts, although the basic sense of them is the same. The two sources are the *Lalita-vistara-sūtra* and the *Mahā-parinirvāṇa-sūtra*. In the former, Buddha is recorded as having said, 'All things are impermanent. Work out your own salvation with diligence.' The latter source gives a much fuller account, and was much more poetically recorded.

4. This and many other stories related to the life of Buddha are found in the *Mūla-sarvāstivāda-vinaya*.

5. Lama Chimpa and A. Chattopadhyaya, *Atiśa and Tibet* (Calcutta: Indian Studies, 1967).

6. W.Y. Evans-Wentz, *Tibet's Great Yogi Milarepa* (Oxford: Oxford University Press, 1928).

7. Tib., *gTer-ston*.

8. There are two main biographies of the First Dalai Lama: *The String of Gems* (Tib., *Nor-bu-'phreng-ba*); and *The Twelve Wondrous Deeds* (Tib., *mDzad-pa-ngo-mtshar-bcu-gnyis*). Both give much the same account of his passing away.

The Death of Gye-re Lama

1. Ten days after the full moon of September 1954.

2. As we shall see later, this is the ordination name of the Gye-re Lama. It is probably a corruption of the Sanskrit name Kumara Sing-ha, or Youthful Lion.

3. This is the hill upon which the town of Kangra is built. Located just a few miles below Dharamsala, Kangra is considered to be one of the twenty-four mystical Heruka sites in India.

4. These are all well-known geographical locations in the Lahoul Valley.

5. Sixteen important disciples of Buddha around whom a magical net of mythology has been spun. These sixteen as a group are a popular theme in Tibetan religious painting. They are supposed to have once visited the cave on Gye-re Mountain.

6. That is, the mid-eighth century. It was Padma Sambhava and his work in Tibet that allowed Shantarakshita to found Samye, Tibet's first monastery.

7. An important twelfth-century mystic who lived in the Lahoul Valley and established numerous monasteries there.

8. A holy mountain in Lahoul.

9. These are all names of sacred pilgrimage spots in Central and Southern Tibet.

10. A sexual form of tantric meditation.

11. A mythological king from Eastern Tibet, similar in character to our own King Arthur. Volumes of stories of his adventures exist in Tibetan.

12. A minor longevity deity in the enormous Tibetan pantheon.

13. Chapter six of our text is one such text in this category.

14. These are the names of people alive and dwelling in Lahoul at the time this text was written.

15. An important Highest Yoga Tantra popular in the Nyingma and Drukpa Kargyu lineages.

16. These refer to the mantras of Avalokiteshvara, Tara and Padma Sambhava, respectively, three of the most popular mantras amongst ordinary Tibetans and Central Asians.

17. Tibetans consider the Muslims to be the epitome of barbarism, due in part to the way the Muslims slaughtered the Buddhists in India during the days of the Mogul invasions.

In Ladakh and the nearby Buddhist valleys such as Lahoul there is the sense of a constant danger from the Muslims due to the way India was rearranged by the British when they left the country in 1947. Ladakh was left under Kashmiri authority and thus is controlled from Muslim Srinagar. The valleys like Lahoul are mainly connected to the world by means of Ladakh.

Chapter Five

Translator's Preamble

1. A glance at the biography of Nagarjuna (see *Taranatha's History of Buddhism in India*, translation by Lama Chimpa and A. Chattopadhyaya, [Simla: Indian Studies, 1970]) will reveal the dual nature of his life. The same holds true for many other of the greatest Indian Buddhist masters, such as Aryadeva, Asanga and Shantideva.

2. Tib., *'Chi-mtshan-rtags-pa-dang-tshe-sgrub-'pho-ba'i-rnam-bshad*

3. Tib., *'Chi-mtshan-rtags-pa.*

4. Skt., *Trivajra-ācala-tantra*.

5. Skt., *Samvara-tantra*.

6. Tib., *Zab-chos-zhi-khro-dgongs-pa-rang-grol.*

7. See note 2 above.

8. This is the same work quoted above.

9. The *I Ching*, German translation by Richard Wilhelm, English version by Cary F. Baynes (Princeton: Princeton University Press, 1950).

10. Dr. Jung goes into this more deeply in *The Structure and Dynamics of the Psyche*, vol. 8 of The Collected Works of C.G. Jung (New York: Pantheon Books, 1953).

Self-Liberation by Knowing the Signs of Death

1. This image is taken from Nagarjuna's *Friendly Letter* (Skt., *Suhṛllekha;* Tib., *bShes-pa'i-spring yig*). By quoting it the author is showing the early Indian lineage.

2. Skt., *gana-chakra;* Tib., *tshogs-kyi-'khor-lo.*

3. Skt., *balim;* Tib., *gtor-ma;* a form of tantric offering.

4. This is the standard Buddhist meditational posture. As Vairochana represents the pure aspect of form, he is used to symbolize this posture.

5. This was discussed earlier in chapter two.

6. Tib., *Ro-sbyin-sreg-du-'bar-ba'i-rgyud.* This work is not found in the standard Tibetan canon.

7. In Buddhism, all life is held as sacred, but the human life is especially so due to the opportunity it provides to achieve enlightenment. In particular, a tantric practitioner, having the ability to accomplish full Buddhahood in one lifetime, has a special responsibility toward the body, which in the Vajrayana is regarded as the temple of a divinity. Therefore one of the fourteen root tantric precepts is to avoid neglecting the body.

8. This is a reference to *The Tibetan Book of the Dead*, to which the text of this chapter is prefatory.

Chapter Six

Translator's Preamble

1. This verse is from the Seventh Dalai Lama's *Songs of Spiritual Change* (my translation) (Ithaca: Snow Lion Publications, 1982).

2. This was pointed out in the preamble to the previous chapter.

3. J. Kelsang, *The Ambrosia Heart Tantra* (Dharamsala: LTWA, 1977).

4. This and the following quotes are from the work by the First Dalai Lama mentioned above.

5. A small work on the Amitayus longevity system appears in the Seventh Dalai Lama's *Lha'i-rnal-'byor* essays.

6. G.C. Chang, *The Hundred Thousand Songs of Milarepa* (New Hyde Park, NY: University Books, 1962).

7. The Evans-Wentz version (*Tibet's Great Yogi Milarepa*) appeared from Oxford University Press in 1928. More recently a new translation by Lobsang P. Lhalungpa has come out, *The Life of Milarepa* (Boulder: Prajna Press, 1982). The French translation by Bacot is also well known and respected.

8. The Second Dalai Lama gives the lineage of transmission toward the end of his explanation of the text. The lives and lineages of these early Indian masters are recorded in Gos-lo-tsa-wa, *The Blue Annals* (Tib., *'Deb-ther-sngon-po*) translated by George Roerich (Calcutta: Motilal Banarsidass, 1949).

9. The findings of these doctors are available through the University of Virginia. A film of the procedures of the tests was also made. The yogis found the tests somewhat humorous and sometimes embarrassing, but they braved through them to the end for the sake of fun and science.

The Longevity Yogas of the Bodhisattva of Life

1. The mantra of emptiness: *OM SVABHAVA SHUDDHOH SARVADHARMA SVABHAVA SHUDDHOH HAM.*

2. A fairly detailed explanation of a similar transformation process can be found in Stephan Beyer, *The Cult of Tara* (Berkeley: University of California Press, 1973).

3. These mantras are not included in the Second Dalai Lama's text, as they are customarily transmitted orally at the time of receiving the initiation. For the same reason I am not including them here.

4. That is, the short Essence Mantra.

5. The legend behind the name of this lineage guru is given in *The Life of Marpa the Translator*, by the Nalanda Translation Committee (Boulder: Prajna Press, 1982).

6. This refers to the nutrient pills used by yogis instead of food. The pills are made of a precise combination of mineral and herbal substances. I knew one yogi who had lived on them for two years, eating nothing but a half dozen of them a day. At first he lost a bit of weight, but after a few months caught his second breath in the practice and gained the pill power, returning to his normal weight for the remainder of the time period.

Chapter Seven

Translator's Preamble

1. These are from the same commentary to the longevity yogas quoted earlier.

2. Tib., *Zab-lam-ni-gu-chos-drug-gi-khrid-yig-ye-shes-mkha'-'gro-ma'i-zhal-lung*, the full title of which is *Instructions of the Wisdom Dakini: A Commentary on the Profound Paths of the Six Yogas of Niguma.*

3. See note 2 above.

4. See note 1 above.

5. The *Lam-dre* (Tib., *lam-'bras*) term indicates the lineage of this specific instruction to be of the Sakya sect.

6. That is, they would share a common source. The lineages are nonetheless significantly different.

The Yoga of Consciousness Transference

1. That is, upon the ability to control the subtle bodily energies and to experience paranormal stages in meditation as explained in chapter two.

2. Tib., *dNgos-grub-rgya-mtsho.*

3. This is given in more detail by the First Dalai Lama in his *Notes on Spiritual Transformation*, which I included in my First Dalai Lama collection, *Bridging the Sutras and Tantras* (Ithaca: Snow Lion Publications, 1982).

4. Skt., *Abhidharma-kośa;* Tib., *Chos-mngon-par-mdzod.*

5. Skt., *Ratna-megha-sūtra;* Tib., *Phags-pa-dkon-mchog-spring.*

6. These names refer to Atisha and Lama Tsongkhapa, respectively. They are not visualized in their ordinary forms but as celestial bodhisattvas. This image is a popular theme in Tibetan religious paintings.

7. Skt., *Madhyamaka-garbha;* Tib., *dBu-ma'i-snying-po.*

8. Skt., *Madhyamakāvatāra;* Tib., *dBu-ma-la-'jug-pa.*

9. Skt., *Mahāyāna-pranidhāna-rāja;* Tib., *Theg-chen-smon-lam-gyi-rgyal-po.*

10. The master referred to here is one of Tibet's greatest philosopher/saints. His numerous compilations of the systems of Indian Buddhist philosophical history have preserved knowledge of much of Buddhist Indian thought that otherwise would have been lost. His *Great Exposition of the Systems of Tenets in Indian Thought* (Tib., *Grub-mtha'-chen-mo*) remains a classic in its field. See Professor Jeffrey Hopkins, *Meditation on Emptiness* (London: Wisdom Publications, 1984).

Chapter Eight

Translator's Preamble

1. Foreword by H.H. the Dalai Lama to Jeffrey Hopkins' *Death, Intermediate State and Rebirth in Tibetan Buddhism* (London: Rider & Co., 1979; rpt. Ithaca: Snow Lion Publications, 1980).

2. See my *Tsongkhapa's Six Yogas of Naropa* (Ithaca: Snow Lion Publications, 1996). Tsongkhapa's commentary to the six yogas is also translated in Chang and Muses, *Esoteric Teachings of the Tibetan Tantras* (California: Falcon's Wing Press, 1961). Unfortunately the rendering is riddled with mistakes, confused by missing passages and disfigured by Chang's footnotes proclaiming his hatred for the Tibetan author, Tsongkhapa. The battle between Chang and Muses in the footnotes re-

minds one more of an Abbot and Costello movie than a serious academic endeavor. In the end Chang returned to Hong Kong in a huff before the publication was complete, leaving final details to Muses, who knew little or no Tibetan.

3. See note 2 to the preamble of chapter seven.

4. This is from his commentary on the Six Yogas of Naropa.

5. The 100-syllable mantra is used in all the tantric systems, being slightly altered in each case to suit the specific family and class of Tantra, and, in the case of Highest Yoga Tantra, being altered to incorporate the name of the principal deity of the mandala.

A Ritual for Caring for the Dead

1. The general nature of the yogas of this tantric system were dealt with earlier in chapter two, where we saw the tradition as a method for self-realization (Tib., *sgrub-thabs*). After developing competence in the practice, one is permitted to take up the activities aspect (Tib., *las*) of practice, which deals with how the method is applied for the benefit of others.

2. This often includes the reading of the long *sadhana*, or generation-stage meditation.

3. Here and elsewhere in the text where mantras are given I have not included the entire mantra, as these are only of use to initiates. My aim here is to show the general nature of the spirituality behind the rite and how it contributes to the Tibetan tradition on death and dying. The mantras have no meaning to the non-initiate. The text itself, however, is rich in the sentiment that Buddhism holds toward the subject of death and shows us the nature of the meditations pursued by the ritualist performing rites for the benefit of the dead. The psychological significance of the text is obvious.

4. Tib., *Bar-do-ngo-sprod*. *The Tibetan Book of the Dead* belongs to this category of literature, and theoretically if it were read would be inserted at this point in the ritual, instead of the brief version given by our author.

Chapter Nine

Translator's Preamble

1. The Sixth Dalai Lama had refused to join the monkhood. His wild life is perhaps the reason for the Seventh's love for simplicity, for the repercussions of the Sixth's unconventional behavior led to unexpected developments and hardships in Central Asia. See *Songs of the Sixth Dalai Lama*, translated by K. Dhondup (Dharamsala, LTWA, 1981).

2. We have seen materials from several of the other Dalai Lamas in the earlier chapters. Amongst the early Dalai Lamas, the First, Third, and Fifth were particularly avid writers. The Ninth through the Twelfth wrote very little, however, all of them being short-lived.

3. The Mongolians under Lhasang Khan had invaded and dethroned the Sixth Dalai Lama, possibly resulting in the Sixth's death. Lhasang Khan continued to hold power in Lhasa until an uprising supported by China forced him to withdraw. This led to the enthronement of the young Seventh Dalai Lama, but with the Chinese seeing the Tibeto-Mongol enmity as an opportunity to gain control of Central Asia themselves.

4. We saw the Atisha lineage of death meditation earlier, in chapter six.

Meditations on the Ways of Impermanence

1. This term, which literally means 'guru as deity' (in the sense of deity as a Buddha), is a literal translation of the classical Sanskrit term *guru-deva*.

2. Skt., *Vajra-kāya*. The idea is that a sage has control over the elements of his/her own body, and thus over his/her own life span. He/she chooses the time of passing. Thus it is a 'death scene,' being a mere show for the benefit of trainees.

3. The Seventh Dalai Lama does not date his poem. Could this verse be a reference to the fierce fighting that arose during the incursions of Lhasang Khan? Or to later years when he himself was exiled to Eastern Tibet?

4. Unfortunately it is difficult to keep the meter consistent in this verse. The meaning is that even the laws of karma—good begets happiness, evil begets suffering, and apathy begets boredom—should remind us of impermanence, and in particular point to the transitory nature of mental experience.

Epilogue

1. It is difficult to say for certain who first coined the term 'lamaism,' but it was mostly popularized by Dr. L.A. Waddell, whose *The Buddhism of Tibet or Lamaism* (London, 1895; reprinted by W. Heffer & Sons, Cambridge, 1939) became a primary source for all further studies on Tibet and its culture. Waddell, unfortunately, seems to have intensely disliked Tibetan Buddhism, and dedicated years of his life to describing aspects of Tibetan culture in one breath and writing them off as degenerate mumbo jumbo with the next. He widely propagated the belief that Tibetan Buddhism or 'lamaism' was Buddhism totally corrupted by Tibetan shamanism. As his works came to be used as source books by later scholars, this bigoted and misplaced belief found its way into the writings of the generation to follow, and still today, more than 100 years later, continues to pop up from time to time. Needless to say, the Tibetan masters consider both the word and the concept behind it extremely offensive.

2. Prof. A.K. Warder gives an account of the Buddhist Sanskrit literature that has come to us in his *Indian Buddhism* (Delhi: Motilal Banarsidass, 1970). Also see Winternitz's *History of Indian Literature* (Calcutta: Motilal Banarsidass, 1927).

3. Elizabeth Kübler-Ross, *On Death and Dying* (New York: Macmillan, 1969).

Bibliography of Texts Translated

Chapter One

Death and the Bodhisattva Trainings
mDo-smed-sku-'bum-byams-pa-gling-dang-lha-ldan-smon-lam-chen-por-tshogs-dgon-du-phebs-skabs-sogs-kyi-gsung-bshad-zags-bsgrigs-'chi-bai'-sgom-tshul-dang byang-sems-slab-bya
Gyalwa Tubten Gyatso (rGyal-ba-thub-bstan-rgya-mtsho), The Thirteenth Dalai Lama

Chapter Two

Tibetan Traditions of Death Meditation
Bod-lugs-nang-chos-'chi-ba-mi-rtags-pa-sgom-tshul
Geshe Ngawang Dargye (dGe-bshes-ngag-dbang-dar-rgyas)

Chapter Three

A Conversation with an Old Man
Nyams-myong-rgan-po'i-'bel-gtam-yid-'byung-dmar-khrid
Lama Gungtang Konchok Tenpai Dronme (bLa-ma-gung-thang-dkon-mchog-bstan-pa'i-sgron-me)

Chapter Four

The Death of Gye-re Lama
sGye-ras-gnas-mchog-blo-sgyud
Terton Dulzhug Lingpa (gTer-ston-'dul-bzhugs-gling-pa)

Chapter Five

Self-Liberation by Knowing the Signs of Death
'Chi-mtshan-rtags-par-rang-sgrol
Terton Karma Lingpa (gTer-ston-kar-ma-gling-pa)

Chapter Six

The Longevity Yogas of the Bodhisattva of Life
  'Tshe-dpags-med-kyi-tshe-sgrub
  Gyalwa Gendun Gyatso (rGyal-ba-dge-'dun-rgya-mtsho), The Second Dalai
  Lama

Chapter Seven

The Yoga of Consciousness Transference
  'Pho-ba'i-dmar-khrid
  Lama Tsechokling Yeshe Gyaltsen (Yongs-'dzin-'tshe-mchog-gling-ye-shes-
  rgyal-mtshan)

Chapter Eight

A Ritual for Caring for the Dead
  rDo-rje-'jigs-byed-rjes-dzin
  Lama Mahasukha (bLa-ma-ma-ha-su-kha)

Chapter Nine

Meditations on the Ways of Impermanence
  'Chi-ba-mi-rtag-pa-sgom-tshul
  Gyalwa Kalzang Gyatso (rGyal-ba-skal-bzang-rgya-mtsho), The Seventh Dalai
  Lama